Cadillac®

MEMORIES

As told by Fleetwood and Brougham owners.

DEDICATION

This book is dedicated to the Cadillac family of owners who graciously agreed to participate in our *Cadillac Memories* program. We invited current owners who purchased a new, rear-wheel-drive Fleetwood or Brougham between 1986 and 1996 to contribute their memories.

Thousands of owners shared their stories and family photographs for inclusion in this very personal tribute. We appreciate their kindness and generosity.

Special thanks to Fleetwood owners Sal Santoro, Kevin Didriksen and Patricia Giantonio who volunteered their time to review the photos and memories submitted by Cadillac owners. Their selections are featured in Chapter One.

We are also grateful to Al Haas, national president of the Cadillac LaSalle Club, for his historical contributions to Chapter Three.

From left to right: Sal Santoro from Rockaway, New Jersey;
Patricia Giantonio from Ridgewood, New Jersey; and Kevin
Didriksen from Tuxedo Park, New York.

CONTENTS

PERSONAL MEMORIES

*A profile of the stories and the cars of Cadillac owners
from around the U.S. and Canada.*

MARGARET *Mayo*

CARUTHERSVILLE, MISSOURI

Minnie Pearl and Teddy Bears

Despite her difficulties, Margaret Mayo loves to drive her Cadillac to nursing homes dressed as Minnie Pearl or Dolly Parton and hand out stuffed animals to the residents. Margaret lost her hearing in 1992, but it hasn't slowed her one bit. Nor has she lost her zest for life.

Margaret's husband, Wesley, bought a new Buick every year. "Nine months after my husband passed away I took the Buick back to the dealer and bought a Cadillac Fleetwood," she said. "I really enjoy my '95 Fleetwood Brougham. It's the only one that I have ever had where the front seats heat up. My little dog, Miss April, loves it, too."

Margaret's best friend, Lorine Burrus, is also a Cadillac owner. "My 1985 Sedan DeVille is so smooth-riding," she said. "It drives like a new one. I'm used to it and it's used to me. I think it would cry if I ever traded it in."

Joe and Kathy Palermo

The Christmas Gift

Kathy Palermo says that 1991 was the best year of her life. After she and Joe were married on February 2, they would drive past the Cadillac dealer every now and then. He'd ask her, "Which car do you like?" and "What's your favorite color?" Kathy thought nothing of it, because the idea of driving a new Cadillac was nothing more than a big dream.

What she didn't know was that Joe had ordered one and stored it at his parents' house.

When everyone gathered for Christmas, Kathy's new mother-in-law gave her a purse, which she had requested. Tucked inside was a small black jewelry case, and inside the case were two gold keys. Joe led her outside where her 1992 Cadillac Brougham d'Elegance was wrapped in a big red ribbon.

"My knees and hands were shaking as I opened the door and sat behind the wheel," she remembered. "I couldn't believe that my husband had been able to do this and keep such a great secret. I was so proud of my husband and the car that we had a license plate made to commemorate the date."

At the age of 19, Archie Nevitt was with the 29th Infantry Division and was in the fourth wave to hit Normandy Beach on D-Day, June 6, 1944. He was wounded the next morning in a church yard in Normandy. When the Germans overran his position, he jumped in a foxhole for safety even though it already held a dead German soldier.

"I was scared to death," he remembers. "I swore to myself that if I ever got out of that foxhole, there were two things I was going to do," Archie said. "The first was to go to Bermuda on my honeymoon and the second was to buy a Cadillac. I eventually did both."

Since he was a sales manager for Nabisco for 40 years, he was always issued a company car, and the promise to own a Cadillac was put off. "After moving around for about 40 years, I said, the heck with the rules, I'm gonna buy a Cadillac," he remembers. "That was in 1978. I bought a Sedan DeVille. I've owned Cadillacs ever since." Today, he loves the comfort of his Cadillac.

ARCHIBALD $\mathscr{N}$EVITT

RADNOR, PENNSYLVANIA

The War Promise

VINCENT FAIOLA

Star Driver

The 1959 Cadillacs, with their soaring fins, represented the height of opulence. Vincent Faiola loved them. Of the 20 cars he has owned, four have been '59 Cadillacs. He still has a '59 Eldorado convertible that he has used to transport celebrities in the annual Hollywood Christmas Parade.

"In 1995, we had two trips down the parade route," Vincent remembered. "We took Halle Berry and Elvira." In the ten years he has been driving the parade route, Vince has transported dozens of stars, from Willie Aames to Pia Zadora. "My favorite was Lee Meriweather," he said. "She was the nicest."

Vince said he bought his 1996 Fleetwood because it was "the last." He likes big comfortable cars. "People of my generation like soft rides," he said.

9

HELEN WOODWARD
MISSISSAUGA, ONTARIO, CANADA

A Life Saver

It was the winter of 1978, and the three Woodward children were headed north from Mississauga, Ontario, to the family ski chalet in Collingwood. Leslie, 18, was driving when the 1972 Eldorado convertible hit black ice.

"Leslie hung onto the wheel as the car hit a pole, slid down an embankment, and finally came to rest a few feet from a rushing river," Helen Woodward said about her children's ordeal. Leslie steered, while brother Jeff, who was sitting in the middle of the front seat, figured he was "toast." "When everyone realized they were all right, they turned off the engine, climbed back up the hill through deep snow and trekked to a nearby gas station for help.

"Naturally we were sentimentally attached to that car," Helen added. "We kept it longer than we normally would. We had it repainted and repaired. That car was our life preserver."

BILL AND ARLENE LACKNER

Kayaks and Cadillacs

Arlene Lackner said her dream car was always a Lincoln Town Car. But Bill Lackner liked Cadillacs. And since their 1993 Brougham probably saved Bill's life when he was hit in the side by a pickup truck, they'll probably keep driving Cadillacs for a long time.

Their 1993 Fleetwood Brougham was totalled in the accident, and Arlene leased a Town Car while Bill was recovering. It gave her the opportunity to drive what had been her dream car. After the experience of driving a Town Car, she decided to buy another Cadillac because she thought "it was a better car."

Bill has completely recovered from the accident. The former American Airlines pilot is back playing golf, kayaking and playing with his grandchildren.

"I transport the kayak on the top of another car," Bill said. "My wife won't let me use the Cadillac. And no, the golf game hasn't improved that much."

11

JOHNNY AND YVONNE HIFER

CHARLOTTE, NORTH CAROLINA

Vacation Memories

You've all heard of people who like to collect things. Johnny and Yvonne Phifer are such people. Johnny fell in love with Cadillacs when friends of his parents drove a 1941 Cadillac on family vacations. Since 1966, he has owned a 1965 Calais coupe, a 1972 Coupe DeVille, a 1976 Seville and a 1984 DeVille, which he still drives. Finally, he bought the last 1992 Brougham that came into Arnold Palmer Cadillac in Charlotte, North Carolina.

Johnny's pride and joy, though, is a 1941 limousine that he bought in 1984. The car had only 16,400 miles on it. Everything was original. The owner had parked it in 1964, and it had not been driven since.

"I had to replace the tires and the fuel tank," Johnny said. "But everything else is original. It now has 17,204 miles. Most of the miles put on the car were when it was in the movie, 'The Color Purple.' This is just a super car. In 1941 I thought it was the prettiest thing ever, and I still do."

12

DALE *Faulkner*

EDMONTON, ALBERTA, CANADA

Our Cadillac Memories Book

Shortly after Dale Faulkner bought his 1989 Brougham d'Elegance, his son, Ken, took the car and said he was going to get it washed. Ken brought the car back after a couple of hours, all clean and shiny.

A week or so after that, "he called and said he was coming over to the house," Dale remembers. "He said he had something for us."

What Ken had done while he was "washing" the car, was take it to some picturesque areas around Edmonton, Alberta, and photograph it. He then assembled the pictures in the Faulkners' own "Cadillac Memories" book.

"Ken and I like cars, period," Dale said. "One of the pictures—which he had blown up and I have hanging in my office—was in front of an extended-care hospital in Edmonton that was built in classic Old Southern architecture. I like that building and the car, so the photograph means a lot to me."

MARK AND LOLITA *L*IPMAN

LANTANA, FLORIDA

Lip-Man and the Lips

When Mark and Lolita Lipman lived in New Jersey, their home was near rock star Bruce Springsteen who had a Cadillac float in his pool in nearby Rumson. Springsteen also recorded a song about a pink Cadillac. Mark had his own seven-piece band, Lip-Man and the Lips, and they played a lot of Springsteen's music.

One day, when Mark was going to pay a bill, he accidentally made a wrong turn and ended up in a used car lot. In front of him was a white 1965 Cadillac convertible. The bill didn't get paid, but the Lip-Man got his Cadillac. A week later, it was painted pink.

"I thought that was very responsible," Mark said of his purchase. "I ended up with a Cadillac, didn't I?"

Mark and Lolita would drive down the street in their pink Cadillac convertible, playing Springsteen's music and cruising into drive-in restaurants. They were even filmed for television playing and singing an original song in their car. When the Lipmans moved to Florida, they sold the pink Cadillac, but they still love to drive their Fleetwood.

14

MICHAEL AND MARGARET *Mc*KINNEY

SHARPSVILLE, INDIANA

Dreams Come True

Michael "Mick" McKinney had always wanted a Cadillac. "But I shouldn't have said anything to my wife," he joked. You see, Margaret McKinney had a little surprise in mind.

"Our children were raised and I had a job," Margaret said. "I thought it might be possible to make his dream of owning a Cadillac come true. I shopped around and found the car he wanted." The purchase was completed in October 1990, but she didn't need the car until February 13, 1991, Mick's 50th birthday. The dealer stored it for her.

"We were to meet at my son's house to go out for dinner," she said. "Mick didn't know we were going to make a stop to pick up his present. The dealer was there with a birthday cake and the keys in his hand." So were about 15 friends and family members, including Michael Jr., who was released from a six-year Navy hitch three days early to make the ceremony. Mick said it was the most memorable birthday he'll ever have because his dream came true.

Mick had a chance for a payback. On Margaret's 50th birthday, he took her to Hawaii to make her dream come true.

15

DAN *Michau*

COLLEGE PARK, MARYLAND

Cadillac on My Keychain

Dan Michau's assignment as a youngster in Ft. Benning, Georgia (his father was a career Army officer), was to keep his father's black 1958 Series 62 Cadillac sedan in "spit-shine" condition. "It wasn't an easy task in a Georgia summer," he said. He earned his driver's license in his father's next Cadillac—a 1960 Fleetwood 60 Special.

"I have owned several Cadillacs since then," Dan said, "but none were Fleetwoods. When I heard that Cadillac wasn't going to build the Fleetwood any more, I realized it was my last chance to own one. I figured it was now or never."

Dan traded in a Buick for a Fleetwood because his Dad's Fleetwood was his pride and joy.

In honor of his father's 1960 Fleetwood, Dan has had the front page of his owner's manual sized to hang from his rear-view mirror on a key chain. "It takes the place of fuzzy dice," he joked.

NETTIE CARVIN

PORT RICHEY, FLORIDA

Surviving the Flood

The "no-name" hurricane of 1993 hit Port Richey, Florida, and Nettie Carvin saw salt water invade her house and 1990 Cadillac Brougham. After the floods subsided, she opened her car door and water poured out. "I had water up to the seats in the front, but to my surprise there wasn't a drop of water in the trunk," she said. She drove the car to her son's house and spent most of the trip dodging debris that was floating down the street.

After Nettie had the car cleaned up, it was hit again by Hurricane Josephine in 1996. "The water was two inches from going in the door again," she remembered. "My son said, 'Mom, we gotta get out.' I got in the car and headed to his house. I was pushing trash all the way.

"I love my car, I really do," Nettie said. "It's a dream. I feel safe in it, too. I was hit twice in the back and I don't know what might have happened in another car."

MARK BURTON

VIRGINIA BEACH, VIRGINIA

A Son's Tribute

Mark Burton grew up in Salt Lake City, where his father, Joseph, was a service manager for the Sharman Auto Company, the local Cadillac distributor. Joseph Burton had learned his trade working for his father, who owned the first Cadillac dealership in Salt Lake City, the Utah Implement Company.

"Almost all the sheep herders in Utah drove Cadillacs in the Twenties and Thirties," Mark remembers. "They were dependable and the only cars that could handle the alleged roads of the time.

"We had Cadillacs and LaSalles all the time when I was growing up," he remembered. "As a child I spent many hours looking at Cadillacs and driving in those 12- and 16-cylinder models. It was a love affair from an early age."

VIVIAN PENNINGTON

ALBUQUERQUE, NEW MEXICO

Worth the Wait

In the early Fifties, R.C. Pennington was an advisor on a government irrigation project in Thailand. Vivian Pennington and their three children drove around in Jeeps and five-ton trucks. "We drove whatever vehicle was available," Vivian remembers.

After Thailand, R.C. worked as a foreign service officer with the State Department. He promised Vivian, "Honey, one of these days I'm going to buy a big Cadillac for you." When he retired in 1976, he was true to his promise. "He bought me a gorgeous 1976 Fleetwood Brougham," Vivian said.

That Fleetwood had experiences that made Thailand and the trucks look tame. "We once drove into a high Rocky Mountain meadow after a rain storm and promptly sank into the soil up to the frame," Vivian said. "My husband told my daughter to shift into low and see what the car would do. That powerful engine plowed us through 200 feet of muck until we reached the pavement."

Today, the car has over 290,000 miles on the odometer and has been made like new. "We're saving it for our grandson, who is now seven," said Vivian.

BILL AND LOIS BELCH

BELLEVILLE, ONTARIO, CANADA

The Birth Day

Bill and Lois Belch were in Toronto, headed for the theatre, when Lois decided that the time had come for daughter, Stephanie, to be born. "Do you want to go to a hospital here or do you want to go home to Belleville?" Bill asked. "Belleville" was the answer.

So their 1960 Persian Sand Cadillac coupe made the 100-mile trip in record time. "We didn't slow down at all," Bill said. After an overnight stay in the hospital, Lois was released with false labor. Stephanie was born six weeks later. Twenty-five years after that, Stephanie made the 1960 Cadillac part of her wedding, as did her sister, Debbie.

"I have lots of visions of the car going to other weddings," Bill said. "We have three granddaughters and two grandsons. This car has always served us well. Now, we just keep it in the garage mostly and drive our Fleetwood, but we drive the '60 every now and then."

OMER AND MONA $\mathscr{P}$OINTER

SNYDER, TEXAS

Teddy Bears in the Trunk

The Colorado Belle Casino in Loughlin, Nevada, is a regular destination for Omer and Mona Pointer. They go there twice a year. In March 1996, they won big.

"You had to win ten jackpots to win a ticket; ten tickets to win a big stuffed bear," Mona said. "We won nine-teen bears. We went back in August and won fifteen stuffed safari animals over the course of seven days. Omer wins and I spend."

For the trip home to Snyder, Texas, the Pointers stuffed the animals everywhere they could in their 1993 Fleetwood Brougham. "Without the roominess of that car, we could have never brought them home to our grandchildren," Mona said. "When we stopped overnight, we had to take all the animals out of the car to get to our luggage."

As soon as Omer and Mona returned home, they had to travel again to distribute the bears to their grandchildren.

Jean Saurette

GRANBY, QUEBEC, CANADA

The Only Cadillac in Town

Jean Saurette dreamed of owning a Cadillac when he was in high school.

Buying it was a challenge, though. "At that time, there was no Cadillac dealer in Granby, Quebec, where I live," he said. "The dealers in Montreal had long lists of customers which made it difficult to order a car. But someone told me that if I would go 'to a certain place,' they had Cadillacs in stock. I bought my '52 and '53 there. In 1955, a dealer opened in Granby and I have bought all my cars since then from him."

Jean imported and built bicycles. He used the Cadillac as a business card. "When I was visiting one of my 500 dealers in eastern Canada, they would know I was around when they saw a Cadillac in front of their store.

"I like the car," Jean said. "I have traveled to Hollywood, Florida, every winter since 1956. I know that I can have the same service on the road that I can have at home, and that's important when you're 80."

RALPH SPECK

Black Cat

Ralph Speck worked for State Farm Insurance. When he bought his first new Cadillac in 1959, he was an agency manager in South Carolina.

In 1962, Ralph traded the '59 for a black '62 Fleetwood Brougham. The black car became his trademark. He called them all "Black Cat." He leased his cars for two years, then bought them at the end of the lease.

"I usually made one trip a month down to the regional office in Jacksonville, Florida, and took agents with me on various training programs," Ralph said. "They all looked forward to the trip in the 'Black Cat' and the foot rests in the back that they referred to as prayer benches."

There aren't many people who will refer to a Cadillac as an "economy car," but Ralph said he feels his Cadillacs have been the most economical cars to own. "They hold their value, and they're not in the garage," he said.

WOODROW VAUGHN

GREER, SOUTH CAROLINA

Felt Like a Millionaire

Life has been good to Woodrow Vaughn. His first Cadillac was a 1952 Coupe DeVille that had over 300,000 miles on the odometer. "That car made me feel like a millionaire," Vaughn said. "I bought it because the doctor told my wife she had to travel in a good heavy car that had a smooth ride. It gave me a good reason to purchase a Cadillac."

His present 1994 Fleetwood Brougham is driven around town and on trips to his in-laws, who live 150 miles away in Orangeburg, South Carolina. "This car was just sittin' out there in the lot and I went in, drove it around the block and bought it," he said. "I'll tell you one thing about this car. Every other car I've owned gave about 15-20 miles per gallon. We'd drive to my in-laws and fill up in Columbia on the way back. With this car, I fill up, go to Orangeburg, and come home, all on a half tank. This car gives me great gas mileage. I didn't get as good mileage from my Model A Ford."

MALCOLM AND ELIZABETH *JARVIS*

PLAINFIELD, CONNECTICUT

Still Dancing Together

Malcolm Jarvis first became interested in Cadillac when he was a chauffeur as a young man in Boston. "I drove for two multi-millionaires," he remembered. "And their cars were always Cadillacs."

Malcolm once took his 1992 Fleetwood to Montreal on a vacation. "I had to watch my speed, because if I wasn't careful I'd be going 75 or 85 miles an hour," he said. "When I got there, I was so relaxed I felt like dancing." One time, he made the mistake of buying a competing brand. On the way home, a gust of wind nearly blew the car off the road. "I brought it back to the dealer the next day and told him, 'This is a car, give me an automobile,'" he remembered. He bought a Cadillac the next day.

"I have owned a lot of cars," he continued. "I bought my first Cadillac from Reedman Motors in Pennsylvania and drove it all the way home to Connecticut."

RAYMOND AND JEAN *K*ENADY

King and Queen of Chicago

Ray Kenady bought his first Cadillac in 1951. "In those days, Cadillac didn't have the competition it has today," he remembers. "But even then, when you had a Cadillac you had a singular automobile."

Ray was an independent insurance agent in South Bend, Indiana. "I didn't use the Cadillac as a business car," he said. "The Cadillac was our family car. My wife used it during the week and it was our 'Sunday go to meeting' car."

All three Kenady daughters learned to drive in Dad's Caddies. Sandra Kenady, the oldest, took the family Caddy out when she and a friend were soliciting ads for the high school yearbook. Sandra was the top salesperson and earned the nickname "Cadillac Kenady."

The most memorable Kenady trip was the first one. Ray and Jean took a trip to Chicago, which was about 90 miles away, to see the musical "Oklahoma" at the Shubert Theatre. They stayed at the Palmer House. "We felt like the king and queen that day," he said.

AL $\mathscr{H}$ENDERSON

APPLE VALLEY, CALIFORNIA

The Gift

"Black Bart" was Al Henderson's 1956 Cadillac that he would leave at the Apple Valley, California, airport for friends to use. "I'd leave the keys with the car," Al said. "They were hidden, of course. The drivers' only obligation was to fill it with gas when they were done so the next person would have enough."

One day in Apple Valley, Al met an entertainer, Bobbejaan Schoepen, who had a theme park in Belgium. "Bobbejaan's park grew from a tent show he and his wife, Josie, would travel around with," Al said. "When their kids got older, they made the show more permanent by building the theme park."

Bobbejaan wanted to buy "Black Bart," but it wasn't for sale. "When I told them 'no' they were disappointed," Al remembered. "Instead, I gave it to them for their son, Jacky. They asked if they could put it on display and I said yes."

Al gave the Schoepens "Black Bart" in April 1993. It was restored and placed in a permanent display as part of one of the rides.

27

CARL *H*UDSON

EATON PARK, FLORIDA

Built Cadillacs for 30 Years

In 1951, Carl Hudson moved from Tennessee to Detroit and went from earning $3.00 a day on the farm to $1.67 an hour on the Cadillac assembly line. He retired in 1981 after 30 years at the Clark Avenue factory in Detroit where every Cadillac from 1921 to 1984 was built.

"I was very proud to work for Cadillac," he said. "We tried to make a car that people would be proud of and not have any trouble with. If a 'bug car' got out and word got back to the department responsible, we had meetings and talks to fix the problem."

Carl and his wife, Dorothy, moved to Florida to give her a warmer climate for her rheumatoid arthritis. After Dorothy passed away in 1994, Carl started thinking that he'd like to have at least one Cadillac before he, too, passed on. In 1995, he bought a new Fleetwood. "I finally own one of those great cars that I had spent my life building," Carl said. "I'm thrilled."

28

TIM *L*EDNUM

ASHEBORO, NORTH CAROLINA

Ad Dreamer

Tim Lednum's eighth grade teacher was boring. "I did not like that teacher," he remembered. "We had closets in the back of the classroom with magazines in them. I would take the magazines out during class and began tearing out the car ads. The Cadillac ads were my favorites."

Over the years, the stack of ads and Tim's love for Cadillacs grew. He began saving his money until he bought his first, a 1977 Coupe DeVille. He named it Amanda because he liked the name.

Tim sold Amanda in 1984, but told the family that bought her, when they wanted to sell it, he'd buy her back. In 1990, he had the opportunity, and she's back in Tim's garage. "She's my hobby car," he said. "She has over 126,000 miles on her."

29

Dwight and Sharon Leister

Tucson, Arizona

Always the First

Sharon Leister's father, Howard, established one of Tucson, Arizona's, first funeral homes in 1928. He bought Cadillac limousines and hearses for the funeral homes as early as 1915.

"My father-in-law always had to have the first of anything," Dwight Leister said. "His 1949 Cadillac was the first with the new V8 engine. He had a V12 Lincoln Zephyr in the Thirties and the first diesel-powered Eldorado."

Dwight said he bought his present 1996 Fleetwood "primarily for my wife's use. Since my father-in-law always had Cadillacs, we wanted to get the last Fleetwood in memory of him."

Dwight ordered a 1997 GMC Suburban, which is being built in the same Arlington, Texas, plant that built the Fleetwood. He ordered it in the same color as the Fleetwood, with the same chrome strip along the bottom. "It'll be nice having the last car built in that plant and the first truck built off that line," Dwight said.

ALRED "BUD" MORROW

A Childhood Dream

In 1926, Bud Morrow was 11 and the oldest of three brothers and two sisters. "When Christmas came around, we were limited to one present each," he remembered. "We were lucky to get an apple."

But Bud had found a picture of a Cadillac open touring car in a magazine and crafted himself a model of the car from a piece of pine and a tin can. "It turned out quite well. As Christmas approached, I decided to make two more models for my younger brothers. They were delighted, and from then on we were a Cadillac family."

Bud worked in the lumber and home improvement business for 45 years, following in the footsteps of his father, who was a carpenter. "Late in life I traded in my Olds 98 for a 1984 DeVille sedan," he said. "My wife, Ruth, said she was embarrassed at first when she took it grocery shopping. I told her to drive it with pride—it was paid for.

"My family provided me with the personalized license plate, '2 x 4,' because of all my years in the lumber business."

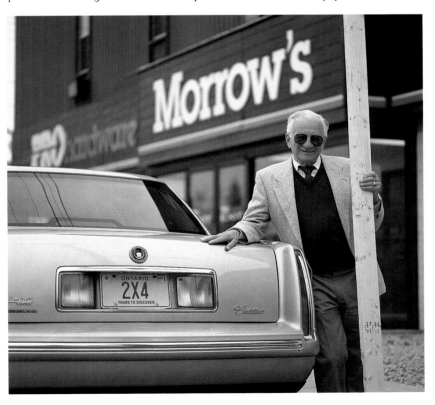

MERLE AND KAY SPINKS

LAKEWOOD, CALIFORNIA

47 States in a Cadillac

"Bessie" was Merle Spinks' 1976 Fleetwood Brougham. "I liked my '75 so much I went out and bought a '76," he remembered. "That was the best car. It never knew the difference between a flat highway and a mountain."

Merle and Kay were married in Las Vegas in 1977, the same year they bought "Bessie." "We took many trips in that car," Merle added. "We went to New Orleans, Florida, Washington, D.C., Philadelphia, New England, Canada—in all, we visited 47 states in that car. Never had a major problem even though we put over 150,000 miles on her.

"We still travel quite a lot," Merle said. "I have always liked the Fleetwood Brougham with all the bells and whistles. The car is worth every penny because you're not always fixing every little thing."

32

HAROLD AND JOYCE $\mathscr{K}$OENIG

Owned Nearly Every Model

Harold Koenig lives in Florida now, but when he was practicing oral and facial surgery in Indiana, he drove over 90,000 miles in one year in his Cadillac.

"That was in 1968," he remembered. "I was named Worthy Grand Patron of the Indiana Grand Chapter of the Order of Eastern Star and traveled to every Masonic Lodge in Indiana. I had no breakdowns, but I hit a bull on a country road once. He was running down the road and I came up behind him. I didn't hurt the car; I'm not sure if I hurt him."

Harold has owned 28 Cadillacs since 1951. "I've had every type except the Cimarron," he said. "One of the finest was the '81 Seville. It must have had stainless steel underneath because there never was any rust."

Connor, who is Harold and Joyce's three-year-old grandson, loves to ride in their '96 Fleetwood Brougham. "He calls me Dad," Harold said, "and he'll say to me, Dad, let's go in the big car."

33

KEITH AND GENNY Turnham

SAN DIEGO, CALIFORNIA

Movie Stars

Keith and Genny Turnham have been Cadillac owners since 1954, when Keith worked for AT&T. He survived a horrific head-on crash in his '66 Coupe DeVille because, as he claims, "it was a substantial car that could withstand the impact and a triple rollover."

The Turnhams are retired and appear in five or six movies, television specials and infomercials a year. Genny played Aunt Belinda in the Ellen DeGeneres movie "Mr. Wrong," and both appeared in the ABC movie, "What Love Sees." As a result, they were invited to a celebrity ski classic. It had snowed the night before their ride up the mountain. "I'm so proud of my '91 Fleetwood," Keith said. "We drove 17 miles on a mountain road and I wouldn't stop for anything. There were 8-10 inches of snow, and the Highway Patrol said there was no way we could have made it if we didn't have this car.

"We also own one of the last 1988 Cadillac Cimarrons and love it," Keith said. "It's carmine red and is one of the most beautiful cars I ever saw in my life. We have over 88,000 miles on it and we haven't had a bit of trouble."

LES *Le*TOURNEAU

PORT ORANGE, FLORIDA

No Problems

Les LeTourneau returned from Europe in 1960 with a 1950 DeSoto. He had transported it to Europe and back, but now he decided he wanted a Cadillac. He bought a 1960 Brougham. "I've had five Cadillacs, and I'm going for my sixth next year," Les said. "I've always liked the big ones.

"My wife, Eve, passed away in January 1996, but she was with me all the time. She loved the Cadillacs as much as I did," Les said. "She'd just sit back and relax in the passenger seat and let the car do everything."

Eve and Les took their brand-new 1960 Cadillac with about 25 miles on the odometer and drove it from Washington, D.C., to his home town of Hibbings, Minnesota, to show it off. "We just took right off," Les remembered. "We didn't have any problems, but you never have a problem with a Cadillac! Any car is only as good as the service you receive, and we've received great service. I have never had to lift the hood for repairs on any of the Cadillacs I've owned."

CHAPTER TWO

CADILLAC OWNERS GALLERY

*A very personal collection of family photographs
through the generations.*

Like many, George Malesich fell in love with the 1959 Cadillac Coupe DeVille the first time he saw one. He was 11 at the time. In 1982, he had an opportunity to buy this 1959 Eldorado Seville with just 48,000 miles on the odometer. "It's a fantastic parade car," he wrote. ▼

GEORGE MALESICH, DENVER, CO

▲ Annette Adams will always remember Christmas 1958. She received a white leather coat, a white poodle she named "Snow Boy" and a white Cadillac. Annette's former husband always bought his cars from Capital Cadillac in Atlanta. This car was the first in 1958.

ANNETTE ADAMS,
DAYTONA BEACH SHORES, FL

"There is no other car like a Cadillac," wrote Everett Wright, who bought his first Cadillac in 1961 because he and his wife, Marie, were going to travel for six months and wanted a comfortable car. In 1964, they bought a 1962 Sedan DeVille and traveled for one full year. ▶

EVERETT & MARIE WRIGHT,
MILTON FREEWATER, OR

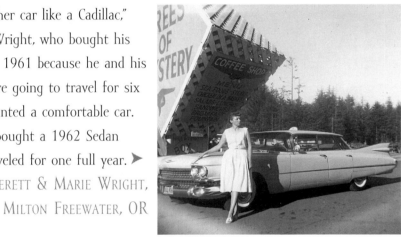

◀ Ben Hansford is driving his 27th and 28th new Cadillacs now, both 1996 Fleetwood Broughams. He bought his first in 1963. Ben also has two 1976 Eldorado convertibles in original condition with less than 20,000 miles on them.

BEN HANSFORD, ELGIN, IL

▲ Albert Becker was working around the house one day in 1956 and impulsively decided to go over to the Cadillac dealer and buy a car. "It was time," he remembered. "I had been saving for a vacation and took that money and bought the car for cash, off the showroom floor." Later, he was able to afford a new Cadillac every two or three years.

ALBERT BECKER, AUDUBON, NJ

▲ Andrew Banyas bought his 1960 Eldorado convertible because he always wanted one. "It was a wonderful car," he wrote, "and lots of fun." Here, his two daughters are ready for a ride in the spacious back seat.

ANDREW BANYAS, LAWRENCE, IN

▲ Car collector Bernard Berman has owned 54 Cadillacs over the years and still owns seven among the 50 cars in his collection. His first was a 1940 LaSalle convertible, above. The photo below is of a 1930 Cadillac Model 353 that Berman (on the right) drove in the Rover FIVA Rally in Scotland in 1996. ▼

BERNARD BERMAN, ALLENTOWN, PA

Barbara Campbell was a territory manager for a coffee company and says "it took a lot of cups of coffee for me to sell to purchase that Cadillac." She wrote that she felt like she finally made it when she got behind the wheel of that car. ➤

BARBARA CAMPBELL, AYR, ONTARIO, CANADA

▲ When Darlene Colburn was four years old, she posed on the fender of her father's 1939 Cadillac coupe. That was the beginning of her love affair with Caddies. Fifty years later, her husband, Clair, bought her a 1991 Brougham for her 54th birthday. "My dream had come true," she said.

CLAIR & DARLENE COLBURN,
STEUBENVILLE, OH

Gordon and Ginny Burroughs gave their granddaughters Cadillacs because their fathers wanted them to learn to drive in big safe cars. One of the girls enjoyed driving her car so much, she took it to Northwestern University, which created a stir in the school paper given her age. ▼   GORDON & GINNY BURROUGHS, ST. LOUIS, MO

Gladys and Preston Fleming owned 17 Cadillacs over 33 years. Preston bought Number 17, a 1994 Fleetwood Brougham, for Gladys' birthday. She had the medallion from Number 16 made into a pendant necklace. ➤

GLADYS FLEMING, ALICE, TX

▲ Devil's Lake, Michigan, is about 80 miles north of Detroit. In 1942, James Cornelius took his mother and their Boston bull terrier, Suzy, on a vacation there in his 1941 Cadillac, where this picture was taken. "I felt great behind the wheel of that car," James writes.

JAMES CORNELIUS, FAIRVIEW PARK, OH

Joseph DeSaro's 1953 Coupe DeVille was his second Cadillac. He lived in Dayton, Ohio, at the time and said he felt as if he was on cloud nine when he drove the car to Springfield Springs Park for the carnival. ▼

JOSEPH DESARO, DAYTON, OH

◀ In Europe, Leonard Cymbalist's 1957 Cadillac Sedan DeVille was unique. "It created such a mystery in England and Scotland that people would inspect the car at stop lights and delay my departure while I answered their questions," he said. "It made me feel like a celebrity."

LEONARD CYMBALIST, SATELLITE BEACH, FL   41

The two most important things in Rudolph Dillon's life are his wife and his 1993 Fleetwood Brougham. Rudolph bought the Fleetwood for Winona's birthday, and she was overwhelmed. He also taught his daughter to drive in the Cadillac because he wanted her to be in a safe car. ▼

RUDOLPH DILLON, CHICAGO, IL

▲ Marian Fanning's first ride in a Cadillac was in her father's 1922 touring convertible. She was 3 when this picture was taken. "We toured many places," she remembers. "One was the Luray Caverns in Virginia. I remember the air brakes on the front wheels."

MARIAN FANNING, NORRISTOWN, PA

Donald Dorward called his '58 convertible "Dagmar" because of the large bumper overriders on the front. This picture was taken on a family vacation trip to Florida where their daughter came down with a case of the mumps. That added several days to the visit with the grandparents, which allowed everyone to spend more time together. ▶

DONALD DORWARD, SARASOTA, FL

"Happiness is washing your Cadillac with your little granddaughter," says Louis Larocque. He bought his 1990 Fleetwood "because I always wanted one." His proudest moment was driving his daughter to church on her wedding day. ➤

LOUIS LAROCQUE, NORTH BAY, ONTARIO, CANADA

◀ Charles Fritz's first Cadillac was a 1955 Azure Blue sedan with a white top. "I accomplished my yearning for a Cadillac," he remembered. His first trip, after visiting an old friend, was to his girlfriend's house. She later became his wife. They took his 1959 DeVille on their honeymoon trip to Niagara Falls and Quebec, as well as on a "wonderful trip" to Yellowstone Park.

CHARLES FRITZ, SEFFNER, FL

George Flint's great-grandfather owned this 1912 Cadillac touring sedan. George's mother took her first ride in that car on June 7, 1912, coming home from the hospital where she was born. George has continued the Cadillac tradition in his family and has owned 21 Cadillacs. ➤

GEORGE FLINT, RENO, NV

43

Ruth and Gurley Garrett have owned 18 Cadillacs over the past 26 years, all Fleetwood Broughams. Their first was purchased in 1971, a particularly happy year for the Garretts. Their only grandchild, Tara, was born that year, and when Ruth and Gurley went on their honeymoon (second marriages for both), the wedding trip was in the 1971 gold Cadillac. ➤ GURLEY GARRETT, BIRMINGHAM, AL

Like many other Cadillac owners, Hoover Wilson taught his son, Mike, to drive in the Cadillac. The only difference is that Mike was eight years old in 1958 when he had his lessons. ▼

HOOVER WILSON, GARDENDALE, AL

▲ Talk about long love affairs. Adam and Vivian Gerres' first ride together in a Cadillac was on their wedding day, July 12, 1947, when this picture was taken. They were leaving the church for the reception at the Lee Plaza Hotel in Detroit. Adam and Vivian have had a love affair with each other and with Cadillacs since then, having owned several, all with personalized license plates reading "Vivann."

ADAM GERRES, CANTON, MI

◄ John Gaylord bought his 1962 Series 62 Cadillac from the original owner in 1978 and had it completely restored to as-new condition. It has been a show winner with the Cadillac LaSalle Club and was one of the display cars when Cadillac introduced its 1992 line at the Renaissance Center in Detroit.

DOROTHY & JOHN GAYLORD, DETROIT, MI

▲ A nine-hour drive anywhere is a chore, but in a 1991 Cadillac Brougham, it's easy. Sondra and Thomas Greer drove from Pittsburgh to Scott's Resort in New York for a ballroom dance exhibition. It was a long trip, but as you can see, Sondra was refreshed after making it.

SONDRA GREER, CECIL, PA

"The most beautiful girl in the world who never talked back" is what Rick Gremer called his first Cadillac, a 1951 convertible. He used it to transport his girlfriend, who was the 1951 Illinois Wesleyan Homecoming Queen. ▼

RICK GREMER, NORMAL, IL

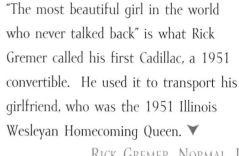

◄ What better way to start a life together than being festooned with dollar bills and riding in a chauffer-driven Cadillac? When Elsie and Brandon Hammond were married in Oak Harbor, Washington, on June 19, 1994, Uncle Lowey Alexander drove them in his car. He dressed for the occasion, wearing chauffeur's livery.

LOWEY ALEXANDER, SAN PABLO, CA

▲ Harold Weiner has owned Cadillacs all his life, beginning with a "1920s" convertible coupe. "There were so many great memories of the wonderful times I've had with my Cadillacs," Harold wrote. He thought the Cadillac was a great automobile in the Twenties and still thinks so. Harold remembers taking Lucille Ball for a ride—before she was famous.   HAROLD WEINER, SARASOTA, FL

When Bob Hart posed in front of his parents' 1959 Cadillac Sedan DeVille, he called the go-kart his "Kiddilac." Little did he realize that in the intervening 37 years, he would own four Cadillacs and his parents would own another twelve. ▼   JEAN HART, DEERFIELD BEACH, FL

Ellen Hines Johnson talks to her 1992 Cadillac Fleetwood Brougham. "I call her my baby," she said. "What a dream! What a car! She begs to be blown out on freeways." ▼

ELLEN HINES JOHNSON, DETROIT, MI

▲ Robert Hosley owned a 1940 LaSalle. When he came home from the Navy after World War II, he asked his wife to order a Cadillac for him. But he had to wait until 1950 to get it because they didn't have the money at the time. He has owned 50 since then.

ROBERT HOSLEY, LANSING, MI

◄ Earl Jones' 1949 Cadillac Model 62 is in complete original condition and has never been restored. Earl and his wife were married in 1949 and bought that car to commemorate their wedding date. "We took the family to Lee State Park in South Carolina to go swimming and celebrate," he said.

EARL JONES, FLORENCE, SC

Les Keesee didn't have much money when he was young, but always wanted to own a Cadillac. His first was a 1960 Sedan DeVille. He took that car to California to see the giant redwood trees and drove through this one, which was later leveled in a storm. ▼

LES KEESEE, DUNCANVILLE, TX

▲ Polly and Ed Kendzior photographed their sons Gary and Rene with friend Sonny Szerborn (in the middle) with their 1950 Cadillac coupe in Youngstown, Ohio. Polly recently sold her Fleetwood and is looking forward to buying another Cadillac.

POLLY & ED KENDZIOR, FRANKLIN, PA

Dorothy Kildoo has had eight Cadillacs in her lifetime, "eight dependable old friends that took me through the highways of life. A personal sense of fulfillment courses through my veins each time I open the door to take my place behind the round wheel of freedom." Here she poses with her 1987, which like all the others was bought at Kelly's of Butler. ▼

DOROTHY KILDOO, BUTLER, PA

▲ George Lemkau was nearly buried alive in a 16-foot ditch while laying a water main in Indiana in 1951. As soon as he recovered from the ordeal, he bought a Cadillac and headed for Leech Lake, Minnesota, for a well-earned vacation with his wife. "After being buried alive," he wrote, "I figured the time had come." He still owns a Fleetwood.

GEORGE LEMKAU, DAVENPORT, FL

Arthur and Mickey LeDuc call Florida home now. When they lived in the Detroit area, he worked for General Motors. They took their 1959 Cadillac convertible to their summer cottage in Strawberry Lake, Michigan, where Mickey sat in the car for this picture. ▶

ARTHUR JEAN LeDUC, INVERNESS, FL

William Alexander said he always admired the "fishtail eight" 1955 Fleetwood because it reminded him of the planes he flew in World War II and Korea. He bought one the first chance he had. He still owns the '55 and probably won't ever let it go. ▼   WILLIAM ALEXANDER, EL PASO, TX

Ed McCanna is 92 and drives his sixth Cadillac, a 1992 Brougham, daily. "I expect it to last as long as I will," he wrote. Here, Ed, his wife and daughter are on the running board of his brother's 1928 two-door. ▼

ED McCANNA, ROCKFORD, IL

▲ Josephine Mauro said she has ridden in cars that cost more than a Cadillac, "but they never gave me the comfort of my Cadillac." When she bought her first Cadillac in 1950, a Buick was $1,500 and a Cadillac $2,000. "Why not go first class?" she asked. In this picture she is standing by her 1957 Brougham.

JOSEPHINE MAURO, ENGLEWOOD CLIFFS, NJ

▲ Carlyle Wells bought "Black Beauty" in the late Eighties. It was original with just a few blemishes. Within several months, Carlyle had the car looking like new and took it to his weekend home on Lake Livingston in Texas, where this picture was taken.

CARLYLE WELLS, HOUSTON, TX   49

▲ The night before Calvin and Norma McInturff arrived at the White Sands of Alamagordo, New Mexico, four inches of snow fell. "We were totally unprepared for snow," Norma wrote, "but the Cadillac drove right through it with no trouble at all."

CALVIN & NORMA McINTURFF, BOYCE, VA

Eugene Rudachuk's 1991 Cadillac Fleetwood Brougham is his seventh Cadillac and his fourth Fleetwood Brougham. He likes Fleetwoods because they make him "feel like a king." He bought this '57 Cadillac convertible in 1970 with only 40,000 miles on it. "It still is the best car I ever owned." ▼   EUGENE RUDACHUK, ST. CATHARINES, ONTARIO, CANADA

◄ Carl Morrison's 1959 Series 62 convertible needed care when he bought it in 1975. He paid only $5,455 for it and brought it home to begin restoration. Two years later, it was finished, only to be T-boned by another car. It's back to original condition now after its second restoration.

CARL & PATTY MORRISON, OWINGS, MD

When Trudy Muller bought her 1960 black and pink Cadillac DeVille—"Shiny black with pink top, black with pink print upholstery trimmed with pink leather"—her mother told her that she felt sorry for her. "Why?" Trudy asked. "Because you'll never want anything else," her mother answered. ➤

GERTRUDE MULLER, PHOENIX, AZ

Like many Cadillac owners, Dorothy Wiebe feels safer in a larger car. Her father, Stanley Merkley, owned a 1929 Cadillac limousine, a 1932 V12-engined Cadillac and a 1955 Cadillac. "I used to drive the '32 to school even before I had my driver's license," she wrote. Dorothy and Abram have owned 12 Cadillacs themselves, and she still owns 1977, 1986 and 1989 Fleetwood Broughams. ➤

DOROTHY AND ABRAM WIEBE, WATERLOO, ONTARIO, CANADA

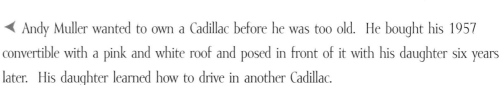

◀ Andy Muller wanted to own a Cadillac before he was too old. He bought his 1957 convertible with a pink and white roof and posed in front of it with his daughter six years later. His daughter learned how to drive in another Cadillac.

ANDY MULLER, DALZELL, SC   51

▲ When Frank Pandolfo traveled 5,500 miles from Alaska to marry Rose DeDonato of Boston, he wanted to leave the church in a black Cadillac. Fifty-two years later, they have eight children and 22 grandchildren, who all love to ride in the family Cadillac. Teenage daughter Lorraine drove Frank to the hospital after he broke his ribs "and handled the Cadillac like a trooper."

FRANK PANDOLFO, WEST YARMOUTH, MA

The little boy enjoying his perch on the back of Harry Peake's 1929 LaSalle convertible is his three-year-old son, Ron. Harry, a clothing salesman for 25 years, said the LaSalle was "one magnificent auto," as were all of the twelve Cadillacs and LaSalles he has owned. Ron apparently agrees. ▼

HARRY PEAKE, GREENSBORO, NC

◄ In August 1941, George Pappas was entrusted by his family to buy a new car to replace one of their current cars. He went to Capitol Cadillac in Washington, D.C., and traded in a 1935 LaSalle for a 1941 four-door Cadillac. Two years later, George was in the Air Force and posed beside the car.

GEORGE PAPPAS, BETHESDA, MD

◄ "I owned a 1957 Cadillac when I saw 'Splashy' (a 1960 Coupe DeVille) in the showroom window," LaVerne Rasmussen wrote. "I made a U-turn, and drove home with a new car." Brenda Rasmussen's 1995 Fleetwood Brougham, "Tuxedo II," sits next to Splashy in the garage. "Splashy is our pride and joy," LaVerne wrote. "The '95 is jealous!"

LAVERNE & BRENDA RASMUSSEN, PINOLE, CA

Hoyn Chan Rim bought a 1987 Fleetwood Brougham as a 17th anniversary gift for his wife. "We felt fantastic," he remembered of the first drive in the car. "We drove the family around Oakton, Virginia." ▼

HOYN CHAN RIM, OAKTON, VA

▲ "I will buy another Cadillac," Jim Roberts wrote. "But I plan on keeping this one for a long time." Jim's favorite trip in his 1955 Fleetwood called "Puddle Jumper" was to Memphis in 1955 when he drove his children to visit their grandparents.

JAMES ROBERTS, SOMERSET, KY

Ero Saccone spent two years as a POW in World War II. Even with resultant back injuries, his first ride in his 1950 Cadillac was a comfortable one, although it was from San Francisco to New York. He and his wife also traveled 80,000 miles touring Europe in the car. ▼ ERO SACCONE, SALINAS, CA

◄ Mathew Schiehsl bought his 1941 Cadillac Fleetwood in 1950 when he was only 17. "I cruised the area of Astoria, Queens, New York," he wrote. "I felt like the king of the mountain. That first car was a standard of excellence to measure all future cars against." He has owned four Cadillacs since then.

MATHEW SCHIEHSL, PALM COAST, FL

Most people save to buy their first Cadillac. Eleanor and Leo Schmoyer won their 1988 Fleetwood Brougham at the Fremont Casino in Las Vegas. The Schmoyers drove their car back home to Crystal, Minnesota, from Las Vegas. Leo drove the Cadillac. He said that was a winning feeling! ➤

LEO SCHMOYER, CRYSTAL, MN

Esther Sulander awoke on Christmas morning 1975 to find a Cadillac Eldorado "under the tree." It was a gift from her husband. Almost as important were the dozen long-stemmed roses added by salesman Oren Ruff. ➤

ESTHER SULANDER, NAPLES, FL

◀ Juanita Stinchcomb's 1990 Fleetwood Brougham will some day belong to her grandson, Jamie. He sat on the armrest of the car when he was little and called himself the King. Juanita's biggest thrill was taking her grandchildren on vacation to Florida and Nashville in her Brougham with an "Elvis" front license plate.

JUANITA STINCHCOMB, CONLEY, GA

◀ Gary Smith always wanted a 1937 Model 90 V16 with the 154-inch wheelbase. He traded his fully restored 1938 Model 90 for this one, which was unrestored at the time. He then set to work restoring it by himself with original parts. At a Classic Car Club of America meet in Indianapolis, he had an opportunity to drive the car around the Speedway.

GARY SMITH, DANVILLE, IN   55

◄ Clayton Tittsworth's 1993 Fleetwood Brougham is his 15th Cadillac in a love affair that began when he bought his 1959 Sedan DeVille. Grandson Kyle enjoys riding in the latest car, while son Michael learned to drive in the first one.

CLAYTON TITTSWORTH, BRANDON, FL

Marcella and Francis Tebo said the most important person Marcella drove in her Cadillac was a deaf nephew who loves cars and trucks. "This one brought a big smile and the OK sign, meaning it was tops with him," Marcella wrote. ▼

MARCELLA TEBO, MENOMINEE, MI

▲ Ira Triplett has had a 77-year love affair with Cadillac that began when he was four years old, sitting behind the wheel of his parents' 1920 seven-passenger touring sedan. His family still has the lap robe that came with the car.

IRA TRIPLETT, LENOIR, NC

▲ "This is my daughter, Sandra and my brother-in-law, David in my father-in-law's Cadillac, a 1942 dark green model with fuzzy-to-the-touch mohair seats," Samuel Wiener wrote. "They are at the bus station waving goodbye to me as I went into the Navy in 1942. The car was the last model made before the assembly line was converted for war production."

SAMUEL WIENER, POMPANO BEACH, FL

J.P. Morton's first Cadillac was a 1946 convertible coupe. It was light blue with a matching leather interior. J.P. used the car to carry family and friends on their 1946 summer vacation to the mountains in upstate New York. ➤

J.P. MORTON, LOS ANGELES, CA

▲ "Some time after we purchased our 1960 Cadillac DeVille, we went on a trip to Daytona Beach," Grace Tucker wrote. "You can see how beautiful the car was on the beach."

GRACE TUCKER, AMISSVILLE, VA

Raymond Volluz bought a Cadillac Superior hearse from a funeral home in Oklahoma and converted it into a family camper. "We needed something heavy enough to pull a horse trailer. The hearse filled the bill." In 1958, his son, Mark, was photographed in front of another hearse/camper, with the caption "Us Texans like 'em long and powerful." ▼

RAYMOND VOLLUZ, AUSTIN, TX

▲ Roy Wilimzig's best vacation was when he took his '57 Coupe DeVille on a 31-day trip through the West and Mexico. In Wyoming, he and three other "cowboys" (Roy is second from the right) posed in front of his car with prized racks.

ROY WILIMZIG, EDWARDSVILLE, IL

CHAPTER THREE

A LOVE AFFAIR WITH CADILLAC

*An historic look at Cadillac
from the early 1900s to today.*

A Love Affair with Cadillac

Founder Henry Leland and grandson circa 1912.

1900-1920
EXCELLENCE FROM THE VERY BEGINNING

The story of Cadillac begins in New England where founder Henry Leland worked in the Springfield Armory during the Civil War as a mechanic and later with Browne & Sharpe as a precision machinist. After moving to Detroit, this entrepreneur started Leland and Faulconer, manufacturing castings, forgings, automotive engines and chassis components.

When the backers of the Detroit Automobile Company wanted to liquidate that company, Leland and his son, Wilfred, were asked to assess the value of the machinery. Leland provided the estimate, but recommended that they not go out of business. Instead, he helped them create the Cadillac Motor Car Company, named after Le Sieur Antoine de la Mothe Cadillac, the founder of the city of Detroit. In just a few months, the very first Model A Cadillac was exhibited at the New York Automobile Show in January 1903.

While the Model A was a good first effort, it was the 1905 Model D that moved Cadillac into prominence. Powered by a four-cylinder engine, the five-passenger touring car had a wood body with an aluminum skin available as an option.

In 1908, three Cadillacs entered the competition for the Dewar Trophy, awarded annually for the most significant automotive advancement. Before this time, parts were hand-fitted by filing and sanding. Cadillacs featured the first interchangeable parts. Three cars were completely disassembled, the parts scrambled and 90 service

1903 Model A runabout

parts exchanged and then put back together. This innovation helped Cadillac endure the 500-mile trial which followed and win the Dewar Trophy.

Another significant milestone happened in 1908 when General Motors made an offer to purchase Cadillac. On July 29, 1909, General Motors acquired Cadillac for $5,969,200. GM President William C. Durant asked the Lelands to continue as managers and to operate the

company as if it were their own.

About the same time, the Fleetwood Metal Body Company was formed in Fleetwood, Pennsylvania. Even then, Cadillac products with sophisticated

Fleetwood custom bodies were built for affluent customers, including movie stars, on chassis supplied by Pierce-Arrow, Packard and, of course, Cadillac. The automobiles they created were masterpieces.

The introduction of the first regular production closed-bodied cars by Cadillac in 1910 was also seen as a benefit to drivers. The self-starter was introduced on 1912 Cadillacs, making it easier for men and women to drive cars because they didn't have to crank start them. Cadillac proudly won the Dewar Trophy a second time, this time for its electric starting-lighting-ignition system.

1912 Model 30 touring

JUST as Cadillac beauty created a vogue car, with its 90-degree, V-type, 8-cylinder engine, in motor car style, so has Cadillac's incomparable can give—performance seemingly unlimited in range performance recreated a vogue for driving. There and variety, so unlabored, so easily controlled, so is an irresistible desire to take the wheel of the zestful yet restful, that once again Cadillac has Cadillac and enjoy what none but a Cadillac-built given the idea of luxury in motoring a new meaning.

More than 50 exclusive body styles by Fisher and Fisher-Fleetwood

CADILLAC

A NOTABLE PRODUCT OF GENERAL MOTORS

1928 advertisement

1920-1930
CARS WITH STYLE AND ELEGANCE

Cadillac production exceeded 20,000 in 1922. Part of that sales success came from the introduction of the Type 61 that came equipped with a standard windshield wiper and rear view mirror. A new era in automobile design was beginning in the Roaring Twenties with the influence of Harley Earl, who established the first styling department by an automobile manufacturer, the General Motors Art and Colour Section, in 1927.

Former General Motors Director of Styling David Holls said, "Before 1927, Cadillac was a good, solid, substantial car. After 1927, the cars had style and elegance."

Earl began his work at Cadillac by designing the smaller, very stylish LaSalle in 1927. Created to fill the gap between Buick and Cadillac in the General Motors lineup, the LaSalle was advertised as a "Companion Car to

1926 Series 314 7-passenger sedan

Cadillac." LaSalle was always considered to be a sportier, more maneuverable Cadillac, similar to the modern Cadillac Catera.

Cadillac LaSalle was the pace car at the 1927 Indianapolis 500. This was the first time a Caddy would pace the race, but certainly not the last. Cadillacs or LaSalles would be the pacesetters five more times, in 1931 (Cadillac Model 370 V12), 1934 (LaSalle), 1937 (LaSalle),

1927 Series 314 dual-cowl phaeton

1973 (Eldorado) and 1992 (Allanté).

In its initial year, LaSalle offered eleven body styles on two wheelbases, plus four Fleetwood designs on a 125-inch wheelbase. LaSalle coupes even had a door on the side that opened to pro-

vide a compartment for golf bags.

Another Cadillac innovation was the first clashless synchromesh transmission in 1929. Now drivers didn't have to double clutch their cars to avoid grinding gears.

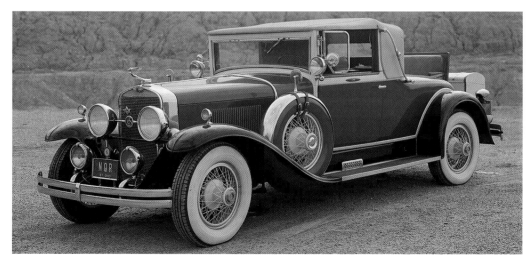

1929 LaSalle 328 convertible coupe

1930 Series 452 5-passenger imperial landaulet by Fleetwood

1930-1940
FOCUSING ON THE DRIVER AND PASSENGERS

The Cadillacs of the Thirties defined classic American sophistication and luxury. With the introduction of V12 and V16 engines, Cadillac led the industry in performance and engineering excellence. Designed by Owen Nacker, the V16 engine powered some of the most exciting Cadillac automobiles. This engine wasn't the only innovative feature, because 1930 V16s also included the first vacuum-assisted "power" brakes. Cadillacs were truly becoming driver responsive!

Cadillac continued to pioneer and exert its leadership in other important engineering advances in this decade. Work began on the automatic transmission at Cadillac in 1932. In 1933, the first independent front suspension appeared on an experimental Cadillac and became a standard feature on the GM lineup for 1934.

1931 Series 452 A dual-cowl phaeton

Bill Mitchell, then only 24 years old, designed the new 1938 Cadillac 60 Special. Bigger than a LaSalle, the 60 Special deleted running boards, featured thin window pillars, chrome-plated door window frames, and was designed to be the transition from chauffeur-driven to owner-driven luxury cars. This car would set styling trends for more than a decade.

1932 Series 370-B V12 Deluxe sport phaeton

65

1940-1950

THE WAR YEARS AND THE GOOD TIMES THAT FOLLOWED

Sophistication, performance and comfort set new standards for the 1941 cars from Cadillac. That year, Cadillac first offered the hydramatic automatic transmission, as well as air conditioning and a gas tank filler cleverly hidden under the left taillight.

Cadillac stopped all civilian automotive production in February 1942 to join the war effort on the homefront. In just 55 days, the first tank powered by two Cadillac V8 engines and two hydramatic transmissions rolled off the line at the Clark Avenue factory in Detroit. Other

1941 Cadillac Fleetwood 60 Special

The 1948 Series 62 coupe was commonly known as a sedanet.

wartime products included M-8 howitzer carriages, the 1944 M-24 light tank and components for the V12 Allison Aircraft engine. Even General Douglas MacArthur's staff car was a Cadillac, a Series 75.

After the war, cars from Cadillac were again ready to create a higher standard for the world. The 1948 Cadillacs had tailfins for the first time, modeled after the Lockheed P-38 fighter plane. Harley Earl had been inspired by that plane's design and couldn't wait to translate the profile to his cars. Because there was so much excitement about this design innovation, dealers would often park cars in their showrooms with the backs facing the window, leaving the taillights on overnight.

The tailfins from these Cadillacs set design trends for decades.

In 1949, Cadillac introduced the high-compression, short-stroke, lightweight "modern" V8. This engine, which was smaller, lighter and very fuel efficient, made Cadillac the fastest, most powerful passenger vehicle in America. At the end of the decade, Briggs Cunningham finished tenth overall in a standard 1950 Cadillac at LeMans.

The Coupe DeVille hardtop was also introduced in 1949, earning Cadillac *Motor Trend*'s first "Car of the Year" award.

1949 Series 62 coupe

1950-1960
The Height of Opulence

1952 Series 62 sedan

Some of the most significant Cadillacs came off the assembly line during this amazing decade. General Motors held its "Mid Century Motorama" at New York City's elegant Waldorf Astoria Hotel in January 1950. Among the featured cars was the Cadillac Debutante, which was inspired by the stage play "The Solid Gold Cadillac." In June of that year,

Fortune magazine held a survey among its readers, asking the question, "What car do you think you will buy next?" Cadillac led the survey and also ranked "best looking" and "best value" among luxury models.

Cadillac celebrated its 50th anniversary in 1952 with a series of "golden anniversary" models. The introduction of power steering as standard equipment was an engineering enhancement that year.

In 1953, Cadillac introduced the Eldorado, which was the first postwar custom luxury car. This was a magnificent machine, with the industry's first wraparound windshield and visors, or "frenched" headlights. Special equipment included a metal convertible boot, cut-down doors, leather upholstery, chrome wire wheels, enhanced styling and signal-seeking radio. The Eldorado sold for $7,750, which was considered a great deal of money at the time, but still an excellent investment.

68 *President Dwight Eisenhower standing in a 1953 Cadillac Eldorado.*

1955 Cadillac Eldorado Brougham show car

Restyling efforts to the 1954 Eldorado featured the "Dagmar" front bumper guard design, named after the voluptuous television star of "Jerry Lester's House Party." Four-way power seats were also introduced that year.

The 1957 Eldorado Brougham was truly a custom Cadillac. This car featured new quad headlights and a pillarless four-door design. The center-opening doors offered unobstructed entry to the front or rear seats. Standard equipment included low-profile tires, a self-opening and closing trunk, air suspension, air conditioning and personal vanities, including a small bottle of Arpege perfume. With a brushed stainless steel roof, the Eldorado Brougham had a look like no other car.

Harley Earl's 1959 Cadillac was the ultimate translation of jet aircraft design. This car has achieved cult status and was the subject of a U.S. Postal Service commemorative stamp in 1996. Fans of the Fifties look to the 1959 Cadillac as a true icon of that amazing decade.

1958 Cadillac Fleetwood 60 Special

1960-1970

REFINEMENT AND INNOVATION

The flamboyant tailfins continued to be refined through 1964 when Cadillac built its three millionth car. However, design enhancements were complemented by several engineering innovations that were introduced in this decade.

In 1962, Cadillac models featured cornering lights and dual circuit braking, both key safety innovations. Also new for 1964 was automatic climate control, which provided "set it and forget it" control of both air conditioning and heating. A welcome cold-weather climate option was electrically heated seats, which first appeared on 1966 models.

In 1967, Cadillac introduced the totally redesigned front-wheel-drive Eldorado. This personal luxury car was built on a completely new chassis. Higher levels of performance were achieved in

Mrs. John F. Kennedy and 1959 Cadillac limousine featuring a custom, transparent roof.

1961 Series 62 Cadillac convertible

1968 with the new 472-cubic-inch engine and again with the 1970 Eldorado, which featured a 500-cubic-inch V8 engine. Track Master anti-skid transistorized rear braking was also available. A magazine survey ranked the Cadillac "most comfortable and easiest to control" among ten German, British and American luxury cars.

A 1961 version of the elegant Cadillac jewelry advertisements.

1964 Cadillac Fleetwood limousine

1970-1980
A WORLD OF
NEW CHALLENGES

Passenger security and environmental protection were the focus of Cadillac innovation in the Seventies. Fuel economy had always been a Cadillac trademark, despite the cars' size and luxury. In this decade, engines were designed for better fuel efficiency and reduced emissions.

In 1971, in order to reduce lead emissions which resulted from the use of premium or high octane gasoline, engines were designed to run on regular fuel. By 1975, the cars were engineered to operate using both regular unleaded fuel and pollution-reducing catalytic converters.

For Cadillac's 70th anniversary year in 1972, many styling refinements were introduced. An improved bumper-crash absorption system was introduced on 1973 Cadillacs. Driver and front seat occupant safety air bags were offered in 1974, 1975 and 1976 models.

The five millionth Cadillac rolled off

1976 Seville by Cadillac

1976 Fleetwood Eldorado convertible

the assembly line in June 1973, and yearly production was running at 300,000 or more.

Cadillac introduced the new internationally sized Seville in May 1975. This car was a more compact and maneuverable Cadillac with generous interior dimensions and enhanced fuel economy. Seville featured electronic fuel injection as standard equipment.

As America celebrated its 200th birthday, Cadillac introduced a bicentennial edition of the Eldorado convertible. This patriotic 1976 model was white with red and blue pinstriping, white leather seating with red piping and wheel discs with white inserts.

The Eldorado for 1979 offered a

combination of engineering features not found in any other car, including front-wheel drive, four-wheel independent suspension and an electronic fuel-injected V8 engine. While shorter in length, head and leg room were greater in the front and rear seats, and there was more usable trunk space.

1977 Fleetwood Brougham d'Elegance

1980 Cadillac Seville Eleganté

1980-1990

NORTHSTAR RISING

The all-new 1980 Seville featured sheer edges and dramatic styling, unlike any other American-built car on the road. For the first time, Seville shared a front-wheel-drive chassis with Eldorado.

John O. Grettenberger, who was named general manager on January 10, 1984, would lead Cadillac for more than 13 years—the longest tenure of any general manager.

As the nation began to enjoy a healthier economic climate, sales of luxury cars increased. Cadillac enjoyed excellent results in 1984, with calendar-year sales of 320,017. The convertible returned to Cadillac that year. Production was limited to 2,000 Eldorado Biarritz convertibles.

The 1987 Allanté luxury two-door convertible was unique in many ways. The body was designed and manufactured by the Italian firm Pininfarina in Turin, Italy. Bodies were flown to Detroit on 747s for assembly of the powertrain and chassis, creating the world's longest assembly line—a distance of 3,300 miles. This front-wheel-drive sports car pioneered many Cadillac innovations, including traction control and the Northstar engine.

In the late Eighties, Cadillac engineering, manufacturing and design staff

1984 Eldorado Biarritz convertible

teamed up to introduce such innovations as the elegant 1989 DeVille and Fleetwood.

At the end of the decade, the 1989 Fleetwood featured a full range of

Cadillac styling cues: a subtle suggestion of fins along with rear fender skirts, long, low protective side molding treatment and a stylish chrome radiator grille and wreath and crest.

1984 Coupe DeVille

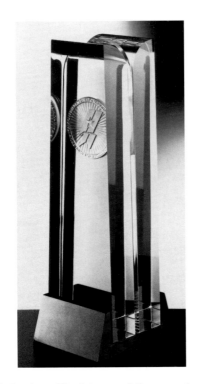

Malcolm Baldrige National Quality Award, 1990

1990-2000
THE CONTINUING REWARDS OF QUALITY

Cadillac was once again recognized as a world leader in quality when the company was awarded the prestigious Malcolm Baldrige National Quality Award in 1990. Cadillac was the first automobile manufacturer to win the Baldrige and, as of 1997, was the only automobile manufacturer to ever receive this honor.

In 1992, the introduction of the totally redesigned Eldorado and Seville received additional worldwide acclaim.

Seville was the recipient of *Motor Trend's* "Car of the Year" honors as well as numerous other awards. A year later, Cadillac again created a higher standard in the area of automotive engineering with the Northstar System. The highly acclaimed Northstar System of power and state-of-the-art technology now provides Cadillac drivers an unparalleled balance of efficiency, power, control and safety.

In 1993, the Fleetwood Brougham was completely redesigned and continued the long-standing Cadillac tradition as the choice for professional car conversions, including the presidential limousine.

In 1996, power output for the Northstar engine was increased to 300 hp in the DeVille Concours, Eldorado Touring Coupe and Seville STS.

For the 1997 model year, Cadillac added StabiliTrak, an exclusive safety technology to the Seville STS, Eldorado Touring Coupe and DeVille Concours. In addition, Cadillac redesigned the DeVille, adding a new model, the d'Elegance, which offers a distinctive expression of classic American luxury and the highest level of comfort and classic luxury amenities. Side airbags were also added to all DeVille models. The Catera, Cadillac's entry luxury sedan, was also introduced for 1997.

1993 Fleetwood Brougham Presidential limousine

As Cadillac moves toward its second century, this innovative car company proudly continues a rich tradition of bringing sophistication, performance, safety and innovative technology to the market.

1997 Cadillac DeVille d'Elegance

CADILLAC OWNERS HONOR ROLL

*The Fleetwood and Brougham owners
who have participated in the Cadillac Memories program.*

A

A. Inc.
16 Cadillacs, Easley, SC

Mr. Leonard A. Aaro
8 Cadillacs, Rochester, MN

Lloyd C. Abbott
1 Cadillac, Hot Springs, AR

Arthur Abel
4 Cadillacs, Hasbrouck Hts., NJ

Mr. Bernard R. Abels
8 Cadillacs, Pittsburgh, PA

Ms. Alice C. Abercrombie
12 Cadillacs, Mobile, AL

Mr. Isaac Aboud
1 Cadillac, Gaithersburg, MD

Loren E. Abrams
1 Cadillac, Webster, NY

Mr. Robert K. Ackerson
1 Cadillac, Niagara Falls, NY

Mr. Milford D. Acrey
Decatur, TX

Mr. Jerry J. Acuff
5 Cadillacs, Satsuma, AL

Bob Adams
5 Cadillacs, El Monte, CA

Harold & Mary Adams
4 Cadillacs, Birmingham, AL

Mrs. Jacqueline C. Adams
3 Cadillacs, Oak Ridge, TN

Ms. Marlene A. Adams, Jr.
6 Cadillacs, Niagara Falls, NY

Mr. Raymond C. Adams
3 Cadillacs, Montgomery, AL

Mr. Richard E. Adams, Jr.
3 Cadillacs, Oklahoma City, OK

Mr. Robert L. Adams
2 Cadillacs, Elkton, KY

Mr. Robert H. Adams
2 Cadillacs, Merrimac, MA

Mr. Wayne L. Adams, Sr.
1 Cadillac, Dolton, IL

Mrs. Catherine H. Addington
15 Cadillacs, Saint John, WA

Mr. Harry L. Addis
3 Cadillacs, Edinburg, TX

Mrs. Margaret Adkins
1 Cadillac, Montgomery, AL

Ms. Willa M. Adkisson
3 Cadillacs, Mount Olive, AL

Mr. Julius J. Adleman
5 Cadillacs, Riverside, CA

Mr. Ardelle R. Adler
2 Cadillacs, Rochester, MN

Mr. Samuel Agolino
West Pittston, PA

Mr. Dennis E. Ahern
8 Cadillacs, Grand Island, NY

Mr. Vern A. Ahlers
8 Cadillacs, Owatonna, MN

Mr. Norman E. Ahlswede
4 Cadillacs, Fort Myers, FL

Mr. Loren W. Aicher
1 Cadillac, Somerset, WI

Ms. Geneva Aide
2 Cadillacs, Mount Hope, WV

Mr. Hugh B. Akers, Jr.
5 Cadillacs, Panama City, FL

Mr. Clifford T. Akey
1 Cadillac, Stillwater, MN

Mr. John A. Akin
10 Cadillacs, Niceville, FL

Mr. John Alba
Albertson, NY

Mr. Richard Alberico
6 Cadillacs, Rome, NY

Ms. Gertrude H. Albert
2 Cadillacs, San Antonio, TX

Mr. E. Pete Albertson
5 Cadillacs, Winnemucca, NV

Mr. Richard H. Albitz
5 Cadillacs, Houston, TX

Janet E. & Harold D. Albright
28 Cadillacs, State College, PA

Allen W. Aldred, M.D.
1 Cadillac, Fort Wayne, IN

Ms. Elizabeth K. Aldridge
1 Cadillac, Rosston, TX

J. Aleksiewicz
1 Cadillac, Calgary, AB

Mr. Frank L. Alexander
1 Cadillac, Independence, MO

Mr. Joe Alexander
18 Cadillacs, Stewartstown, PA

Mr. Lowey Alexander
4 Cadillacs, San Pablo, CA

Ms. Mirian B. Alexander
3 Cadillacs, Columbia, MD

Mr. Velda B. Alexander
2 Cadillacs, San Antonio, TX

Mr. William H. Alexander, Jr.
4 Cadillacs, El Paso, TX

Mr. Willis P. Alexander
4 Cadillacs, Coushatta, LA

Mr. Gaylon K. Alfrey
8 Cadillacs, Sedalia, MO

Mr. Tom F. Alioto
3 Cadillacs, Punta Gorda, FL

Mr. D. Allan
2 Cadillacs, Surrey, BC

Norman Allard
3 Cadillacs, N. Providence, RI

Mrs. Charlie Mae Allen
4 Cadillacs, Houston, TX

Mr. Clifford O. Allen
2 Cadillacs, Appleton, MN

Ms. Dorothy E. Allen
7 Cadillacs, Nashville, TN

Mr. Ellis B. Allen
1 Cadillac, Jackson, MI

Mr. Fred E. Allen
11 Cadillacs, Mt. Pleasant, TX

Mr. Kenneth W. Allen
2 Cadillacs, Gaylord, MI

Mr. Raymond L. Allen
1 Cadillac, Buffalo, NY

Sherwood Allen
9 Cadillacs, Saginaw, MI

William Allen
8 Cadillacs, Hollywood, FL

Mr. Murry Allewitz
15 Cadillacs, Houston, TX

John B. Alley
4 Cadillacs, Carson, CA

William Alley, Jr.
2 Cadillacs, Wichita, KS

Mr. Alexander V. Allis
28 Cadillacs, San Antonio, TX

Mrs. Vivian Alls
14 Cadillacs, Daleville, VA

Mr. Harry & Nellie Alspach
21 Cadillacs, Merrillville, IN

Mr. Lewis C. Alston
3 Cadillacs, Dayton, OH

Mr. William Alsup
4 Cadillacs, Gary, IN

Anthony & Angela Altadonna
8 Cadillacs, Saint Louis, MO

Ms. Dorothy Altier
3 Cadillacs, New Lexington, OH

Judith Altomonte
3 Cadillacs, North York, ON

Eugene Alverson
3 Cadillacs, Chester, SD

Mr. John T. Alvey
14 Cadillacs, Sioux City, IA

John B. Alwran
2 Cadillacs, Orange Park, FL

Mr. Manuel Amaro
1 Cadillac, Wichita, KS

J. Amatuli
1 Cadillac, Flushing, NY

Elvin & Lucile Amen
9 Cadillacs, Bartlesville, OK

Mr. Sylvan Ames
12 Cadillacs, Lincoln, IA

Mr. Frank S. Amico
4 Cadillacs, Flushing, NY

Mr. Henry C. Ammons
3 Cadillacs, Asheboro, NC

Morton Amon
6 Cadillacs, Havertown, PA

Dr. Anthony F. Amorosi
8 Cadillacs, Springfield, PA

Mr. Kenneth A. Amundson
1 Cadillac, Minneapolis, MN

Lawrence Amyotte
3 Cadillacs, Mississauga, ON

Mr. Walter Anders
1 Cadillac, Winnipeg, MB

Mr. Lloyd Andersen
2 Cadillacs, Naples, FL

Mr. Alan D. Anderson
3 Cadillacs, Savannah, GA

Mr. Albert W. Anderson
9 Cadillacs, Travelers Rst., SC

Mr. Arthur Anderson
10 Cadillacs, Finley, ND

Ms. Betty L. Anderson
12 Cadillacs, Indian Wells, CA

Mrs. Betty Augusta Anderson
3 Cadillacs, Willingboro, NJ

Buford S. Anderson
7 Cadillacs, Herndon, VA

Mr. Charles B. Anderson
1 Cadillac, Sun City Center, FL

Mr. Don D. Anderson
3 Cadillacs, Midland, TX

Mr. Donald Anderson
4 Cadillacs, Ontario, CA

Mr. Donald A. Anderson
3 Cadillacs, Albion, NY

Mr. Elmer V. Anderson
13 Cadillacs, Key West, FL

Mrs. Emerene Anderson
12 Cadillacs, Tremonton, UT

Ms. Ethel W. Anderson
1 Cadillac, Knoxville, TN

Mr. Floyd Anderson
4 Cadillacs, Oshkosh, WI

James D. Anderson
2 Cadillacs, Pampa, TX

Dr. L.T. & Janet Anderson
2 Cadillacs, Cherryville, NC

Mr. Lowell M. Anderson
4 Cadillacs, Linden, MI

Ms. Lucille Anderson
2 Cadillacs, Santa Monica, CA

Mr. Melvin G. Anderson
5 Cadillacs, Ludington, MI

Norval Anderson
2 Cadillacs, Scarborough, ON

Mr. Robert K. Anderson
4 Cadillacs, Denver, CO

Robert S. Anderson
2 Cadillacs, Waukegan, IL

Robert C. Anderson
3 Cadillacs, Middletown, NJ

Thomas Anderson
10 Cadillacs, Saint Louis, MO

Ms. Truth J. Anderson
2 Cadillacs, Las Cruces, NM

Mrs. Vernon Anderson
3 Cadillacs, Radford, VA

Ms. Beryl A. Anding
11 Cadillacs, Arena, WI

Ms. Kathryn A. Andraski
10 Cadillacs, Scottsdale, AZ

Debra Lynn Andres
1 Cadillac, North Ridgeville, OH

Travis Andress
2 Cadillacs, Enterprise, AL

Mr. Bliss Andrews
4 Cadillacs, Rosemount, MN

C.H. Andrews
3 Cadillacs, Starkville, MS

Mr. Gordon C. Andrews
1 Cadillac, Columbus, OH

Mr. Henry D. Andrews
1 Cadillac, Vicksburg, MS

Mr. William M. Andrews
7 Cadillacs, Bahama, NC

Mr. Carl C. Andrus
3 Cadillacs, Orange, TX

Mr. Victor Andujar
Elmont, NY

Gary R. San Angelo
4 Cadillacs, W. Covina, CA

Mr. Florian Angelwicz
30 Cadillacs, Algonac, MI

V. Angiuli
1 Cadillac, Montreal, QC

Wallace P. Ansardi
2 Cadillacs, Meraux, LA

Mr. Patrick Anselmo
1 Cadillac, Staten Island, NY

Mr. Robert A. Antrobius
3 Cadillacs, Tallmadge, OH

Mr. Winfred P. Appelt
3 Cadillacs, Pasadena, TX

Mr. Theodore Appleby
6 Cadillacs, Harrisburg, PA

Mr. Erskine G. Arbeiter
3 Cadillacs, Corvallis, OR

Mr. Gerald G. Arbes
5 Cadillacs, Owego, NY

Herman & Monteize Archer
2 Cadillacs, Arlington, TX

Ms. Margaret Armatage
10 Cadillacs, W. Vancouver, BC

Mr. Kenneth D. Armbrust
2 Cadillacs, Cudahy, WI

Mr. Liston Armentrout
3 Cadillacs, Toledo, OH

Armelia & Thomas C. Armsterd
2 Cadillacs, Godfrey, IL

Ms. Almetta Armstrong
3 Cadillacs, Candor, NC

Mr. Edwin M. Armstrong
1 Cadillac, Mauldin, SC

Mr. Howard J. Armstrong
2 Cadillacs, Grafton, WV

Robert & Gloria Armstrong
Bailey, CO

Mr. Clifford M. Arneson
1 Cadillac, Tolley, ND

Ms. Jean N. Arnette
3 Cadillacs, San Antonio, TX

Mr. George E. Arnold
3 Cadillacs, Berkshire, NY

Mr. James Arnold
4 Cadillacs, Oakland, CA

Mr. William N. Arnold
1 Cadillac, Perry, GA

Marie Arnone
1 Cadillac, Rochester, NY

Mr. W. Arnott
6 Cadillacs, Brampton, ON

Martin Arribi
2 Cadillacs, Quebec, QC

Mr. Joe Q. Arro
5 Cadillacs, Caseyville, IL

Mr. Gilbert E. Artman
1 Cadillac, Winter Springs, FL

Mr. Al Artuso
8 Cadillacs, Henderson, NV

Mr. Stanley H. Arvey
2 Cadillacs, Athens, WV

Ms. Helen W. Asbury
2 Cadillacs, McDonough, GA

Mr. William P. Asplen, Jr.
14 Cadillacs, Cambridge, MD

Thomas Astarita
7 Cadillacs, Hernando Beach, FL

Edgar & Carol Ater
13 Cadillacs, Parrish, FL

Mrs. Sue A. Atha
9 Cadillacs, Catlin, IL

Mr. Donald G. Atkins
9 Cadillacs, Merritt Is., FL

Mr. Nathaniel R. Atkins
2 Cadillacs, Fresno, CA

George E. & Doris W. Atkinson
14 Cadillacs, Erie, PA

Mr. Joseph J. Atkociunas
27 Cadillacs, Destin, FL

Mr. Thomas Audia
3 Cadillacs, Lombard, IL

Mr. Willis R. Auer
1 Cadillac, Canton, TX

Mr. & Mrs. Sterling N. Augustine
2 Cadillacs, Sullivan, IL

Mr. Clarence Austin
4 Cadillacs, Lynchburg, VA

Mr. Claude B. Austin
4 Cadillacs, Taylorsville, NC

Mr. Robert V. Avant
1 Cadillac, Marshall, TX

Mr. Harry Avedisian
1 Cadillac, Fowler, CA

Mr. Joseph L. Aven
3 Cadillacs, Mountain Brook, AL

Ms. Lynne S. Averett
2 Cadillacs, Houston, TX

Ms. Louise H. Avery
4 Cadillacs, Opelika, AL

Mr. Andrew Avila
7 Cadillacs, Glendale, CA

Ms. Eva Avinger
3 Cadillacs, Pittsburgh, PA

Mr. Clarke G. Axelson
1 Cadillac, Van Buren, AR

Mrs. Raechel H. Axmear
1 Cadillac, Keswick, IA

Wavelene Ayres
1 Cadillac, Orlando, FL

Mr. Richard Azar
8 Cadillacs, Atlanta, GA

B

Mr. Nova V. Babb
Springfield, MO

Mr. Robert S. Babin
1 Cadillac, Rncho. Pls. Vrd., CA

Mr. William L. Babineau
5 Cadillacs, Rice Lake, WI

Mr. Jerry Back
4 Cadillacs, Arcadia, IN

Mr. R.C. Backus
28 Cadillacs, Mexico, NY

Mr. Charles Badgett
4 Cadillacs, Clarksville, TN

Mr. B. Badoor
1 Cadillac, Windsor, ON

John Baganakis
14 Cadillacs, Williamsburg, VA

Kenneth R. Bagatelle
8 Cadillacs, Freeport, NY

Mr. Raymond G. Bagby
7 Cadillacs, Villa Ridge, IL

Mr. Roy L. Baggett
13 Cadillacs, Killeen, TX

Raymond M. Baggiani
8 Cadillacs, San Mateo, CA

Colonel Kenneth R. Baile
7 Cadillacs, Columbus, OH

Bailey-Kirk Funeral Home
4 Cadillacs, Princeton, WV

Ms. Edith Bailey
2 Cadillacs, Mitchellville, IA

Mr. Garrison B. Bailey
4 Cadillacs, Agua Dulce, TX

Mr. Robert E. Bailey
3 Cadillacs, Redwood City, CA

Toya I. Bailey
13 Cadillacs, Starkville, MS

Mr. William C. Bailey
1 Cadillac, Lockhart, SC

Mr. Richard Bailly
3 Cadillacs, West Orange, NJ

Mr. Clarence D. Bain, Jr.
20 Cadillacs, Destin, FL

Mr. Carl D. Bainbridge
1 Cadillac, Kingsport, TN

Mr. Joseph Bair
3 Cadillacs, Mount Laurel, NJ

Mr. Harry P. Baisley
2 Cadillacs, Monsey, NY

Mr. Ancil D. Baker
3 Cadillacs, San Rafael, CA

Mr. Edwin G. Baker
3 Cadillacs, West Columbia, SC

Mr. Fred P. Baker
6 Cadillacs, Fountain Vly., CA

Mr. Hubert M. Baker
11 Cadillacs, Poplar Bluff, MO

Ms. Irene R. Baker
5 Cadillacs, Carthage, NC

Mr. Leo Baker
2 Cadillacs, Augusta, GA

Mr. Robert C. Baker
2 Cadillacs, Buckhead, GA

Ronald E. Baker, Jr.
6 Cadillacs, Westfield, MA

Mr. William K. Baker
4 Cadillacs, Gaithersburg, MD

Mr. William R. Baker
2 Cadillacs, Knox City, TX

Mr. Carrol M. Bakken
1 Cadillac, Garner, IA

Mr. Gordon P. Bakken
6 Cadillacs, Fergus Falls, MN

Mrs. M. Bakken
1 Cadillac, Weyburn, SK

Ms. Lillian Baldassari
4 Cadillacs, San Francisco, CA

Mr. Daune H. Baldwin
5 Cadillacs, Edmond, OK

Mr. George H. Baldwin
Bridgeport, IL

Mr. Herbert Baldwin, Jr.
7 Cadillacs, Frankfort, IN

Mrs. Hallie V. Ball
5 Cadillacs, S. Charleston, WV

Mr. James C. Ballard
5 Cadillacs, Henderson, NV

Mr. Cletus E. Ballweg
3 Cadillacs, Saint Marys, OH

Mrs. Beatrice Balsam
8 Cadillacs, Clementon, NJ

Mr. Richard N. Bamburg
4 Cadillacs, Calhoun, LA

Mr. William T. Bame
3 Cadillacs, Sebastian, FL

Ms. Genevieve K. Banas
1 Cadillac, St. Petersburg, FL

Stanley Banas
33 Cadillacs, Chicago, IL

Mr. Albert Banasky
3 Cadillacs, Portsmouth, VA

Mrs. Anna R. Bandsma
3 Cadillacs, Port Neches, TX

Greg & Midge Banister
4 Cadillacs, Arnold, MD

Mr. William Banks
1 Cadillac, Redding, CA

Willie Banks
16 Cadillacs, Kansas City, MO

John Bannan
1 Cadillac, Buckhorn, ON

Mr. Robert C. Banta
10 Cadillacs, Phoenix, AZ

Mr. Andrew Banyas
10 Cadillacs, Indianapolis, IN

Bernice Barber
50 Cadillacs, Washington, DC

Mr. Walter Barber, Jr.
2 Cadillacs, Bennington, VT

Nello R. & Shirley Barbieri
1 Cadillac, Clarksdale, MS

Mr. Kenneth E. Barbour
2 Cadillacs, Hampton, VA

Mr. James J. Barca
14 Cadillacs, Berwyn, IL

Mr. Harold Bare
8 Cadillacs, York, PA

Pete C. Barengo
6 Cadillacs, Reno, NV

Mr. George Barenick
3 Cadillacs, Indiana, PA

Mr. James E. Barham
7 Cadillacs, Springfield, IL

Mrs. Agnes Barilich
2 Cadillacs, South Bend, IN

J.D. Barkley
5 Cadillacs, Sharpsburg, NC

Mr. Leon Barlas
5 Cadillacs, Petaluma, CA

Mr. Gene R. Barnes
11 Cadillacs, Hamilton, OH

J. Darrel Barnes,
1 Cadillac, Estes Park, CO

Pearl E. & Leona Barnes
4 Cadillacs, Preemption, IL

Mr. Peter Barnesky
3 Cadillacs, Windsor, ON

Mr. Ellis L. Barr
9 Cadillacs, Gainesville, FL

Mr. Charles M. Barrack
10 Cadillacs, Trinidad, CO

Mr. Carl Barrett
5 Cadillacs, Holly Springs, GA

Colonel James E. Barrett
16 Cadillacs, Fort Myers, FL

Svea N. Barrish
1 Cadillac, Redding, CT

Mr. Paul V. Barron
1 Cadillac, Lubbock, TX

Mr. William C. Barron
7 Cadillacs, Hyattsville, MD

Ms. Virginia Barry
3 Cadillacs, Fort Calhoun, NE

Kathleen M. Barta
2 Cadillacs, Brunswick, OH

Mr. Robert R. Bartel
8 Cadillacs, Youngstown, OH

Mr. Manuel C. Barthelemy
5 Cadillacs, Pt. A. La Hache, LA

Mr. Robert N. Bartholomew
2 Cadillacs, Littleton, CO

Mr. Richard E. Bartlebaugh
4 Cadillacs, Coshocton, OH

Ms. Ella D. Bartlett
5 Cadillacs, Detroit, MI

Mr. Lewis D. Barton
4 Cadillacs, Bowie, MD

Loren & Luella Bartzat
26 Cadillacs, Phoenix, AZ

Mr. Burton Barzelay
6 Cadillacs, Boynton Beach, FL

Mari Jo Basford
2 Cadillacs, Philipsburg, PA

Mr. Benny R. Basile
12 Cadillacs, Sarasota, FL

Ms. Alene L. Bass
8 Cadillacs, Tampa, FL

Hobart J. Bastian
Goleta, CA

Mr. William Bataille
2 Cadillacs, Clark, NJ

Mr. George H. Bates
3 Cadillacs, Burt, NY

Ms. Iva B. Bates
6 Cadillacs, Traverse City, MI

Mr. John B. Bates
6 Cadillacs, Hoover, AL

Mortimer B. Bates
4 Cadillacs, Quincy, FL

Myrtle Bateson
6 Cadillacs, Auburn, MI

Nicholas P. Battista
11 Cadillacs, Lake Zurich, IL

Ms. M.C. Battle
4 Cadillacs, Altadena, CA

Mr. Joseph M. Batyski
15 Cadillacs, Salem, OH

Mr. Ernest T. Bauer
5 Cadillacs, American Fls., ID

Mr. Kenneth E. Bauer
20 Cadillacs, Davis, IL

Mr. Larry D. Bauer
3 Cadillacs, Encino, CA

Mr. Robert D. Bauerle
5 Cadillacs, Sausalito, CA

Mr. Robert M. Baughn
3 Cadillacs, Florissant, MO

Mr. Raymond A. Bausch
4 Cadillacs, St. Petersburg, FL

Mr. Robert C. Bausman
12 Cadillacs, Safety Harbor, FL

Mr. Anthony D. Baviello
3 Cadillacs, Mamaroneck, NY

Inderjit Bawa
4 Cadillacs, West Chester, OH

Mr. William D. Bayer
6 Cadillacs, Fort Myers, FL

Mr. George C. Bayless
5 Cadillacs, Lake City, FL

Mr. Bernard Bazemore
10 Cadillacs, Savannah, GA

Mr. Robert C. Beach
6 Cadillacs, Holiday, FL

Bert B. Beadle
22 Cadillacs, Greenwood, IN

Mr. Ralph Bealer
1 Cadillac, Norristown, PA

Opal M. Beall
4 Cadillacs, N. Little Rock, AR

Mr. John R. Beam
3 Cadillacs, North Augusta, SC

Homer Bean
2 Cadillacs, Findlay, OH

Mr. Elby L. Beard
6 Cadillacs, Brackettville, TX

Ms. Maggie K. Beard
Rockingham, NC

Ms. Jess W. Beasley
10 Cadillacs, Hendersonville, TN

Mrs. Sylvia B. Beasley
3 Cadillacs, Aberdeen, MS

C.J. Beauchamp
2 Cadillacs, Omaha, NE

Mr. Guy J. Beaulieu
2 Cadillacs, Surfside Bch., SC

Gerald Beaupre
2 Cadillacs, Dundas, ON

Mr. D.G. Bechtel
6 Cadillacs, Springfield, MO

Mr. Clyde Beck
10 Cadillacs, Evansville, IN

Richard Beck
1 Cadillac, Lehigh Acres, FL

Mr. Albert E. Becker
17 Cadillacs, Key Col. Bch., FL

Mrs. Hallie S. Beckerdite
5 Cadillacs, Clemmons, NC

Mr. William W. Beckett
14 Cadillacs, Lakeland, FL

Mr. Donald E. Beckman
Sebring, FL

John O. & Ruth D. Beckman
Delhi, IA

Mr. W. Beckman
1 Cadillac, Lethbridge, AB

Ms. Edna Becton
2 Cadillacs, Mobile, AL

Mr. Paul Bedenbaugh
15 Cadillacs, Saginaw, MI

Mr. Stanley A. Bednarz
3 Cadillacs, Warren, MI

Ms. Bobbie G. Bego
2 Cadillacs, Goliad, TX

Mrs. Myra E. Behm
2 Cadillacs, Neenah, WI

Mr. Harry K. Beitsch
13 Cadillacs, Orlando, FL

Mr. Amos E. Belardo
2 Cadillacs, Delray Beach, FL

Mr. Jack A. Bell
1 Cadillac, Mt. Pleasant, SC

Mr. John D. Bell, III
16 Cadillacs, No. Palm Beach, FL

Mr. Richard W. Bell
4 Cadillacs, Cedar Rapids, IA

Mr. Robert S. Bell
2 Cadillacs, Springfield, OH

Dr. Spencer Y. Bell
7 Cadillacs, Knoxville, TN

Mr. Lester E. Bellinger
6 Cadillacs, Fort Collins, CO

Vincent A. & Virginia H. Bellomo
4 Cadillacs, Satellite Bch., FL

R. Belluomini
Fremont, CA

Mr. Daniel T. Belmont
2 Cadillacs, Covington, KY

George Belson
10 Cadillacs, Kalamazoo, MI

Mr. Arthur V. Bender
10 Cadillacs, Sun City West, AZ

Mrs. Olga R. Bender
5 Cadillacs, Mesa, AZ

Mr. Norman L. Bendinger
12 Cadillacs, Long Beach, CA

Ms. Helen Bendler
14 Cadillacs, Indianapolis, IN

Reginald Beneby
22 Cadillacs, East Elmhurst, NY

Ms. Clara E. Benecki
2 Cadillacs, Newark, DE

Ms. Diane Benedetto
3 Cadillacs, Boca Raton, FL

Mr. Salvatore J. Benelli
9 Cadillacs, Boca Raton, FL

Mr. James Benes
3 Cadillacs, Saugatuck, MI

Gailard C. Benham
3 Cadillacs, Weatherford, TX

Mr. William F. Benneke
10 Cadillacs, Redwood City, CA

Mrs. Francis Bennett
5 Cadillacs, Clyde, TX

James L. Bennett
3 Cadillacs, Winchester, KY

Mr. Noel Bennett
Irvington, NJ

Rose Marie Bennett
5 Cadillacs, San Antonio, TX

Wallace Bennett
2 Cadillacs, North York, ON

Dr. Robert A. Benninger
6 Cadillacs, Cape Coral, FL

Patricia Benoist
1 Cadillac, Natchez, MS

Mr. Foster W. Bens
15 Cadillacs, La Mirada, CA

Ms. M. Bensette
24 Cadillacs, Calgary, AB

Mr. George H. Benson
3 Cadillacs, Albany, NY

Mr. Gerald L. Benson
19 Cadillacs, Lodi, OH

Ms. Ethel G. Benton
5 Cadillacs, Huntsville, AL

Dr. George W. Bentzel
1 Cadillac, York, PA

Mr. Don Berchem
2 Cadillacs, La Porte, IN

Denfred J. Bergeaux
5 Cadillacs, Houston, TX

Mr. Alex Berger
30 Cadillacs, Mission, KS

Mrs. Thelma Berger
11 Cadillacs, Lynn, MA

Ms. Anita L. Berglund
23 Cadillacs, Sun City, AZ

Robert Bruce Bergmann, M.D.
5 Cadillacs, Massapequa, NY

Richard Bergquist
6 Cadillacs, Litchfield, CT

Mr. Bernard Berman
59 Cadillacs, Allentown, PA

Mr. Philip I. Berman
57 Cadillacs, Allentown, PA

Mr. Shepherd Berman
3 Cadillacs, Manhasset, NY

Mrs. D. Bernachi
1 Cadillac, Amherstburg, ON

Mr. Francis L. Bernarde
1 Cadillac, Binghamton, NY

Mr. Leslie M. Bernstein
5 Cadillacs, Bronxville, NY

Mrs. Verne C. Bernstein
1 Cadillac, Boynton Beach, FL

Mr. Nolan P. Bernucho
2 Cadillacs, Morgan City, LA

Mr. Roy J. Berrier, Sr.
1 Cadillac, Lexington, NC

Mr. Jack Berry
21 Cadillacs, Anderson, IN

Mrs. Sunshine M. Berry
10 Cadillacs, High Springs, FL

Ms. Elizabeth Bersaw
3 Cadillacs, Wallingford, VT

Ms. Barbara Z. Bertenshaw
4 Cadillacs, Glenwood, IL

Mr. Charles P. Bertland
26 Cadillacs, Charlotte, NC

Alan Bertling
3 Cadillacs, Port Charlotte, FL

E. Bertsch
3 Cadillacs, Calgary, AB

Mr. Teddy Bertuca
McAllen, TX

Mr. James E. Berven
1 Cadillac, Montevideo, MN

Ms. Erma S. Besbeck
6 Cadillacs, La Jolla, CA

Mr. Walter G. Besser
1 Cadillac, Slidell, LA

Mr. Joseph A. Besso
5 Cadillacs, Largo, FL

Edward Best
1 Cadillac, Thorndale, ON

Ms. Deborrah A. Bethel
2 Cadillacs, S. Charleston, OH

Mr. James L. Bethurum
2 Cadillacs, Colorado Spgs., CO

Mr. J. Betik
2 Cadillacs, Guelph, ON

Mr. John J. Bevan
28 Cadillacs, Hilton Head, SC

Mr. William Bevins
2 Cadillacs, Georgetown, KY

Mr. Jeffrey Bianco
1 Cadillac, Playa Del Rey, CA

Douglas Whitfield Biddle
4 Cadillacs, Sicklerville, NJ

Anthony Biegler
1 Cadillac, Moose Jaw, SK

R. Biehler
4 Cadillacs, Brantford, ON

Mr. Harold F. Bielfeldt
3 Cadillacs, Bloomington, IL

Colonel Bernard Big
3 Cadillacs, Hampton, VA

Mr. Robert R. Bigelow
Buffalo, NY

Mr. Jack D. Bigham
1 Cadillac, Killeen, TX

Mr. Real Bigras
4 Cadillacs, Sarnia, ON

Ms. Alma Biles
3 Cadillacs, Nashville, TN

Mrs. Berneita A. Bill
2 Cadillacs, Madelia, MN

Mr. Galen Billings
15 Cadillacs, Winston Salem, NC

Les Bilwacks
1 Cadillac, Addison, IL

Bruno Binelli
1 Cadillac, Scarborough, ON

Ms. Muriel J. Binette
4 Cadillacs, Berlin, NH

Mr. Kermit Binger
4 Cadillacs, Loysville, PA

Mr. A. Binnie
1 Cadillac, Scarborough, ON

Mr. Louis J. Birchem
1 Cadillac, Saint Paul, MN

Mr. Elry C. Bird
7 Cadillacs, Hemphill, TX

Mr. William H. Bird
Ft. Lauderdale, FL

Ms. Bettie R. Birdsall
2 Cadillacs, Norman, OK

Mrs. Eleanor J. Birdwell
4 Cadillacs, Tyler, TX

Mr. E. Birimcombe
1 Cadillac, Midhurst, ON

Mr. Albert C. Bisher
6 Cadillacs, Cincinnati, OH

Arabela G. Bishop
Zapata, TX

Mr. Ralph L. Bishop
2 Cadillacs, Bridgewater, MA

Mr. Roy F. Bishop
4 Cadillacs, Ankeny, IA

Dr. G. Donald Bissell
2 Cadillacs, Batesville, AR

Mr. Clay B. Bittinger
35 Cadillacs, Lake Worth, FL

Mr. Harry D. Bivens
3 Cadillacs, Cleveland, TN

Mr. Bobby G. Black
7 Cadillacs, Euless, TX

Mr. Donald Black
3 Cadillacs, Scarborough, ON

Mr. Gladstone S. Black
3 Cadillacs, Hartford, AL

Lester Black
2 Cadillacs, Scotch Plains, NJ

E. Blackman
2 Cadillacs, St. Catharines, ON

Mr. Fred L. Blackwell
2 Cadillacs, Griffin, GA

Mrs. Sara Blackwell
3 Cadillacs, Sheffield, AL

Mr. Robert Blaha
2 Cadillacs, Indianapolis, IN

Mr. Alfred J. Blair
25 Cadillacs, Noblesville, IN

Mr. Armand E. Blair
8 Cadillacs, Altamonte Spg., FL

Mr. George E. Blaise, Sr.
5 Cadillacs, Terrytown, LA

Ms. Doris Blake
3 Cadillacs, Indianapolis, IN

Mr. J.S. Blake
1 Cadillac, Keller, TX

O.L. & Phyllis Blake
5 Cadillacs, Portland, TX

Mr. Roy M. Blake
6 Cadillacs, Nacogdoches, TX

Mr. Harold B. Blalock
4 Cadillacs, Jackson, MS

Mr. Robert A. Blanchette
2 Cadillacs, Lewiston, ME

Mrs. Patricia Blandford
3 Cadillacs, Pittsburgh, PA

Mr. & Mrs. Morry Blank
4 Cadillacs, West Palm Bch., FL

Mr. Norbert Blaskowski
24 Cadillacs, Lake Forest, CA

Mr. Raymond Blaszky
8 Cadillacs, Westbury, NY

Ms. Mildred P. Bledsoe
2 Cadillacs, Kingsport, TN

Mr. Carl Blessing
5 Cadillacs, Reading, PA

U. Alfred Blevens
4 Cadillacs, Louisville, KY

Mrs. Diane Blier
1 Cadillac, Val-Belair, QC

LaVonne Blikre
Wahpeton, ND

Karen Block
2 Cadillacs, Bloomfield, NJ

Mr. P. Block
9 Cadillacs, Abbotsford, BC

Sanford Block
3 Cadillacs, Bloomfield, NJ

Mr. Morris G. Blocker
1 Cadillac, Benoit, MS

Jerry Bloom
41 Cadillacs, Sun City West, AZ

Mr. Robert E. Bloom
9 Cadillacs, Warren, OH

Mr. Sheldon S. Bloomfield
9 Cadillacs, Los Angeles, CA

Edward S. Blumenthal
30 Cadillacs, North Miami, FL

Mr. Frank C. Blumeyer, Jr.
3 Cadillacs, Saint Louis, MO

Mr. S. Bobaljik
1 Cadillac, Windsor, ON

Mr. Robert J. Boehlert
3 Cadillacs, Utica, NY

Mr. Lee R. Boehme
4 Cadillacs, Orange, TX

Mr. Harold Boerboom
6 Cadillacs, Villard, MN

Charles Boerner
3 Cadillacs, Pilot Point, TX

Mr. Kenneth O. Boers
7 Cadillacs, Green Bay, WI

Mr. Adelbert Boettcher
5 Cadillacs, Appleton, WI

Mr. Byron Boettcher
11 Cadillacs, Indio, CA

R.E. Bogardus
4 Cadillacs, Fresno, CA

J. Bogdanski
1 Cadillac, Kitchener, ON

Mr. Victor Boger
1 Cadillac, Philadelphia, PA

Mr. Eugene Boggiatto
2 Cadillacs, Castroville, CA

Dr. Alfred J. Bogush, Jr.
2 Cadillacs, Huntsville, AL

Mr. William Bolden
1 Cadillac, Birmingham, AL

Ms. Mary G. Bollinger
Crookston, MN

Mr. Joseph G. Bomber
1 Cadillac, Marinette, WI

Ms. Constance T. Bompadre
10 Cadillacs, West Chester, PA

Anthony Bonales
6 Cadillacs, Fogelsville, PA

Mr. John Bonds
1 Cadillac, Philadelphia, PA

Mr. Melvin Bonebrake
1 Cadillac, Indianapolis, IN

Mr. Paul G. Bonin
2 Cadillacs, Sanford, NC

Richard Bonnell
10 Cadillacs, Lady Lake, FL

Beddie Bonner
5 Cadillacs, Charleston, SC

H. Bonnetta
1 Cadillac, Port Perry, ON

Mr. Boyd J. Bonzer
2 Cadillacs, Mesa, AZ

Mr. Marvin W. Boode
5 Cadillacs, Tucson, AZ

Mr. John R. Booker, Sr.
1 Cadillac, Richmond, VA

Mr. Daniel L. Boone
3 Cadillacs, Sylacauga, AL

Mr. Joe A. Booth
Lawton, OK

Lester & Elsie Boothe
6 Cadillacs, Tallahassee, FL

Kenneth R. & Cecelia T. Bordeaux
1 Cadillac, Raleigh, NC

Mr. Tom Borden
3 Cadillacs, Portales, NM

Ms. Mira L. Bordin
7 Cadillacs, Scarsdale, NY

Ms. Anna S. Borges
3 Cadillacs, Somerset, MA

Mr. Edward Boron
7 Cadillacs, Clearfield, PA

Mr. Stanley Borowski
8 Cadillacs, N. Kensington, PA

Mr. George J. Borre
4 Cadillacs, Scottsdale, AZ

Mr. Ralph L. Borriello
2 Cadillacs, Berlin, CT

Ms. Linda A. Bosco
2 Cadillacs, New Castle, DE

Mr. Forest D. Bose
2 Cadillacs, Indianapolis, IN

Mrs. Elizabeth Bosi
24 Cadillacs, West Memphis, AR

Mr. Joseph W. Bossi
1 Cadillac, Nixa, MO

Mr. Jay S. Bost
42 Cadillacs, Rockwell, NC

Mr. William H. Boston
2 Cadillacs, Marion, OH

Mr. Wells M. Bothwell
3 Cadillacs, Mooresville, MO

Frank Bott
5 Cadillacs, Rochester, NY

Mr. Leyman I. Bott
16 Cadillacs, Bradenton, FL

Mr. Leo A. Bottari
7 Cadillacs, Glendora, CA

Mr. Armand E. Bouchard
11 Cadillacs, Grants Pass, OR

Mr. & Mrs. Ray Bouchard
32 Cadillacs, Portage, MI

Mr. Leonard Boucher
8 Cadillacs, Thief Rvr. Fls., MN

Peter A. Boukidis
7 Cadillacs, Los Angeles, CA

Mrs. Sylviane Boulay
7 Cadillacs, Repentigny, QC

Mr. Russell Bouman
2 Cadillacs, Holland, MI

Mr. Roger Bousquet
2 Cadillacs, S. Sioux City, NE

Mr. Philip F. Bova
6 Cadillacs, Belleville, IL

George Bow
4 Cadillacs, Homosassa, FL

Willie E. Bowden
1 Cadillac, Atlanta, GA

Mr. Henry Bowdoin
7 Cadillacs, Sacramento, CA

Mrs. Lucille Bowen
11 Cadillacs, Palestine, IL

Ms. Mildred L. Bowker
5 Cadillacs, Saugus, MA

Ms. Charlotte M. Bowles
1 Cadillac, Cleburne, TX

Ms. Lurline M. Bowles
5 Cadillacs, Jackson, TN

Mr. Mayfield Bowles
1 Cadillac, Detroit, MI

Mr. Robert L. Bowman
1 Cadillac, Greensboro, NC

Mr. Winton E. Bowman
5 Cadillacs, Atlanta, GA

Ivor Boyagoda
1 Cadillac, Oshawa, ON

Mr. Frank L. Boyce
5 Cadillacs, Sioux Falls, SD

Mr. George F. Boyd
Kansas City, MO

Mr. Thomas G. Boyd
5 Cadillacs, Moline, IL

Mr. Albert R. Boye
20 Cadillacs, Arlington, TX

Mr. Lloyd Boyles
5 Cadillacs, Mead, WA

Mr. Robert L. Boynton
Murfreesboro, TN

Mr. & Mrs. Lawrence Brachtenbach
4 Cadillacs, Sidney, NE

Mr. William D. Brackett
1 Cadillac, Falmouth, ME

Mr. Clifford Braden
Cobden, IL

H. Lee Bradford
Dallas, TX

Mr. Hope L. Bradford
Dallas, TX

Reverend Milton G. Bradley
6 Cadillacs, Sweetwater, TX

Mr. Raymond L. Bradley
1 Cadillac, Macomb, IL

Mr. Silas L. Bradley
3 Cadillacs, Belhaven, NC

Mr. Fred C. Bradshaw
6 Cadillacs, Lima, OH

Mr. George E. Bradshaw, Jr.
3 Cadillacs, Rochester, NY

Mr. William T. Bradshaw
Writsvlle. Bch., NC

Glen Bramble
11 Cadillacs, Easton, MD

Mr. William A. Bramel
Decatur, IL

Ms. Billie J. Bramlett
8 Cadillacs, Baytown, TX

Frank C. Branch
6 Cadillacs, Amelia, OH

Ms. Joanna Branch
6 Cadillacs, Richmond, VA

Mr. Keith R. Brandeberry
18 Cadillacs, Gallipolis, OH

Mr. John D. Brandenhorst
7 Cadillacs, San Diego, CA

Ms. Jean C. Brandon
3 Cadillacs, Quitman, TX

Mr. John Brandon
2 Cadillacs, Fort Wayne, IN

Frances Maurice Brantley
2 Cadillacs, Montgomery, AL

Barbara & Richard Brasen
2 Cadillacs, Jericho, NY

Ms. Marjorie R. Brashier
3 Cadillacs, Florence, AL

A. Brasteh
1 Cadillac, Bashaw, AB

Ms. Verna D. Braswell
1 Cadillac, West Palm Bch., FL

Mrs. Alice T. Bratcher
18 Cadillacs, Fort Worth, TX

Mr. Gerald L. Bratsch
8 Cadillacs, Saint Louis, MO

Mr. Paul Bratz
5 Cadillacs, McMurray, PA

Mr. Peter Braun
5 Cadillacs, Alexandria, VA

Ms. Dorothy S. Brawley
1 Cadillac, Burlington, NC

Mr. Roland E. Brazeau
5 Cadillacs, Bristol, CT

Mr. William B. Brazel, Jr.
1 Cadillac, Geneva, AL

Mr. Milton A. Breakie
2 Cadillacs, San Juan, TX

Ms. Annette L. Breaux
26 Cadillacs, Lockport, LA

James R. Brecheen
3 Cadillacs, El Paso, TX

Mr. Dewey M. Bredemeyer
2 Cadillacs, Omaha, NE

Mr. William M. Breeden
1 Cadillac, Chillicothe, MO

Mr. Charles D. Breeding
2 Cadillacs, Waskom, TX

Mr. James D. Breedlove
8 Cadillacs, San Antonio, TX

Mr. Lee A. Breeland
9 Cadillacs, Canton, MS

Mr. Robert E. Breen
12 Cadillacs, Orange Park, FL

Mr. Melvin E. Breidecker
4 Cadillacs, Florissant, MO

Ms. Dorothy Breitenfeldt
1 Cadillac, Antigo, WI

Mamie Lee L. Breitenfield
4 Cadillacs, Glenview, IL

John Brennan
6 Cadillacs, Rotonda West, FL

Mr. Robert Brennan
12 Cadillacs, Bellevue, WA

Louis Brent
18 Cadillacs, Springfield, PA

Ms. Martha T. Brescia
4 Cadillacs, Silver Spring, MD

Joseph Breslin
4 Cadillacs, Malvern, PA

Clinton F. Brethold
4 Cadillacs, Hillsboro, MO

Pearl A. Kohler Brethold
4 Cadillacs, Hillsboro, MO

Mr. Paul E. Brette
10 Cadillacs, Bucyrus, OH

Mr. John W. Breusing
1 Cadillac, Victor, NY

Mr. Clyde O. Brewer
11 Cadillac, Chattanooga, TN

Ms. Helen Brewster
4 Cadillacs, East Meadow, NY

Ms. Rebecca Brewster
2 Cadillacs, Los Angeles, CA

Mr. Samuel Brewster
1 Cadillac, Oshawa, ON

Mr. Joe L. Brickner
2 Cadillacs, Shepherd, MI

Ms. Ann Bridges
2 Cadillacs, Ft. Washington, MD

Mr. Orel Bridges, Jr.
10 Cadillacs, Lafayette, LA

Ms. Patricia C. Brien
6 Cadillacs, Racine, WI

Mr. Perry Briggs
2 Cadillacs, Richmond, VA

Wayne & Marian Briggs
1 Cadillac, Logansport, IN

Ms. Reva Brin
2 Cadillacs, Highland Park, IL

Joseph C. Brinkley
4 Cadillacs, Jacksonville, FL

Jim & Betty Brinkman
4 Cadillacs, Huron, SD

Ms. Patsy E. Brinkoetter
5 Cadillacs, Decatur, IL

Ms. Mabel Bristol
3 Cadillacs, Grosse Pointe, MI

James W. Broadnax
1 Cadillac, Ridge Spring, SC

Mr. & Mrs. Robert H. Brock
1 Cadillac, San Angelo, TX

Mr. Bengt H. Broderman
9 Cadillacs, Cambridge, IL

Mr. Billy G. Brodt
1 Cadillac, Salt Lake Cty., UT

Mr. Elwin V. Bromley
8 Cadillacs, Avoca, MI

Mr. Charles Bronstad
2 Cadillacs, Aurora, CO

Mr. Eugene H. Brooke
4 Cadillacs, Denton, MD

Mr. Howard B. Brookins, Jr.
3 Cadillacs, Chicago, IL

Ms. Georgia Brooks
3 Cadillacs, Atlanta, GA

Mr. Noland Brooks
8 Cadillacs, Cedar Hill, TX

Mr. Rodger Brooks
2 Cadillacs, Abilene, TX

Alex Broomfield
1 Cadillac, Scarborough, ON

Mr. David T. Brothers
1 Cadillac, Alameda, CA

Mr. Ernest Brothers, Jr.
4 Cadillacs, Bowling Green, KY

Ms. Arlene E. Brown
8 Cadillacs, Pharr, TX

C. Brown
2 Cadillacs, Halifax, NS

Charlie Brown
1 Cadillac, Aiken, SC

Mr. Clarence E. Brown
2 Cadillacs, Lima, OH

Ms. Claudine M. Brown
2 Cadillacs, San Jose, CA

Mr. David F. Brown
12 Cadillacs, Meridian, MS

Mr. David C. Brown
5 Cadillacs, Richardson, TX

Mr. Eldon N. Brown
5 Cadillacs, Kankakee, IL

Mrs. Florence Brown
3 Cadillacs, Detroit, MI

Mr. Frank Brown
2 Cadillacs, Bartlett, IL

G. Brown
6 Cadillacs, Pointe-Claire, QC

Mr. Glendon D. Brown
2 Cadillacs, Madison Heights, MI

Mr. Hadred L. Brown
2 Cadillacs, Paducah, KY

Mr. Isaac C. Brown
1 Cadillac, Columbia, SC

Mr. James F. Brown
5 Cadillacs, Tucson, AZ

Mr. John E. Brown
3 Cadillacs, Elgin, IL

Mr. Le Roy A. Brown
1 Cadillac, Arp, TX

Ms. Mary G. Brown
3 Cadillacs, Greensboro, NC

Mary M. & Frank D. Brown
3 Cadillacs, Lexington, TX

Mrs. Nellie C. Brown
6 Cadillacs, Springville, TN

Mrs. Nina Brown
23 Cadillacs, Little Rock, AR

Mr. Paul Brown
7 Cadillacs, Chicago, IL

Paul Brown
13 Cadillacs, Lincoln, NE

Raymond Brown
13 Cadillacs, Margate City, NJ

Mr. Ronald H. Brown
6 Cadillacs, St. Petersburg, FL

Ms. Silvia Brown
2 Cadillacs, Franklin, KY

Mr. Walter J. Brown
17 Cadillacs, Hartsville, SC

Mr. Wilbur H. Brown
5 Cadillacs, Saint Louis, MO

Ms. Blanche A. Browne
8 Cadillacs, Canaan, NH

Mr. M. Browne
1 Cadillac, Cardston, AB

Mr. Vern L. Brownell
2 Cadillacs, Marion, IA

Mr. Cecil O. Browning
5 Cadillacs, Greenwood, SC

Mr. Moss C. Browning
18 Cadillacs, Huntington, WV

Felix Adrian Bruce
1 Cadillac, Madisonville, KY

Mr. Joseph Brumberg
29 Cadillacs, Margate, FL

Mr. Thomas Brumfield
3 Cadillacs, Ringwood, OK

Kenneth A. & Shirley M. Brunelli
7 Cadillacs, Pewaukee, WI

Shirley Mae Brunelli
7 Cadillacs, Pewaukee, WI

Mr. Ned C. Bruner
1 Cadillac, Butte, MT

Charles Brunje
3 Cadillacs, River Edge, NJ

N. Brunk
1 Cadillac, Kitchener, ON

Mr. Paul J. Brunner
3 Cadillacs, Cincinnati, OH

Mr. & Mrs. Robert E. Bruns
2 Cadillacs, Radford, VA

Melvin Brussow,
8 Cadillacs, Madison, WI

Mr. Vincent Brust
4 Cadillacs, Scranton, PA

Mr. Albert Bruzzini
3 Cadillacs, Melrose Park, IL

Albert V. Bruzzini, Sr.
3 Cadillacs, Northlake, IL

Ms. Sharon L. Bryan
2 Cadillacs, Cottage Grove, WI

Barbara J. Bryant
4 Cadillacs, Peru, IL

Mr. Carlie Bryant, Jr.
12 Cadillacs, Enterprise, AL

Mr. Curtis O. Bryant
58 Cadillacs, New Albany, MS

Ms. Geraldine E. Bryant
3 Cadillacs, Dayton, OH

Mr. Francis Buchannan
5 Cadillacs, Blowing Rock, NC

Harold Buchholz
4 Cadillacs, Margate, FL

Mr. Fred Buckhalter, Jr.
3 Cadillacs, Oakland, CA

Mr. Thomas J. Buckley
9 Cadillacs, Deltona, FL

Mrs. B. Budd
2 Cadillacs, Mt. Pleasant, PA

Mr. William C. Budge, Jr.
3 Cadillacs, Bemidji, MN

Judge William L. Buenzli
2 Cadillacs, Madison, WI

Berith Wilma Buffaloe
3 Cadillacs, Victoria, TX

Mr. Robert E. Buffum
6 Cadillacs, Portsmouth, NH

Dortha H. Buie
4 Cadillacs, Tyler, TX

Robert Builta
Le Roy, IL

Mr. Perlin A. Bull
3 Cadillacs, Phoenix, AZ

Mr. Theron W. Bull
3 Cadillacs, Inverness, FL

Mr. Guy S. Bullard, Jr.
4 Cadillacs, Winston Salem, NC

Rev. L.B. Bullock
2 Cadillacs, Hattiesburg, MS

Ms. Linda K. Bullock
1 Cadillac, Ruston, LA

Mr. Carol E. Bunn
17 Cadillacs, Arlington Hts., IL

Mr. John T. Burdett
3 Cadillacs, Princeton, IL

Mrs. Mildred G. Burdette
1 Cadillac, Salisbury, NC

Ms. Marjorie E. Burdo
3 Cadillacs, Clare, MI

Mr. George J. Burger
2 Cadillacs, Tucson, AZ

Mrs. Anne M. Burgess
6 Cadillacs, N. Myrtle Bch., SC

Mr. Jesse B. Burgess
1 Cadillac, Amarillo, TX

Mark Burgessporter
2 Cadillacs, Honolulu, HI

Ray Burgoon
3 Cadillacs, Spring Hill, FL

Mr. Ernest Burgs
6 Cadillacs, Garfield, NJ

Mr. Alfred Burke
3 Cadillacs, Cap-Pele, NB

Mr. Charles B. Burke
1 Cadillac, North Platte, NE

Mr. William R. Burke
2 Cadillacs, San Antonio, TX

Mr. Homer H. Burkett
3 Cadillacs, San Antonio, TX

Mr. Rufus L. Burkhalter
5 Cadillacs, Savannah, GA

Mr. Alfred O. Burkhardt
14 Cadillacs, Denver, CO

Mr. Guenter H. Burkhardt
4 Cadillacs, Lancaster, NY

Mr. Maurice W. Burkhart
Circleville, OH

Mr. James L. Burleson
3 Cadillacs, Panama City, FL

Mr. H. Burley
2 Cadillacs, Odessa, ON

Mr. Marvin L. Burlison
4 Cadillacs, Plano, TX

Mr. Henry C. Burnam, Jr.
2 Cadillacs, Iraan, TX

Ms. Billie Burnett
5 Cadillacs, Memphis, TN

Mr. Claude Burnett
8 Cadillacs, Hale Center, TX

Mr. Walter G. Burnett
3 Cadillacs, Parksley, VA

Mr. Arthur O. Burnette
1 Cadillac, Barnesville, GA

Mr. Joseph M. Burnik
5 Cadillacs, Joliet, IL

Ms. Betty D. Burns
3 Cadillacs, Bath, NY

Mr. Edward L. Burns
1 Cadillac, Mohawk, NY

Mr. Thomas Burns, Jr.
4 Cadillacs, Elizabeth Cty., NC

Mr. Grady Burrell
1 Cadillac, Roanoke, VA

Hairston & Carolyn Burrell
6 Cadillacs, Winston Salem, NC

G. Gordon Burroughs
11 Cadillacs, Glen Carbon, IL

Mr. Robert F. Burroughs
5 Cadillacs, Portville, NY

Mr. William Burrows
3 Cadillacs, Birchwood, WI

Mr. Frank Bursick
4 Cadillacs, Pittsburgh, PA

Mr. Curtis M. Burton
7 Cadillacs, Detroit, MI

Mr. John T. Burton
6 Cadillacs, Somerset, KY

Ms. Mary E. Burton
4 Cadillacs, Cookeville, TN

Ms. Shirley E. Burton
5 Cadillacs, San Jose, CA

Mr. George L. Buscaglia
3 Cadillacs, Depew, NY

Mr. Joseph Buscavage
5 Cadillacs, Bound Brook, NJ

Mr. Robert C. Busch
7 Cadillacs, McCormick, SC

Mr. Thomas Busch
6 Cadillacs, Long Beach, CA

Mr. William J. Buscher
11 Cadillacs, Thorofare, NJ

Ms. Alma J. Bush
6 Cadillacs, Clara City, MN

Mr. Herman S. Bush
Tonawanda, NY

Sharon L. Bush
5 Cadillacs, Altamonte Spg., FL

Mrs. Audrey C. Buskirk
2 Cadillacs, Circleville, OH

Mr. Delbert Bussey
4 Cadillacs, Vancouver, WA

Mr. Joseph O. Bussey
12 Cadillacs, Apache Jct., AZ

Mr. Fred M. Butalla, Jr.
7 Cadillacs, Orland Park, IL

Mrs. Carolyn Butler
1 Cadillac, Charlotte, NC

Ms. Irene L. Butler
1 Cadillac, Big Spring, TX

Mr. Russell Butler
2 Cadillacs, Holden, WV

Mr. Michael Butorovich
6 Cadillacs, Great Falls, MT

Mr. Fred Butry, Jr.
6 Cadillacs, Yorktown, VA

Mr. Harvey R. Butts
4 Cadillacs, Largo, FL

Mr. R. Byfield
5 Cadillacs, Delta, BC

Mr. Ben F. Byrd
3 Cadillacs, Clearwater, FL

Mr. Marshall L. Byrd
5 Cadillacs, Toney, AL

Mr. Thaddeus H. Bysiek
1 Cadillac, Norridge, IL

Mr. John A. Bystry
3 Cadillacs, Princeton, IL

C

Ms. Catherine E. Cable
1 Cadillac, Prospect, KY

Mr. Kent Cabral
5 Cadillacs, Clayton, CA

Kenneth Edwin Cade
1 Cadillac, Kansas City, MO

Mr. Frank J. Cademartori
11 Cadillacs, Mesa, AZ

Mr. Thomas W. Cadigan
8 Cadillacs, Fort Myers, FL

Mrs. Hazel J. Cadle
1 Cadillac, Aiken, SC

Mr. T. Cadman
2 Cadillacs, Tillsonburg, ON

Ms. Ann B. Cadovich
5 Cadillacs, Farmington, MI

LaVerne Cadwell
3 Cadillacs, El Paso, TX

Pauline & Pat Cafaro
2 Cadillacs, Spokane, WA

Mr. Gene N. Cage
9 Cadillacs, Olathe, KS

Mr. Anthony V. Caggiano
8 Cadillacs, Floral Park, NY

Mr. Ethyl A. Cain
1 Cadillac, Philadelphia, MS

Albert Cairo
1 Cadillac, West Islip, NY

Mr. Anthony N. Cairo
7 Cadillacs, Westchester, IL

Mr. Sam J. Calcione
23 Cadillacs, Rockford, IL

Mr. C.H. Calder
1 Cadillac, Wyckoff, NJ

Ned G. Calderone
7 Cadillacs, Plainfield, IL

Mr. James E. Caldwell
4 Cadillacs, St. George, UT

Walter L. Caldwell
15 Cadillacs, Pittsburgh, PA

Mr. John F. Calhoun
3 Cadillacs, Deering, MO

E. & C. Louise Califano
10 Cadillacs, Fort Pierce, FL

Mr. Joe Caliguire
4 Cadillacs, Lksid. Marblhd., OH

Mr. Charles W. Call
1 Cadillac, Painesville, OH

Dr. William M. Callaham
14 Cadillacs, Richmond, VA

Mr. Frank Callahan, Jr.
4 Cadillacs, Jackson, TN

Mr. James A. Callahan
8 Cadillacs, Hitchcock, TX

Mr. Brant Callaway
8 Cadillacs, Nashville, TN

Mr. Leland Callaway
5 Cadillacs, Nacogdoches, TX

Mr. William Calloway
8 Cadillacs, Glen Daniel, WV

Mr. Allan K. Cameron
3 Cadillacs, Tucson, AZ

Mr. Ernie W. Cameron
7 Cadillacs, Chicago, IL

Mr. Emile Camire
2 Cadillacs, New Bedford, MA

Mr. Richard O. Camp
6 Cadillacs, Hartselle, AL

Mr. Bob Campbell
11 Cadillacs, Parsons, KS

Mr. Douglas Campbell
2 Cadillacs, Burnaby, BC

Mr. Frank W. Campbell, Sr.
8 Cadillacs, Huntsville, AL

Harlen J. Campbell, Sr.
7 Cadillacs, Rio Rancho, NM

Mr. John B. Campbell
2 Cadillacs, Chatsworth, CA

Mr. John F. Campbell
6 Cadillacs, Fernandina, FL

Mr. F. Campeau
1 Cadillac, Dalhousie Station, QC

Mr. Anastacio Campos
1 Cadillac, Elizabeth, NJ

Mr. Felix Campos
2 Cadillacs, Lawton, OK

Mr. Alton Z. Canady
9 Cadillacs, Winston Salem, NC

Mary & Pete G. Canakes
16 Cadillacs, Waterloo, IA

Mr. Vicente Candales
2 Cadillacs, Miami, FL

Mr. William Cane
3 Cadillacs, Oshawa, ON

Mr. Winton J. Canfield
2 Cadillacs, Nacogdoches, TX

Ms. Mary S. Cannon
8 Cadillacs, Metairie, LA

Mr. Robert P. Cannon
1 Cadillac, El Reno, OK

Mr. Wilford W. Cannon
4 Cadillacs, Saint George, UT

Mr. Valentine R. Cano
5 Cadillacs, Jacksonville, FL

Lloyd L. Canterburry
4 Cadillacs, Austin, TX

Mr. Henry A. Canterbury, Jr.
2 Cadillacs, Mullens, WV

Mrs. Maymee M. Cantrell
5 Cadillacs, Waverly, TN

Mr. Robert J. Cantrill
2 Cadillacs, El Paso, TX

Mr. Barry L. Caouette
6 Cadillacs, Key West, FL

Ms. Dianne R. Capin
11 Cadillacs, Las Vegas, NV

Mr. Gregory Capito
4 Cadillacs, Warren, OH

Mr. James Capobianco
West Orange, NJ

Mr. Joseph Caponegro
1 Cadillac, Tenafly, NJ

Ann & Geno Cappadoro
3 Cadillacs, Hallandale, FL

Bruno & Irene Cappy
4 Cadillacs, Seven Hills, OH

Mr. Antonio Ruiz Caraballo
Willingboro, NJ

Mr. Antonio Carannante
2 Cadillacs, Pottstown, PA

Mr. Anthony Carbone
2 Cadillacs, Rochester, NY

Mr. Clair A. Carden
1 Cadillac, Tyler, TX

Mr. James R. Carden
6 Cadillacs, Englewood, CO

Mr. Meyer M. Cardin
10 Cadillacs, Baltimore, MD

Mr. Anthony S. Cardoni
7 Cadillacs, Lyndhurst, OH

Mr. Charles M. Cardwell
1 Cadillac, Salt Lake Cty., UT

Ms. Marjorie E. Carey
14 Cadillacs, Peabody, MA

Mr. Richard J. Carey
1 Cadillac, Longmeadow, MA

Dr. John L. Carkeet
20 Cadillacs, Ind. Hbr. Bch., FL

Mr. Carl B. Carlson
9 Cadillacs, San Antonio, TX

Elmer Carlson
3 Cadillacs, Agoura, CA

Ms. Hinda Carlson
9 Cadillacs, La Grange, IL

Mr. Cloid & Elma Carmichael
7 Cadillacs, Valparaiso, IN

Mr. Richard E. Carney
12 Cadillacs, Kansas City, MO

Mr. Sidney F. Carney
4 Cadillacs, Anadarko, OK

Ms. Ruthie H. Carpenter
8 Cadillacs, Pittsview, AL

Mr. Serge A. Carpenter
4 Cadillacs, Port St. Lucie, FL

Mr. Charles J. Carper
1 Cadillac, Zephyr Cove, NV

Ms. Anne E. Carr
5 Cadillacs, Dover, DE

Janet Carr
2 Cadillacs, Moose Jaw, SK

Mr. Robert E. Carr
2 Cadillacs, Carmi, IL

Mrs. Frances M. Carrico
2 Cadillacs, Maceo, KY

Mr. & Mrs. L.J. Carroll
6 Cadillacs, Glen Ridge, NJ

Mr. Thomas K. Carroll
7 Cadillacs, Norfolk, VA

Scott Carruthers
2 Cadillacs, Tallahassee, FL

Mr. Carl Carson
22 Cadillacs, Wellsboro, PA

Ms. Bessie M. Carte
10 Cadillacs, West Plains, MO

Ms. Doris M. Carter
3 Cadillacs, Bradenton, FL

Mr. Fred Carter
3 Cadillacs, Birmingham, AL

Mr. Laurence S. Carter
7 Cadillacs, Sanford, NC

Mrs. Leo Carter
4 Cadillacs, Albany, GA

Marie F. Carter
1 Cadillac, San Antonio, TX

Mr. Velvin Carter
6 Cadillacs, Fort Worth, TX

Mr. Walter E. Carter
3 Cadillacs, Potomac, MD

William & Ella Carter
37 Cadillacs, Martinsville, VA

Mr. Robert W. Carts
5 Cadillacs, Belvidere, IL

K. Cartwright
1 Cadillac, Peachland, BC

Ms. Joan M. Caruso
7 Cadillacs, Marshfield, MA

Ms. Nettie Carvin
3 Cadillacs, Port Richey, FL

Mr. Tony Casadidio
12 Cadillacs, Colonial Hgts., VA

Mr. Anthony D. Cascio
5 Cadillacs, East Meadow, NY

Mr. Travis J. Cash, Jr.
8 Cadillacs, Greenville, SC

Mr. Richard B. Cashwell
6 Cadillacs, Bristol, TN

Mr. Edwin A. Casler
4 Cadillacs, Lakeland, FL

Mr. Fred C. Cassel, Jr.
10 Cadillacs, Navasota, TX

Mr. John W. Cassell
6 Cadillacs, Cape Coral, FL

Mr. Chester Catalano
2 Cadillacs, Myrtle Beach, SC

Mr. Ralph J. Catalano, Jr.
15 Cadillacs, Everett, MA

Mr. George A. Cataldo
15 Cadillacs, Port Richey, FL

Paul Catania
1 Cadillac, Etobicoke, ON

J. Cates
1 Cadillac, Etobicoke, ON

Jim Cates
13 Cadillacs, Silverton, OR

Mr. Joe Cates, Jr.
4 Cadillacs, Baytown, TX

Mr. Junious Cates
1 Cadillac, Anniston, AL

Mr. Don P. Catron
3 Cadillacs, Lk. Providence, LA

Mr. Lyle Cattnach
5 Cadillacs, Castro Valley, CA

Mr. Nicholas Catucci
8 Cadillacs, Washington, DC

Johnie Stanley Caudill
5 Cadillacs, Ashland, KY

Mr. Maxwell Cauthen, Jr.
3 Cadillacs, Spartanburg, SC

Mr. Rea K. Cauthen
4 Cadillacs, Rock Hill, SC

Mr. Dario P. Cavarzan
2 Cadillacs, Redding, CA

Mr. & Mrs. John E. Caverly
1 Cadillac, Winthrop, ME

Irvin M. Cederlind, M.D.
8 Cadillacs, Bellingham, WA

Mrs. Louise A. Cefali
7 Cadillacs, Hobart, IN

Mr. Alfred & Stella Centrella
2 Cadillacs, Pittston, PA

Mr. Michael Cephas
2 Cadillacs, Passaic, NJ

Mr. Jerry V. Cerabona
1 Cadillac, Chicago, IL

Mr. Fred V. Cercone
2 Cadillacs, Follansbee, WV

Mr. Anthony Ceriale
3 Cadillacs, Addison, IL

Mr. S. Cerisano
7 Cadillacs, North Bay, ON

Thomas J. Cerkez
10 Cadillacs, La Grange Pk., IL

Mr. David M. Cerul
3 Cadillacs, Sudbury, MA

Mr. Louis A. Cervi
26 Cadillacs, Ocean Springs, MS

Mr. Carmello Cervino
Garden City, NY

Mr. Edward L. Ceski
6 Cadillacs, St. Petersburg, FL

Mr. Guido P. Cetrone
6 Cadillacs, Newton, MA

R. Chabot
1 Cadillac, Mattice, ON

Krishna Chadalavada
2 Cadillacs, Sterling, IL

Ms. Vera Chaffin
6 Cadillacs, Shamrock, TX

Mr. Norman Chakir
3 Cadillacs, Great Bend, KS

Mr. Eugene Chambers
5 Cadillacs, Houston, TX

Mrs. F.M. Chambers
10 Cadillacs, Maplesville, AL

N. Chan
2 Cadillacs, Edmonton, AB

Tony & Astherine Chan
1 Cadillac, Mundelein, IL

Mrs. Phyllis C. Chana
3 Cadillacs, Daytona Beach, FL

Mrs. Beverly J. Chancy
3 Cadillacs, Pensacola, FL

Juan Jose Chanin
1 Cadillac, McAllen, TX

Mr. Joseph J. Chapla
30 Cadillacs, South Holland, IL

Mr. Boyd Chapman
6 Cadillacs, Friday Harbor, WA

Mrs. Charlotte J. Chapman
1 Cadillac, Normal, IL

Mr. John Harold Chapman
7 Cadillacs, Lubbock, TX

Richard Chapman
5 Cadillacs, Woodland Hls., CA

Mr. Elmer Chappell
3 Cadillacs, Chesapeake, VA

Mr. P. Chappell
7 Cadillacs, Oshawa, ON

Mr. F. Charest
3 Cadillacs, St. Georges, QC

Mr. James Charlton
1 Cadillac, Weyburn, SK

Mr. Paul Charneski
10 Cadillacs, Tacoma, WA

Ms. Pauline Charping
26 Cadillacs, Waveland, MS

Mr. George N. Chatham
8 Cadillacs, Roanoke, TX

Ms. Polly I. Chatham
8 Cadillacs, Raleigh, NC

Mr. Robert E. Chatman
2 Cadillacs, Flint, MI

Mr. Fred Chavis, Jr.
4 Cadillacs, Winston Salem, NC

Ms. Leatrice J. Check
6 Cadillacs, Manitowoc, WI

Mr. Lorrin & M. Chee
2 Cadillacs, Huntington Bch., CA

Mr. William Cheesman
4 Cadillacs, Burlington, NJ

Mr. Albert Cheety
3 Cadillacs, Pt. Charlotte, FL

Mr. Shiu H. Chen
2 Cadillacs, Monterey Park, CA

Ms. Anna C. Chennault
1 Cadillac, Washington, DC

Mr. Harold R. Chenoweth
3 Cadillacs, Lathrop, MO

Dr. N.A. Chetta
4 Cadillacs, Gretna, LA

Mr. H. Cheung
1 Cadillac, Kanata, ON

Virgil D. & Kathryn I. Cheyne
6 Cadillacs, Mesa, AZ

Kuk Chi
Pasadena, CA

Alfred Chiarolanzio
9 Cadillacs, Madison, NJ

Mr. Arthur R. Chidester
1 Cadillac, Highland, UT

Mr. Charles B. Childers
2 Cadillacs, Pleasant Grv., AL

Mr. John Chilingerian
2 Cadillacs, Waltham, MA

Mr. Cecil W. Chinn
5 Cadillacs, Owensboro, KY

Mr. Daniel A. Chisarick
2 Cadillacs, Binghamton, NY

Ms. Myrtle W. Chitwood
3 Cadillacs, Safety Harbor, FL

Mr. Jang Choe
1 Cadillac, Honolulu, HI

Ms. Genevieve J. Chominski
11 Cadillacs, Chicago, IL

Mr. Robert E. Chopp
9 Cadillacs, Woodinville, WA

Mr. D. Chopra
1 Cadillac, Halifax, NS

Mr. Roger J. Choquette
4 Cadillacs, Lancaster, NH

Mr. Milo Chozen
3 Cadillacs, Spirit Lake, IA

Mr. John E. Christen
13 Cadillacs, Lady Lake, FL

Mr. Lloyd Christensen
6 Cadillacs, Tulsa, OK

Mr. Lyle G. Christensen
1 Cadillac, Sioux Falls, SD

Mrs. Norma Christian
6 Cadillacs, Midlothian, VA

Mrs. R.M. Christian
12 Cadillacs, Bridgeport, TX

Mayo Christianson
5 Cadillacs, Sun City West, AZ

Mr. Mayo Christianson
5 Cadillacs, Fargo, ND

Eugene Christmas, Sr.
6 Cadillacs, Waukegan, IL

Mr. M.E. Christopherson
16 Cadillacs, Easley, SC

Mr. William R. Chroszy
1 Cadillac, Highland Park, IL

Mr. Carl Churchman
5 Cadillacs, Lake Charles, LA

Mr. Anthony Cibel
Washington, DC

Comonaldo Cicerone
5 Cadillacs, Sarasota, FL

Mr. & Mrs. Stephen J. Cichron, Jr.
1 Cadillac, Meriden, CT

Mrs. Josephine Cino
2 Cadillacs, Rockville Ctr., NY

Mr. Battista P. Cioni
1 Cadillac, East Peoria, IL

Mr. Vince T. Circhio
1 Cadillac, New Windsor, NY

Mrs. Jennie B. Cirelli
20 Cadillacs, S. Yarmouth, MA

Mr. James J. Ciriaco, Sr.
1 Cadillac, New Castle, DE

William J. Cirrito
6 Cadillacs, Sanibel, FL

Ms. Mavis G. Cisneros
12 Cadillacs, Kenly, NC

Mr. Italo Citarella
1 Cadillac, Youngstown, OH

Mrs. Donna G. Civello
1 Cadillac, Metairie, LA

Mr. John A. Clairmont
1 Cadillac, Gladstone, MI

Mrs. Lena Clark-Moore
4 Cadillacs, Powhatan, VA

Mr. John G. Clark
4 Cadillacs, Charleston, SC

Mr. Ollie S. Clark
1 Cadillac, Irvington, AL

Dr. Raymond C. Clark
4 Cadillacs, San Antonio, TX

Mr. Robert L. Clark
3 Cadillacs, Louisville, MS

Mr. Robert R. Clark
5 Cadillacs, Memphis, TN

Robert H. Clark
1 Cadillac, Petersburg, VA

Mr. Theodore M. Clark
1 Cadillac, Arvada, CO

Mr. William Clark
3 Cadillacs, Lakeview, AR

Carlton & Margie Clary
5 Cadillacs, Prince George, VA

Mr. Roger H. Claus
2 Cadillacs, Arcadia, CA

Mr. Abe D. Clayman
12 Cadillacs, W. Des Moines, IA

Mr. James D. Clemens
5 Cadillacs, Dearborn, MI

Mrs. Barbara J. Clement
4 Cadillacs, Apopka, FL

Mr. Lucien Clement
1 Cadillac, Orleans, ON

Ignazio V. Clemente
10 Cadillacs, Smithtown, NY

Ms. Ella M. Clements
Mineola, TX

Mr. William Clements
20 Cadillacs, Enid, OK

Mr. Wayne O. Clevenger
4 Cadillacs, Moline, IL

Mr. George Cline
3 Cadillacs, Lake Charles, LA

Mr. Martin W. Cline
3 Cadillacs, Bradenton, FL

Mr. H. Clumpus
1 Cadillac, Scarborough, ON

Frank J. Cmelik
2 Cadillacs, Marengo, IA

Faith K. Coachman
6 Cadillacs, Saint Petersburg, FL

E. Cobb
3 Cadillacs, Los Angeles, CA

Mr. Howard Cobb
3 Cadillacs, Suffolk, VA

Mr. Robert Coffman
13 Cadillacs, Seymour, IN

Mr. Allan Cohen
3 Cadillacs, Minneapolis, MN

Mr. Budd Cohen
5 Cadillacs, Pompano Beach, FL

Mr. Donald N. Cohen
6 Cadillacs, Jupiter, FL

Mr. Gil Cohen
7 Cadillacs, Lincolnshire, IL

Mr. Herbert Cohen
8 Cadillacs, Mims, FL

Mr. Louis Cohen
5 Cadillacs, Topeka, KS

Mr. Rudolph R. Cohen
7 Cadillacs, Atlanta, GA

Mrs. Doris L. Coker
7 Cadillacs, Fouke, AR

Ella Jean Coker
4 Cadillacs, Knoxville, TN

Clair M. & Darlene L. Colburn
1 Cadillac, Steubenville, OH

Handferd L. Colden
9 Cadillacs, Waupaca, WI

Mr. Allan Cole
1 Cadillac, Severn Bridge, ON

Mr. Elbert L. Cole
2 Cadillacs, Petersburg, WV

Mr. Fred Cole, Jr.
1 Cadillac, Lehighton, PA

Mr. John Cole
11 Cadillacs, Dunedin, FL

Mr. Richard G. Cole
2 Cadillacs, Lansing, MI

Shirley J. Cole
3 Cadillacs, Dunedin, FL

Ms. Victoria R. Cole
5 Cadillacs, Melbourne, FL

William Howard Cole
4 Cadillacs, Scottsville, KY

Mr. Arcangelo Colello
2 Cadillacs, Middletown, NY

Mr. Alwin B. Coleman
1 Cadillac, Holland, MI

Ms. Christie Coleman
3 Cadillacs, Saint Charles, IL

Ms. Emma J. Coleman
4 Cadillacs, Jackson, MS

Mrs. Jeanette Coleman
4 Cadillacs, Thomson, GA

Mr. Julius C. Coleman
3 Cadillacs, Mascoutah, IL

Lanie Mae Coleman
3 Cadillacs, Carbondale, IL

Mr. Roger Coleman
1 Cadillac, East Hartford, CT

Mr. Gabriel Coles
1 Cadillac, Flushing, NY

Mr. Dominic P. Colianni
6 Cadillacs, Minneapolis, MN

Mr. Lloyd Collacutt
19 Cadillacs, Oshawa, ON

Ernest Collett
1 Cadillac, Reading, OH

Mr. Vincent Colletta
13 Cadillacs, Rockford, IL

Mr. Andrew J. Colletti
2 Cadillacs, Hampton Bays, NY

Mr. Nicholas D. Colling
6 Cadillacs, De Pere, WI

Mr. Paul J. Collingsworth
1 Cadillac, Arlington, TX

Mrs. Betty Jean Collins
4 Cadillacs, Mount Vernon, WA

Blanard R. Collins
2 Cadillacs, Kingsport, TN

Ms. Claudia J. Collins
2 Cadillacs, Tampa, FL

Mr. Malvin E. Collins
16 Cadillacs, Jacksonville, NC

Mr. Walter J. Collins
2 Cadillacs, Crisfield, MD

Ms. Wanda Collins
2 Cadillacs, Fulshear, TX

Mr. & Mrs. Wendell F. Collins
4 Cadillacs, Keithville, LA

Mr. Russell F. Collum
4 Cadillacs, Fort Myers, FL

Mr. Kenneth F. Collyer
13 Cadillacs, Medford, MA

Kermit Lee Colson
3 Cadillacs, Appleton City, MO

Mr. Calvin C. Combs
2 Cadillacs, N. Wilkesboro, NC

Ementha R. Combs
3 Cadillacs, Fort Worth, TX

Ms. Sallie C. Combs
5 Cadillacs, Hindman, KY

Ms. Evelyn J. Commers
6 Cadillacs, Minneapolis, MN

Mr. Ranis Compton
2 Cadillacs, Roanoke, VA

Mr. James A. Conerly
5 Cadillacs, Shreveport, LA

John Confrey
4 Cadillacs, Fort Pierce, FL

Mr. V.E. Conn
3 Cadillacs, Punta Gorda, FL

Mr. Harold D. Conner
2 Cadillacs, Fort Worth, TX

Mrs. Mary Ann Connors
Madison, WI

Mr. Walter C. Conover
1 Cadillac, Concord, NC

Mrs. Margaret M. Conrad
2 Cadillacs, Westwood, MA

Mr. Anthony J. Constantine
7 Cadillacs, Lehigh Acres, FL

Ms. Concetta D. Conte
4 Cadillacs, Northfield, NJ

Mr. Joseph L. Conti, Jr.
1 Cadillac, Victoria, TX

Ms. Alice K. Conway
9 Cadillacs, New Prt. Rchy., FL

Mr. Charles L. Conyers
4 Cadillacs, Richmond, VA

Alphonsa Cook
3 Cadillacs, Middletown, RI

Mr. Billy D. Cook
1 Cadillac, Russell, KY

Ms. Eula R. Cook
3 Cadillacs, Winston Salem, NC

Mr. & Mrs. Freddy W. Cook
2 Cadillacs, Jonesboro, LA

Mr. George H. Cook
7 Cadillacs, Port Richey, FL

Mr. Jeter W. Cook
Temple, TX

Ladda B. Cook
3 Cadillacs, Laurelton, NY

Mrs. M.G. Cook
2 Cadillacs, San Antonio, TX

Odis & Juanita Cook
3 Cadillacs, Muldrow, OK

Robert Cook
5 Cadillacs, Hendersonvlle, TN

Ms. Ruth M. Cook
4 Cadillacs, Gretna, LA

Mr. Warren D. Cooke
6 Cadillacs, Baldwinsville, NY

Mr. Charles Cookson, Jr.
1 Cadillac, Alamogordo, NM

Mr. James Cooley
8 Cadillacs, San Diego, CA

Corydon Coombs
5 Cadillacs, Wilmington, MA

Blynn Cooper
6 Cadillacs, Anacortes, WA

Mr. Charles J. Cooper
8 Cadillacs, Alexandria, LA

Mr. Charles F. Cooper
2 Cadillacs, Elkhart, TX

Mr. Elliott E. Cooper, Sr.
3 Cadillacs, Forest City, IA

Mr. George C. Cooper
4 Cadillacs, Moncks Corner, SC

Mr. Jack C. Cooper
8 Cadillacs, Corvallis, OR

Patty & Howard Cooper
2 Cadillacs, Beloit, KS

Mr. Samuel Cooper
20 Cadillacs, Key West, FL

William Cooper
40 Cadillacs, Albuquerque, NM

Mr. R. Cope
1 Cadillac, Burnaby, BC

Ms. Geneva E. Coplin
8 Cadillacs, Burbank, CA

Leon & Delores Coppedge
13 Cadillacs, Portsmouth, VA

Myrtle C. Copper
2 Cadillacs, Baton Rouge, LA

T. Corbierre
1 Cadillac, Little Current, ON

Mr. Harold K. Corbin
3 Cadillacs, Auburn, MI

Mr. Joseph Cordo
6 Cadillacs, Toms River, NJ

Mr. Ricardo Cordova
2 Cadillacs, El Paso, TX

Ms. Doris G. Corn
2 Cadillacs, Tyler, TX

Mr. & Mrs. Gary G. Cornelius
4 Cadillacs, Salisbury, MD

Mr. James H. Cornelius
7 Cadillacs, Fairview Park, OH

Mr. John P. Cornell
6 Cadillacs, Wilmington, DE

Mr. Wallace W. Cornell
5 Cadillacs, Massena, NY

Mr. J. Corp
3 Cadillacs, Baltimore, MD

A. Corrent
2 Cadillacs, Windsor, ON

Ms. Shirley H. Corson
4 Cadillacs, Olean, NY

Mr. Ernie Cortez
3 Cadillacs, Hayward, CA

Mr. Robert D. Cory
3 Cadillacs, Bondurant, IA

Mr. Charles E. Cosby
3 Cadillacs, St. Petersburg, FL

Ms. Leanor D. Costello
2 Cadillacs, Calabash, NC

Edward F. Costigan, Jr.
2 Cadillacs, Chappaqua, NY

Ms. Bobbie D. Cothern
3 Cadillacs, Lumberton, TX

Mr. Billy C. Cothran
2 Cadillacs, Rock Hill, SC

Mr. Michael A. Coto
11 Cadillacs, Casselberry, FL

Ruth Cottingim
4 Cadillacs, Apple Valley, CA

Clyde Cottom
3 Cadillacs, Jeanette, PA

Mr. James H. Couch
1 Cadillac, N. Little Rock, AR

Mr. Monroe Couch
Norton, VA

Mr. James Coulter
7 Cadillacs, Clearfield, PA

P.C. Coulter, Jr.
3 Cadillacs, Collins, MS

Mr. Herbert G. Councill, Jr.
1 Cadillac, Canandaigua, NY

Mr. Wallace D. Counselman
14 Cadillacs, San Antonio, TX

Mr. Thomas K. Countryman
3 Cadillacs, Elmhurst, IL

Mr. Edward C. Coupland
El Paso, TX

Mr. G. Courey
1 Cadillac, Richmond Hill, ON

Mr. Waverly Cousin, Jr.
5 Cadillacs, Cascade, VA

Ms. Louise M. Coutre
1 Cadillac, Addison, IL

Mr. Elias W. Covington
7 Cadillacs, Alexandria, VA

Mr. Robert Cowan
6 Cadillacs, Bristol, VA

Mr. Clyde L. Cox
2 Cadillacs, Houston, TX

Ms. Louise Cox
3 Cadillacs, Wellington, TX

Ms. Mary L. Cox
1 Cadillac, Mount Carmel, IL

Mr. Robert A. Cox
4 Cadillacs, Shrewsbury, MA

Mrs. Sammie Cox
1 Cadillac, Oglethorpe, GA

Mr. Wyatt H. Cox, Sr.
1 Cadillac, Dallas, TX

Mr. Ernie Coyle
2 Cadillacs, Burkburnett, TX

Lynn Coyle
3 Cadillacs, Sugar Land, TX

Mr. Adolph A. Cozzie
5 Cadillacs, Fennville, MI

Carrol Crabb
31 Cadillacs, Muncie, IN

Mike Cracolice
5 Cadillacs, Hollister, CA

Alvin A. Cradduck
9 Cadillacs, Ada, OK

Mr. Oscar P. Craft
4 Cadillacs, Duncan, SC

Elizabeth M. Crafton
10 Cadillacs, Blytheville, AR

Mr. Harold Craig
3 Cadillacs, Corbin, KY

Irvin B. Craig
10 Cadillacs, Diamond Bar, CA

James Craig
2 Cadillacs, Sarnia, ON

Henry G. Cramblett, M.D.
4 Cadillacs, Columbus, OH

Mrs. Patricia R. Cranford
4 Cadillacs, Tampa, FL

Mr. Rufus T. Cranford
4 Cadillacs, Jonesboro, GA

Millicent Cranford
1 Cadillac, Brooklyn, NY

James F. Crankshaw
12 Cadillacs, Riviero Beach, FL

Adam Crapanzano
2 Cadillacs, Holmdel, NJ

Dr. S.M. "Dutch" Craumer
3 Cadillacs, Corning, NY

Ms. Annie M. Crawford
3 Cadillacs, South Holland, IL

Mr. Calvin Crawford
6 Cadillacs, Cleveland, TN

Mr. John P. Crawford
2 Cadillacs, Marion, KY

Mrs. Lois A. Crawford
7 Cadillacs, Saint Louis, MO

Ms. Sandra M. Crawford
1 Cadillac, Flint, MI

Mr. Brent M. Crawley
4 Cadillacs, Hartshorne, OK

Mr. James W. Cray
9 Cadillacs, Meadville, PA

Col. Robert W. Creamer
8 Cadillacs, Pearland, TX

Ms. Virginia M. Creech
4 Cadillacs, Temple, TX

Mr. John W. Cremer
1 Cadillac, Naples, FL

Mrs. Hertisene Crenshaw
1 Cadillac, Wetumpka, AL

Mr. Norris L. Crenshaw, Jr.
14 Cadillacs, Clearwater, FL

Geneva Crisp
5 Cadillacs, Bonita Spgs., FL

Mrs. Anna A. Crispino
10 Cadillacs, Ft. Lauderdale, FL

Mr. Frank J. Crispo
21 Cadillacs, Chicago, IL

James Crockatt
1 Cadillac, Etobicoke, ON

Mr. Johnie Crocker, Jr.
2 Cadillacs, Beaumont, TX

Elizabeth A. Crockett
4 Cadillacs, Stamford, TX

Maurice Crockett
Tallahassee, FL

Walter P. Croft
3 Cadillacs, Aiken, SC

Cron-Cheney Funeral Home
13 Cadillacs, Troy, OH

Ms. Ernestine M. Crook
6 Cadillacs, Mer Rouge, LA

Mrs. Eulalie Prell Crosland
14 Cadillacs, Brazoria, TX

Ms. Connie Cross
2 Cadillacs, Yakima, WA

Ms. Dorothy I. Cross
9 Cadillacs, Avon Park, FL

Mr. E. Cross
1 Cadillac, Brampton, ON

Mr. Henry Crouch
4 Cadillacs, Agoura Hills, CA

Mr. Howard J. Crouch
13 Cadillacs, Thousand Oaks, CA

Mrs. Marjorie E. Crouch
5 Cadillacs, Bryan, TX

Mr. James R. Croucher
6 Cadillacs, Fair Lawn, NJ

Mr. Charles E. Crow
1 Cadillac, Huntington, WV

Mr. Donald Crowe
1 Cadillac, Brampton, ON

James Crowe
1 Cadillac, Warsaw, ON

K. Wayne Crowell
1 Cadillac, Hermitage, TN

Mr. Charles Crump
1 Cadillac, Cornwall, ON

Mrs. Christine V. Crute
2 Cadillacs, Richmond, VA

Ms. Connie E. Cruz
20 Cadillacs, Dallas, TX

Mr. Olan B. Cryer
5 Cadillacs, Apopka, FL

Ms. Ruth S. Crymes
2 Cadillacs, Colorado City, TX

Mr. Emeric Csengeri
1 Cadillac, New York, NY

Glenna Cuccarolo
1 Cadillac, Mississauga, ON

Peter Culhane
2 Cadillacs, Scarborough, ON

Dr. Oscar Z. Culler
15 Cadillacs, Gulfport, MS

Mr. Robert Cummins
3 Cadillacs, Houston, TX

Mr. Carl Cumpton
2 Cadillacs, Wilson, OK

Dominic F. Cundari
2 Cadillacs, Kearny, NJ

Ms. Johanna M. Cundari
3 Cadillacs, Sandusky, OH

Mrs. Albert Cunningham
6 Cadillacs, Snyder, OK

Mr. Chester O. Cunningham
2 Cadillacs, Vienna, WV

Geneva Cunningham
5 Cadillacs, Youngstown, OH

Mr. Homer W. Cunningham
8 Cadillacs, Virginia Bch., VA

Mr. Philip J. Cunningham
5 Cadillacs, Jackson, MI

Mr. William C. Cunningham
9 Cadillacs, Huntsville, AL

Mr. & Mrs. Hartwell B. Curd
3 Cadillacs, Pomeroy, OH

Mr. Harry Curlee, Jr.
7 Cadillacs, Rock Hill, SC

Mr. Albert Curley
4 Cadillacs, Junction City, KS

Mr. F. Curreri
9 Cadillacs, North York, ON

Ralph Currie
1 Cadillac, Toronto, ON

Vearl M. Curry
3 Cadillacs, Abilene, TX

Alberta B. Curtis
3 Cadillacs, San Jose, CA

Mr. Gerry D. Curtis
1 Cadillac, Madison, WI

Mr. John F. Curtis
1 Cadillac, Coronado, CA

Ms. Laverne A. Curtis
6 Cadillacs, Cooperstown, NY

Mr. Wilbur N. Curtis
3 Cadillacs, San Jose, CA

Mr. Benjamin F. Cutcliffe
7 Cadillacs, Rcho. Sta. Marg., CA

Ms. Cora C. Cuthertson
2 Cadillacs, Fort Worth, TX

Mr. Richard W. Cutler
3 Cadillacs, Rhinelander, WI

Grace M. Cwiok-Pelka
5 Cadillacs, Chicago, IL

L.D. & Joyce Cymbalist
5 Cadillacs, Satellite Bch., FL

Mr. Wilfred J. Cyr
3 Cadillacs, Redwood Vly., CA

Mr. Robert J. Cyrog
8 Cadillacs, Sun City West, AZ

D

G. Dagostini
1 Cadillac, Fort Frances, ON

Mr. Douglas J. Dahl
3 Cadillacs, Tampa, FL

Mr. G.J. Daidone
2 Cadillacs, South Holland, IL

Dr. Roy J. Daigle
Sulphur, LA

Mr. Harold Daily
1 Cadillac, Norwalk, CA

Mrs. James W. Daisey
7 Cadillacs, Harrington, DE

Mr. William M. Daley
1 Cadillac, Co. Bluffs, IA

Mr. John R. Dalholtz
2 Cadillacs, Grand Jct., CO

Ms. Barbara B. Dallam
9 Cadillacs, Saint Louis, MO

Mr. Carl W. Dallape
1 Cadillac, Fayetteville, AR

Mr. Calvin Dalton
8 Cadillacs, Ridgeway, VA

W.C. Dalton
1 Cadillac, Hephzibah, GA

Mr. Richard Daly
2 Cadillacs, Mt. Prospect, IL

Mr. William Dampier
5 Cadillacs, Lakeland, FL

Bledsoe L. Daniels
3 Cadillacs, Newton, TX

Mr. Jesse B. Daniels
3 Cadillacs, Bolingbrook, IL

Mr. William L. Daniels
8 Cadillacs, Minneapolis, MN

Mr. Paul Danker
5 Cadillacs, East Moline, IL

Mr. Frank Dante
5 Cadillacs, Bellwood, IL

Mr. Robert Darden
2 Cadillacs, Muncie, IN

Mr. John W. Darnel
5 Cadillacs, Hutchinson, KS

Mr. Joseph D. Darr
1 Cadillac, Joplin, MO

Mr. Guilford F. Darst
9 Cadillacs, Ashland, NE

Mrs. Gladys L. Darville
3 Cadillacs, Riviera Beach, FL

James Dattoma
3 Cadillacs, West Haven, CT

Mr. Benjamin G. Daugherty, Jr.
1 Cadillac, Sikeston, MO

Ms. Martha E. Davan
9 Cadillacs, Englewood, CO

Mr. Leo F. Davey
3 Cadillacs, Aurora, CO

Ms. Eve D. David
7 Cadillacs, Youngstown, OH

Mr. Charles J. Davidson
1 Cadillac, Brockville, ON

Dr. Eli Davidson
2 Cadillacs, Liberty, TX

Mr. Isidore Davila
3 Cadillacs, Smyrna, GA

Mr. Albert H. Davis
7 Cadillacs, Clearwater, FL

Mr. Arvil Davis
17 Cadillacs, Wichita Falls, TX

Mr. Bernard Davis
Spanish Fort, AL

Mr. Beverly Davis
3 Cadillacs, Whitby, ON

Mr. Charles H. Davis
2 Cadillacs, Montgomery, AL

Mr. Dale Davis
2 Cadillacs, Garden City, KS

Mr. Dan W. Davis
12 Cadillacs, Florence, AL

Mr. Gerald A. Davis
2 Cadillacs, Marshallberg, NC

Mr. Gerald Davis
2 Cadillacs, Springfield, VA

Mr. Homer R. Davis
2 Cadillacs, Wilbraham, MA

Mr. Horace A. Davis
6 Cadillacs, Sullivan, IL

Mr. Johnnie Davis
12 Cadillacs, Tallahassee, FL

Mr. Joseph F. Davis
8 Cadillacs, Kingsport, TN

Mrs. Lillie M. Davis
5 Cadillacs, Universal City, TX

Mrs. Lois Davis
Savannah, GA

Mr. Louis Davis
2 Cadillacs, Lake Charles, LA

Mr. Norman Davis
4 Cadillacs, Reading, PA

Mr. Otis Davis
8 Cadillacs, Miami, FL

Ms. Pauline M. Davis
3 Cadillacs, Newton, TX

Mrs. R.H. Davis
8 Cadillacs, Lavonia, GA

Mr. Robert J. Davis
3 Cadillacs, Marion, IN

Robert & Donna Davis
18 Cadillacs, Janesville, WI

S. Stanton & Eloise Davis
10 Cadillacs, Madison, WI

Ms. Sarah Davis
5 Cadillacs, Covington, GA

Mr. Thomas A. Davis
3 Cadillacs, Colonial Hgts., VA

Mr. William L. Davis
7 Cadillacs, Maple Grove, MN

Mr. William E. Davis
19 Cadillacs, Nanticoke, PA

Mr. Willis H. Davis
4 Cadillacs, Colorado Spgs., CO

Mr. Elvin W. Davison
16 Cadillacs, St. Augustine, FL

Mr. Edwin F. Dawes
7 Cadillacs, Johnstown, NY

Hugh Dawkins
1 Cadillac, Phenix City, AL

Mr. Glenn A. Dawley
5 Cadillacs, Liverpool, NY

Mr. Daniel Dawson
1 Cadillac, Buffalo, NY

Edwin F. Dawson
1 Cadillac, Butte, MT

Mr. Josh Dawson
6 Cadillacs, Savannah, GA

Ms. Ann F. Day
2 Cadillacs, Ridgeland, MS

Gert Day
1 Cadillac, Edmore, MI

Judith & Ronald L. Day
3 Cadillacs, Michigan City, IN

Mack Day
2 Cadillacs, Hermitage, TN

Mr. V. Dayment
1 Cadillac, Nepean, ON

Charles De Bourbon
3 Cadillacs, Markham, ON

Mr. Robert A. De Pree
3 Cadillacs, Indianapolis, IN

Mr. Anthony F. De Sorbo
6 Cadillacs, Albany, NY

Mr. William R. Deacon
4 Cadillacs, Barrington, IL

George & Elizabeth Dean
6 Cadillacs, Athens, GA

Mrs. Norma G. DeAngelis
1 Cadillac, Mattapoisett, MA

Mr. Russell W. Dearing
7 Cadillacs, Martinsburg, WV

Mr. Milton B. Deas
4 Cadillacs, Chicago, IL

Dr. Allen G. Debus
6 Cadillacs, Deerfield, IL

Mr. & Mrs. Emerald Dechant
4 Cadillacs, Hays, KS

Mr. A Dock D. Decker
13 Cadillacs, Rancho Mirage, CA

Ms. Carol T. Decker
3 Cadillacs, Ridgefield, CT

Mr. John Dedecko
2 Cadillacs, Fort Myers, FL

Mr. Eugene P. Dediego
8 Cadillacs, Tampa, FL

Mr. John J. Dee
3 Cadillacs, East Hartford, CT

Mr. John F. Deeley
5 Cadillacs, Margate, FL

Mr. Louis J. DeFelice, Sr.
12 Cadillacs, Bridgeport, CT

Mr. William D. DeFer
1 Cadillac, Tucson, AZ

Mrs. Ednamae Defrance
1 Cadillac, Fairfield, TX

Mrs. Vinnie DeFranco
2 Cadillacs, Wheeling, IL

Mr. Henry A. DeFries
3 Cadillacs, Clearwater, FL

Fred DeGeronimo
Massapequa Pk., NY

Ms. Thelma L. Degoede
1 Cadillac, Kalamazoo, MI

Howard DeGraffenreid
2 Cadillacs, Mt. Pleasant, TX

Mr. M. Deir
2 Cadillacs, Cambridge, ON

Mr. Hubert D. DeJaynes
4 Cadillacs, Tucson, AZ

Mrs. Margaret A. Del
7 Cadillacs, Bucyrus, OH

Mr. Curtis G. Delamont
12 Cadillacs, Glendale, AZ

Robert & Diane DeLessio
2 Cadillacs, Roslyn Heights, NY

Mr. Leon DeLoach
1 Cadillac, Athens, LA

Mark & Katharine Delorean
27 Cadillacs, Westlake, OH

Mr. Maurice DeLorenzo
Sarasota, FL

Mr. Donald E. Delp, Sr.
15 Cadillacs, Columbus, OH

Mr. August F. DeLuca
14 Cadillacs, Silver Spring, MD

Mr. Wilbur Demarest
9 Cadillacs, Newburgh, IN

Ms. Lillian Dembik
2 Cadillacs, Buffalo, NY

Mr. Norman J. Demers
9 Cadillacs, Haverhill, MA

Mr. Norman W. Demers
2 Cadillacs, Gorham, NH

Mr. Carl Demoe
4 Cadillacs, Omemee, ON

Mr. James W. DeMore
4 Cadillacs, Brooklyn, NY

Mr. Vincent Denaples
1 Cadillac, Edmond, OK

Ms. Pauline L. Deniston
1 Cadillac, Kansas City, MO

Ms. Catherine L. Denney
6 Cadillacs, Mt. Pleasant, SC

Patrick H. Dennis, Sr., M.D.
4 Cadillacs, Charleston, SC

Mr. Harold C. Deno
8 Cadillacs, Portage, IN

Mrs. Norma Denton
8 Cadillacs, Pana, IL

Mr. Bobby R. Denwood
8 Cadillacs, Saint Louis, MO

Mr. George F. DePriest, Jr.
7 Cadillacs, Nashville, TN

Mary Ann Derby
1 Cadillac, Nacogdoches, TX

Gladys Deresch
3 Cadillacs, Grove, OK

Mr. Ralph F. Dereus
2 Cadillacs, Davenport, IA

Ms. Elaine Derman
Surprise, AZ

Charles L. Dermott
5 Cadillacs, Omaha, NE

Mr. Randall L. Derry
1 Cadillac, Canton, IL

Mr. Russell J. Derx
1 Cadillac, Scottsdale, AZ

Mr. Frank DeSalvo
9 Cadillacs, Chelsea, MA

Mr. Joseph V. DeSaro
14 Cadillacs, Dayton, OH

Roland Descormiers
1 Cadillac, Fleurimont, QC

Mr. Joseph Desiato
5 Cadillacs, Greenacres, FL

Mr. Robert J. Deskovich
1 Cadillac, Akron, OH

Mr. John F. Desris
2 Cadillacs, Rib Lake, WI

Mr. Bart Dethomas
5 Cadillacs, Placitas, NM

Mr. Enoch E. DeVeaux
4 Cadillacs, Eastover, SC

Mr. Donald Dever
2 Cadillacs, Naples, FL

Mr. Francis C. DeVinck
24 Cadillacs, Superior, WI

Mr. Carl A. DeVito
Aventura, FL

Mr. Frank DeVries
8 Cadillacs, Cedar Lake, IN

Mr. Oliver H. Dew
5 Cadillacs, Lancaster, OH

Mr. Raymond W. Dew, Jr.
2 Cadillacs, Raleigh, NC

E. Orval DeWeerth
5 Cadillacs, Rock Falls, IL

Mr. John H. DeWerth, M.D.
10 Cadillacs, Friendship, WI

Paul Dewhirst
4 Cadillacs, Folsom, CA

Mr. Albert J. Di Bella
1 Cadillac, Galveston, TX

James Di Perri
2 Cadillacs, Boston, MA

Mrs. Esie Di Troia
1 Cadillac, Lynn, MA

Robert M. Diamant
9 Cadillacs, Ft. Lauderdale, FL

Mr. Harvey E. Diamond
1 Cadillac, Humboldt, MN

Osvaldo Diaz, M.D.
13 Cadillacs, Miami, FL

Frank Dicanio
1 Cadillac, Hudson, FL

I. Ian Dick
4 Cadillacs, Homewood, IL

Marham A. Dickson
3 Cadillacs, Shreveport, LA

Mr. Thomas A. Dickson
14 Cadillacs, Shreveport, LA

Mr. John S. DiDomenico
5 Cadillacs, St. Petersburg, FL

Frank M. Didway
5 Cadillacs, Charleston, IL

Mrs. Hilda Diehl
5 Cadillacs, Gary, TX

Loren J. Dierkhissing
3 Cadillacs, Everett, WA

Mrs. Vincent Digangi
9 Cadillacs, Norwich, CT

Mary Ann Dillingham
5 Cadillacs, Warrensburg, MO

Mr. Joe R. Dillman
2 Cadillacs, Ellettsville, IN

Mr. Albert Dillon
4 Cadillacs, Salem, OR

Mr. Rudolph Dillon
2 Cadillacs, Chicago, IL

Mr. John T. Dimanno
7 Cadillacs, W. Hartford, CT

Mr. Jovo P. Dimic
2 Cadillacs, Harper Woods, MI

Ms. Patricia A. Dinger
5 Cadillacs, Grand Blanc, MI

Mr. James A. Dingwerth
1 Cadillac, Kansas City, MO

Mr. John E. Dinnsen
5 Cadillacs, Clearwater, FL

Gino DiPace
20 Cadillacs, Clinton Twp., MI

Mr. Anthony R. DiPietro
8 Cadillacs, Lynnfield, MA

Ms. Carmine E. DiPietro
4 Cadillacs, Falmouth, ME

Mr. Robert B. Dirlam
4 Cadillacs, Cortez, FL

Mr. Sam A. Disclafani
3 Cadillacs, Mechanicsville, MD

Mr. Robert H. Dittenber
10 Cadillacs, Gladwin, MI

Mr. Mike Divizie
16 Cadillacs, Merrittstown, PA

Mr. Ovie Dixon
12 Cadillacs, Jasper, TX

Mr. Wilford A. Dixon
2 Cadillacs, Harkers Is., NC

Mr. Milan Djurkovic
1 Cadillac, Mission, TX

Ms. Virginia Dobbins
Anderson, SC

Mrs. Frances K. Dobkowski
2 Cadillacs, St. Augustine, FL

Mr. Leo L. Dobrolonski
7 Cadillacs, Toledo, OH

Mr. O.C. Dobynes
2 Cadillacs, Selma, AL

General Joseph B. Dodds
2 Cadillacs, Colorado Spgs., CO

Dr. Jeffrey E. Dodge
4 Cadillacs, Attleboro, MA

Mr. Ray W. Dodson
7 Cadillacs, Camden, AR

Mr. George P. Doern
2 Cadillacs, Gladstone, OR

Mr. Fred Domaratz
3 Cadillacs, Cheswick, PA

Mr. James H. Donahue
7 Cadillacs, Clearville, PA

Mr. Claude C. Donaldson
4 Cadillacs, Ashland, IL

Mr. Larry J. Donaldson
5 Cadillacs, Houma, LA

Mr. Mark H. Donaldson
3 Cadillacs, Wilmington, DE

Ms. Barbara A. Donelon
5 Cadillacs, Houston, TX

Mr. Earl E. Donges
5 Cadillacs, Hamilton, OH

Mr. James R. Donham
1 Cadillac, Cashmere, WA

Mr. Robert B. Donnelly
8 Cadillacs, Zephyrhills, FL

Sis & Les Dooley
7 Cadillacs, Beloit, WI

Mr. Thomas H. Dooley
10 Cadillacs, Wells, ME

Mr. Cornelius L. Doorn
6 Cadillacs, Grand Rapids, MI

Mr. Richard M. Dorn
13 Cadillacs, Port Richey, FL

Ms. Dorothy M. Dorsey
5 Cadillacs, Santa Maria, CA

Ms. Joyce R. Dorsey
2 Cadillacs, Groves, TX

Mr. Donald A. Dorward
3 Cadillacs, Sarasota, FL

Geraldine Dotson
9 Cadillacs, Highland Bch., FL

Mr. Max A. Doty
4 Cadillacs, Tulsa, OK

Mr. George Douchkess
3 Cadillacs, New York, NY

Ms. Alma Doughman
5 Cadillacs, Alexandria, VA

Mr. George N. Doughty
5 Cadillacs, Cape Charles, VA

Mr. George T. Douglas
4 Cadillacs, Niceville, FL

Mr. Donald G. Douglass
17 Cadillacs, Pine City, MN

Mr. Robert A. Douty
1 Cadillac, Monroeville, PA

Mr. Fred E. Dove
8 Cadillacs, Warrior, AL

Mr. Doran R. Dover
6 Cadillacs, Portland, TX

Mr. Dwight Dover
7 Cadillacs, Kirksville, MO

Mr. Winfred G. Dovey
3 Cadillacs, Decatur, AL

A. Dow
1 Cadillac, Charlottetown, PE

Mr. William Downey
3 Cadillacs, San Diego, CA

Ms. Helen E. Downham
12 Cadillacs, Wilmington, DE

Mr. Edward L. Downs, Sr.
18 Cadillacs, Cpe. Girardeau, MO

Mr. John W. Downs
3 Cadillacs, Greenwood, MS

Mr. Conrad J. Doyle
8 Cadillacs, San Diego, CA

Mr. Dean L. Doyle
5 Cadillacs, Beatrice, NE

Mrs. Ann K. Draeger
3 Cadillacs, Westlake, OH

Mr. J. Drago
2 Cadillacs, Sudbury, ON

Mr. John R. Drago
6 Cadillacs, Scottsville, NY

Mr. Howard M. Dragomer
5 Cadillacs, Ft. Lauderdale, FL

Mr. Vernon Dragt
15 Cadillacs, Fullerton, CA

Mr. Stanley B. Dranoff
10 Cadillacs, Wyncote, PA

Mr. John P. Drao
7 Cadillacs, Daytona Beach, FL

Raymond Dreezer
8 Cadillacs, Boca Raton, FL

Mr. Albert & Lorriane F. Dress
Sun City, AZ

Mr. John Dresslar
3 Cadillacs, Mercer Island, WA

Mrs. Edward R. Drexler
6 Cadillacs, Clearwater, FL

Mr. Wilson C. Driggs
16 Cadillacs, Dallas, TX

Mr. Robert E. Driscoll
2 Cadillacs, Papillion, NE

Mr. Arthur J. Drivas
4 Cadillacs, Andover, MA

Edward W. Droege
5 Cadillacs, Saint Louis, MO

Mr. Clyde Droll
4 Cadillacs, Ina, IL

Mr. James A. Drone
1 Cadillac, Ridgway, IL

James Droney
4 Cadillacs, Lake Ariel, PA

Mr. Casey S. Druan
6 Cadillacs, Albuquerque, NM

Carson M. Drumheller, Jr.
Fort Defiance, VA

Preston Drummer
10 Cadillacs, Jacksonville, FL

Harold A. Druschke
2 Cadillacs, Milwaukee, WI

Mr. Victor E. Drussell
5 Cadillacs, Seattle, WA

Mr. A. Druxerman
1 Cadillac, Toronto, ON

Mr. Robert A. Dublis
13 Cadillacs, Ft. Lauderdale, FL

Betty DuBois-Jackson
3 Cadillacs, Waco, TX

Mr. John C. DuBrava
Chenango Fks., NY

Dr. Howard C. Duckett
2 Cadillacs, Jacksonville, FL

Ms. Mildred Duesenberg
3 Cadillacs, Fort Worth, TX

Leveret G. Duggan
1 Cadillac, Folsom, CA

Mr. James G. Dugger
4 Cadillacs, Fort Collins, CO

Mr. George W. Duke, Jr.
5 Cadillacs, Gulf Shores, AL

Mrs. Robert Dummitt
1 Cadillac, Uxbridge, ON

Mr. Lanny L. Dunahoo
2 Cadillacs, Davison, MI

Louis & Cleo Dunaway
4 Cadillacs, San Antonio, TX

Ms. Florence W. Dunbar
2 Cadillacs, Orlando, FL

Mr. James L. Duncan
8 Cadillacs, Monroe, LA

Rebecca Duncan
2 Cadillacs, Beachwood, OH

Mr. Richard Duncan
1 Cadillac, Savannah, GA

Mr. Robert C. Duncan
7 Cadillacs, Oak Lawn, IL

Mr. William B. Duncan
1 Cadillac, Columbus, GA

Ms. Dolores Dungey
20 Cadillacs, Indianapolis, IN

Ms. Neva P. Dunham
4 Cadillacs, Montour, IA

Byron J. & Dorothy Dunkley
3 Cadillacs, Mesa, AZ

Mr. Glen R. Dunlap
2 Cadillacs, Ozark, AL

Isabel Dunlop
1 Cadillac, Richmond Hill, ON

James H. Dunn
2 Cadillacs, Southaven, MS

Raymond & Betty Dunn
2 Cadillacs, Camden, AR

Mr. Steven Dunn
1 Cadillac, Aurora, ON

Mr. George J. Dunne
7 Cadillacs, S. Lake Tahoe, CA

Ms. Clara C. Dunnington
5 Cadillacs, Rainbow City, AL

Mr. Johnny Duran
3 Cadillacs, Grand Prairie, TX

Lena P. Durant
4 Cadillacs, Dallas, TX

Mr. Elmer N. Durivage
2 Cadillacs, Eden, VT

Berline Durley
3 Cadillacs, Dallas, TX

Mr. Eldridge J. Durocher
6 Cadillacs, Thibodaux, LA

William J. Durr
Elwood, IN

Mr. Frank Dushatinski
1 Cadillac, Auburn, NY

Mr. Robert W. Dussault
8 Cadillacs, Fall River, MA

Capt. R.N. Dussell, Ret.
15 Cadillacs, Arlington, VA

Ms. Lois Dust
3 Cadillacs, Rockford, IL

Mr. Adam B. Duszynski
8 Cadillacs, Mt. Prospect, IL

Mr. Harold J. Dvorak
6 Cadillacs, Sun City, AZ

Brenda Dyck
1 Cadillac, Niagara, ON

Mr. Lewis F. Dye
6 Cadillacs, Belpre, OH

George & Beverly Dyer
1 Cadillac, Dalton, MA

Mr. Gordon W. Dyer
5 Cadillacs, Battle Creek, MI

Mr. William Dyk
Ripon, CA

Lloyd Dykeman
4 Cadillacs, Bridgewater, NS

Mrs. Liz Dykes
1 Cadillac, Amory, MS

Mr. Fred Dysard
2 Cadillacs, Conway, SC

Mr. Harold G. Dyvad
1 Cadillac, Buda, TX

E

Mr. Charles W. Eades
15 Cadillacs, Browder, KY

Mr. Donald Eakin
6 Cadillacs, Albuquerque, NM

Mr. & Mrs. Leonard A. Earring
3 Cadillacs, Bella Vista, AR

Mr. & Mrs. Carl W. Eastridge, Sr.
6 Cadillacs, San Diego, CA

Mr. Gerald A. Eaton
1 Cadillac, Whitman, MA

William V. Eaton
7 Cadillacs, Wichita, KS

Mr. Gerald L. Ebersole
1 Cadillac, Clear Spring, MD

Mr. Paul Ecenia
1 Cadillac, Tampa, FL

Ms. Clara H. Echols
5 Cadillacs, Virginia Bch., VA

Mr. Donald W. Eck
4 Cadillacs, Whitesboro, NY

Mr. Kenneth E. Ecker
2 Cadillacs, Tonawanda, NY

Mr. William R. Edgar
3 Cadillacs, Arlington, VA

Mrs. Carol C. Edgin
3 Cadillacs, San Marcos, CA

Mr. George R. Edgington
3 Cadillacs, White Lake, MI

Robert W. Edland, M.D.
4 Cadillacs, La Crosse, WI

John (Jack) Edmister
8 Cadillacs, Whitney Point, NY

Mrs. Velma Edmiston
3 Cadillacs, Gansevoort, NY

Mr. Robert Edmondson
8 Cadillacs, Pampa, TX

Dr. Clarence L. Edmunds
1 Cadillac, East Tawas, MI

Mr. Benjamin J. Edmundson
8 Cadillacs, Gretna, LA

Mr. Soren Edsberg
Provo, UT

Mr. Blaine H. Edson
1 Cadillac, Sherrill, NY

Mr. Charles Edwards
16 Cadillacs, St. Petersburg, FL

Mrs. Edythe W. Edwards
6 Cadillacs, Florence, AL

Ms. Faye G. Edwards
4 Cadillacs, Columbia, SC

Mrs. Hazel Edwards
1 Cadillac, Kinston, NC

Mr. James M. Edwards
2 Cadillacs, Tyler, TX

Mr. John L. Edwards
4 Cadillacs, Florence, SC

Mr. Sidney B. Edwards
6 Cadillacs, Cincinnati, OH

Sidney & Agnes Edwards
6 Cadillacs, Cincinnati, OH

Mr. W. Edwards
1 Cadillac, Midland, ON

Mr. W.B. Edwards
14 Cadillacs, Lubbock, TX

Mr. William J. Edwards
14 Cadillacs, No. Palm Beach, FL

Mr. William T. Edwards
Las Vegas, NV

Ms. Ann M. Eggleston
2 Cadillacs, Plover, WI

Mr. Robert F. Egler
2 Cadillacs, Arlington, TX

Mr. Darrell C. Egner
8 Cadillacs, Jacksonville, FL

Mr. Gustave R. Egner
2 Cadillacs, Independence, MO

Mr. Harry M. Ehle, Jr.
30 Cadillacs, Marco Island, FL

Mr. Kevin H. Eich
1 Cadillac, Grand Haven, MI

Mr. Harris C. Eichen
12 Cadillacs, Severna Park, MD

Mr. John D. Eickmeyer
2 Cadillacs, Chesterfield, MO

Mr. Gerald H. Eide
2 Cadillacs, Redmond, WA

Mr. Jack D. Eirwin, Sr.
4 Cadillacs, Whitesville, KY

Mr. Le Roy D. Eland
2 Cadillacs, Burlington, IA

Ms. Dianne N. Elges
1 Cadillac, Marathon, FL

Ms. Zerline Elgin
3 Cadillacs, Arlington, TX

Mr. Cecil A. Eli
4 Cadillacs, Kansas City, MO

Mr. Daniel J. Elias
15 Cadillacs, Washington, DC

Sam D. Elias
2 Cadillacs, Orange, CA

Mr. Norman L. Elie
1 Cadillac, Gladstone, OR

Jimmy Elkins
13 Cadillacs, Nashville, TN

Ms. Linda P. Elkins
4 Cadillacs, Hindman, KY

Nahed E. Elkordy
2 Cadillacs, Raleigh, NC

Mr. & Mrs. D.P. Elliott, Jr.
1 Cadillac, Pinewood, SC

William T. Elliott
5 Cadillacs, Ellenton, FL

Mr. Carl & Carolyn Ellis
5 Cadillacs, Kokomo, IN

Mr. Charles Ellis
1 Cadillac, Warner Robins, GA

Mr. Charles M. Ellis
10 Cadillacs, Florence, SC

Mr. Emery E. Ellis
6 Cadillacs, Youngstown, OH

Mr. Jake Ellis
1 Cadillac, Roosevelt, NY

Mrs. Jean G. Ellis
1 Cadillac, Warminster, PA

Mr. Robert A. Ellis
5 Cadillacs, Bonita Spgs., FL

Mr. Robert Ellis
1 Cadillac, Ottawa, ON

Mr. James A. Ellison
5 Cadillacs, Oden, AR

Mr. John H. Ellison, Sr.
7 Cadillacs, Columbus, OH

Mr. Robert A. Ellison
4 Cadillacs, Atlanta, GA

Mr. R. Elpers
4 Cadillacs, Fort Branch, IN

Ms. Margaret L. Emde
12 Cadillacs, Morris, MN

Ms. Gloria Emens
4 Cadillacs, Bayfield, CO

Don A. Emerson
6 Cadillacs, Cumberland, MD

Mr. Harry Emerson
14 Cadillacs, Cathedral Cty., CA

Mrs. Marian G. Emerson
40 Cadillacs, Clinton, KY

Mrs. Mary L. Emerson
2 Cadillacs, Puryear, TN

Mr. Emmett Emmett
8 Cadillacs, El Paso, TX

Guilman Emond
2 Cadillacs, Campbellton, NB

Mr. Robert E. Emory
7 Cadillacs, Las Vegas, NV

Vera Endahl
Lincoln, NE

Mr. Loren S. Endsley
1 Cadillac, Port Arthur, TX

Ms. Venice L. Endsley
1 Cadillac, Huntington, IN

Ms. Ruth M. Enfinger
Atlanta, GA

Mrs. Nettina Engel
1 Cadillac, West Palm Bch., FL

Blair-Alexander Engineering
4 Cadillacs, Denver, CO

Mr. Clark A. English
3 Cadillacs, Marion, IL

Miss M. English
1 Cadillac, North York, ON

Mr. Marvin W. Englund
6 Cadillacs, Alamo, TX

Mrs. Mildred Enis
1 Cadillac, El Dorado, AR

Mr. Donald S. Enterline
3 Cadillacs, Abilene, TX

Mrs. Ann F. Entrekin
3 Cadillacs, Pawleys Isl., SC

Eldon & Pat Epperson
1 Cadillac, Garland, TX

Mr. George B. Epperson
4 Cadillacs, Co. Bluffs, IA

Mrs. Anita Eppert
Columbus, OH

Mr. Robert Epstein
12 Cadillacs, Framingham, MA

Mr. David A. Epting
1 Cadillac, Columbia, SC

Mr. Wilbur F. Erck
4 Cadillacs, Alice, TX

Mr. Francis E. Erdmann
6 Cadillacs, Washington, DC

Mr. Frank C. Erdmann
6 Cadillacs, Boca Raton, FL

Mr. Thomas A. Erickson, Jr.
21 Cadillacs, Clear Lake, IA

Mr. John C. Ernst
3 Cadillacs, Muskegon, MI

Ms. Joyce J. Ernst
2 Cadillacs, Neenah, WI

Mr. George K. Erp
Sun City Center, FL

Mr. C. Esbaugh
1 Cadillac, Waterloo, ON

Col. & Mrs. Edmundo Escudero
San Antonio, TX

Mr. Luis Espinosa
20 Cadillacs, Chula Vista, CA

John Esposito
New York, NY

Sam A. Estelle
3 Cadillacs, Saint Louis, MO

Mr. Bernard E. Estes
3 Cadillacs, Saint Joseph, MO

Mr. Everett Estes
2 Cadillacs, Harrisburg, IL

Albert Ethier
4 Cadillacs, Montreal, QC

Mr. Alexander V. Evans
4 Cadillacs, Scotia, NY

Mr. Charles W. Evans, Jr.
11 Cadillacs, Dayton, OH

Mr. Ed Evans
3 Cadillacs, Lake Ozark, MO

Mr. Edwin C. Evans
7 Cadillacs, Ft. Walton Bch, FL

Mr. Harold L. Evans
22 Cadillacs, Chelmsford, MA

Mr. & Mrs. J.T. Evans
1 Cadillac, Ft. Lauderdale, FL

Mr. Jarrate P. Evans
17 Cadillacs, Oak Park, MI

Jarrate Pete Evans
1 Cadillac, Oak Park West, MI

Mr. Walter B. Evans, Jr.
6 Cadillacs, Middletown, OH

Mr. Freddie Everett
6 Cadillacs, Miami, FL

H. LaVerne Everett
1 Cadillac, Kempner, TX

Mr. Thornton Everett
1 Cadillac, Longview, TX

Mr. Casimer K. Evinski
3 Cadillacs, Grand Blanc, MI

Ms. Ann H. Evridge
3 Cadillacs, Galveston, TX

Mr. Charles R. Ewert
2 Cadillacs, Brookfield, WI

Mr. Robert D. Ezell
6 Cadillacs, Brentwood, TN

F

Ms. Eileen M. Faber
5 Cadillacs, Lennon, MI

Kenneth L. Faber
8 Cadillacs, Mount Morris, MI

Mr. Frederick B. Fabi
5 Cadillacs, Indian Rk. Bch., FL

Mr. Arthur Fabre
2 Cadillacs, Napa, CA

Mr. John Fader
2 Cadillacs, Mollusk, VA

Jerald Fagelbaum
6 Cadillacs, Flushing, NY

Mr. Ben W. Fagen
2 Cadillacs, Littleton, CO

Mr. Dwaine L. Fagler
6 Cadillacs, Lincoln, NE

Mr. Robert C. Fahl
9 Cadillacs, Springfield, MO

Mr. Theodore L. Fairbanks
1 Cadillac, Manchester, CT

Garould Fairhead
4 Cadillacs, Merriman, NE

Mr. Millard A. Fairley, Jr.
3 Cadillacs, Spencerport, NY

Ms. Theresa Falbo
1 Cadillac, Hillside, NJ

Mr. Stephen Falcione
3 Cadillacs, Ormond Beach, FL

Bernard N. Falkowski
4 Cadillacs, West Seneca, NY

Mrs. Helen N. Faller
1 Cadillac, Erie, PA

Gregory Fallon
3 Cadillacs, Phoenix, AZ

Mr. Willard G. Falls
8 Cadillacs, Houston, TX

Mr. & Mrs. Arthur E. Fanning
6 Cadillacs, Norristown, PA

Johnnye & Dorothy Fant
3 Cadillacs, Anderson, SC

Katharyn S. Farina
5 Cadillacs, Hawthorne, NJ

Mr. John Farkas
8 Cadillacs, Erie, PA

Leo C. & Dorothy Farmer
5 Cadillacs, Dallas, TX

Mr. Chauncey F. Farnach
1 Cadillac, Canastota, NY

Mr. Richard W. Farndale
6 Cadillacs, Prophetstown, IL

Mr. Lorimer D. Farnsworth
5 Cadillacs, Shenandoah, IA

Mr. Anthony Faro
1 Cadillac, River Edge, NJ

Richard Farrell
3 Cadillacs, Edwardsville, IL

Mrs. Evelyn E. Farrer
18 Cadillacs, Salt Lake Cty., UT

Ms. Karen J. Farris
1 Cadillac, Juneau, AK

Mr. Patrick A. Fasciale
1 Cadillac, North Brunswick, NJ

Mr. Bryan Faulkner
1 Cadillac, Nepean, ON

Mr. John Faulkner
1 Cadillac, Longford Mills, ON

Mr. Luther F. Faulkner
3 Cadillacs, Alexandria, VA

Mr. Michael Favet
6 Cadillacs, Chicago, IL

Mr. Larry D. Favors
3 Cadillacs, Fort Worth, TX

Mr. Edward Feddersen
San Diego, CA

Mr. John Fedor
2 Cadillacs, Clairton, PA

Mr. D.D. Fee
2 Cadillacs, Long Beach, CA

Mrs. K. Fee
2 Cadillacs, Peterborough, ON

Mr. Jerry S. Feeney
2 Cadillacs, Independence, MO

Earl L. & Betty L. Feiss
5 Cadillacs, Princeton, WV

Joseph C. Feldkircher, Sr.
12 Cadillacs, Westlake, OH

Mr. Allan Feldman
3 Cadillacs, North York, ON

Mr. Wallace H. Feldmeier
10 Cadillacs, Ashtabula, OH

Mr. Emmanuel L. Fellouzis
9 Cadillacs, Largo, FL

Mrs. Grete S. Fellows
3 Cadillacs, San Antonio, TX

Anne Felton
4 Cadillacs, Tallahassee, FL

Ms. Lois W. Fenton
14 Cadillacs, Centralia, MO

George Fenwick
3 Cadillacs, Washington, DC

Mrs. Helen G. Fenza
5 Cadillacs, Lake Park, FL

Mr. Howard J. Ferguson
New Port Richey, FL

Mr. Loy V. Ferguson
6 Cadillacs, Birmingham, AL

Ms. Margaret I. Ferguson
3 Cadillacs, Walnut Creek, CA

Mr. Richard B. Ferguson
5 Cadillacs, Tacoma, WA

Mr. Charles L. Ferko
2 Cadillacs, Trent Woods, NC

Ms. Betty Ferrante
3 Cadillacs, Johnston, RI

Mr. Joseph G. Ferrara
6 Cadillacs, Mansfield Ctr., CT

Dr. Roger & Malba Ferrec
4 Cadillacs, Venice, FL

Ms. Fern Ferrell
4 Cadillacs, Hermitage, AR

Ms. Hattie L. Ferrell
15 Cadillacs, Robertsdale, AL

Mr. Royce T. Ferrell
1 Cadillac, Sweetwater, TX

Mr. Raymond C. Ferris
Mission Viejo, CA

Commander David E. Ferrucci
2 Cadillacs, Palm Coast, FL

Mr. Leo E. Ferry, Jr.
9 Cadillacs, Arlington, MA

Mr. Joseph Feuer
4 Cadillacs, Pepper Pike, OH

Thomas Fezzey
4 Cadillacs, Allen Park, MI

Mr. Felix Fezzuoglio
6 Cadillacs, Voorhees, NJ

Mr. Joe Fiedler
1 Cadillac, Timpson, TX

Mr. James P. Fields
1 Cadillac, Shawnee Msn., KS

Mr. Marlon T. Fields
2 Cadillacs, Tucson, AZ

Mrs. Virginia G. Fields
1 Cadillac, Anderson, IN

Mr. Louis J. Filardo
Lyndhurst, NJ

Ms. Leona F. Filkins
1 Cadillac, Colorado Spgs., CO

Mr. Tony W. Fillman
2 Cadillacs, Sherman, TX

Robert Fillmore
1 Cadillac, Lakewood, OK

Mr. Donald L. Finch
5 Cadillacs, Arcadia, CA

Mr. Robert C. Findlay
1 Cadillac, Arlington, TX

Ms. Marie Finelli
4 Cadillacs, Altoona, PA

Mr. Roger P. Finger
4 Cadillacs, Troy, NY

Mr. Herbert C. Fingerhut
6 Cadillacs, Hinsdale, IL

Donald E. & Shirley M. Fink
7 Cadillacs, Nelsonville, OH

Mr. Earl H. Fink
5 Cadillacs, Harbor Spgs., MI

Mr. Stanley Finkel
12 Cadillacs, Wernersville, PA

Mrs. Betty Finkelstein
5 Cadillacs, Woodbridge, NJ

Robert E. Finken
2 Cadillacs, Austin, TX

Mr. Jack L. Finley
2 Cadillacs, Albuquerque, NM

Lucille Z. Finn
3 Cadillacs, Houston, TX

Mr. Casimiro Fiorentino
13 Cadillacs, Philadelphia, PA

Jeffrey O. Firestone
1 Cadillac, Bay Village, OH

Ms. Carmine C. Fischetti
4 Cadillacs, Kings Park, NY

Mrs. Mary Fiser
21 Cadillacs, Elaine, AR

Cecil F. Fisher
2 Cadillacs, Wichita, KS

Mr. Howard J. Fisher
1 Cadillac, Elmira, NY

Mr. Hughes B. Fisher
7 Cadillacs, Ft. Walton Bch., FL

Mr. John A. Fisher
15 Cadillacs, McConnelsvle., OH

Mr. Melvin Fisher
2 Cadillacs, Columbia, MO

Mr. Ted R. Fisk
3 Cadillacs, Grayville, IL

Mr. Maxwell Fiske
14 Cadillacs, Nokomis, FL

Mr. Richard L. Fite, Jr.
5 Cadillacs, Sarasota, FL

Mr. James A. Fitts
1 Cadillac, Urbandale, IA

Harold Dean Fitzgerald
3 Cadillacs, Clinton, IL

Mr. Richard F. Fitzner
1 Cadillac, Hermiston, OR

W. Burke Fitzsimmons
2 Cadillacs, Hilton, NY

Mr. Frank Fiur
10 Cadillacs, Miami, FL

Mr. Daniel J. Fix, Sr.
2 Cadillacs, Cedar Falls, IA

Mr. Henry L.L. Fjellman
3 Cadillacs, Dubuque, IA

Robert C. Flanders
5 Cadillacs, Melbourne, FL

Mr. James Flatt
37 Cadillacs, Anderson, IN

Mr. Raymond Flaville
8 Cadillacs, Philadelphia, PA

Mr. Orville Fleetwood
31 Cadillacs, Columbus, IN

Mr. Paul J. Fleischmann
10 Cadillacs, Sussex, WI

Mr. Jacob R. Fleming
1 Cadillac, Elizabeth, PA

Mrs. Preston Fleming
17 Cadillacs, Alice, TX

Wallis T. Fleming
4 Cadillacs, Glendale, AZ

Mr. Edward Flemmer
4 Cadillacs, Bismarck, ND

George Flint
21 Cadillacs, Reno, NV

Mr. Robert P. Floeter
18 Cadillacs, Saginaw, MI

Mr. Melvin R. Flom
1 Cadillac, Minneapolis, MN

Mrs. Jean A. Flood
1 Cadillac, Crystal Falls, MI

Dr. Rafel Florez
1 Cadillac, Meridian, MS

Mr. Frank J. Florio
6 Cadillacs, Warren, OH

Mr. Loren B. Floyd
1 Cadillac, Hope Mills, NC

Mr. C. Flynn
4 Cadillacs, Trenton, ON

Mr. Herbert J. Flynn
21 Cadillacs, Boca Raton, FL

Ms. Eleanor H. Flynt
1 Cadillac, Houston, TX

Mr. Edward J. Focke
Cincinnati, OH

Mr. Wayne H. Fogelman
8 Cadillacs, Tiffin, OH

Ronald Fogler
3 Cadillacs, Las Vegas, NV

Mr. Loyal Folden
11 Cadillacs, Venice, FL

Mr. Ralph E. Foos
20 Cadillacs, Bellevue, OH

Mr. Floyd G. Forcade
2 Cadillacs, Smithton, IL

Mr. Ralph M. Ford, Jr.
10 Cadillacs, Georgetown, SC

Mrs. Richard & Virginia Ford
4 Cadillacs, Houston, TX

Mr. James Fordyce
3 Cadillacs, Gloucester Cy., NJ

Mr. Allen W. Fore
4 Cadillacs, Silver Spring, MD

Mr. H.L. Foreman
5 Cadillacs, Crowley, LA

Mr. Ernest H. Forest
19 Cadillacs, Tewksbury, MA

Mr. Michael J. Forgione
5 Cadillacs, Copiague, NY

Mr. Philip Forman
4 Cadillacs, Stoughton, MA

Mr. Theodore B. Fornetti
1 Cadillac, Iron Mountain, MI

Mr. William F. Forrest
2 Cadillacs, Grimstead, VA

Mr. Argel B. Forrester
4 Cadillacs, Norcross, GA

Mr. Delmer V. Forsberg
33 Cadillacs, Beaver Falls, PA

Archibald F. Forster, M.D.
10 Cadillacs, Long Beach, CA

Milton Forster
14 Cadillacs, Coral Gables, FL

Mr. Richard B. Fort
14 Cadillacs, Nashville, TN

Mr. Andre P. Fortier, MD
3 Cadillacs, Biddeford, ME

Mr. Roland Fortin
4 Cadillacs, Rutland, VT

Mr. Donald Foss
6 Cadillacs, Tacoma, WA

Ms. Amy C. Foster
1 Cadillac, Dunnellon, FL

Dr. Donald J. Foster
2 Cadillacs, San Diego, CA

Mr. Elmer J. Foster
2 Cadillacs, Detroit, MI

Ms. Lucy S. Foster
3 Cadillacs, Sparta, GA

Mr. Ulysses W. Foster
3 Cadillacs, N. Wilkesboro, NC

Mr. Paul E. Fournier
1 Cadillac, Amesbury, MA

Ms. Dorothy F. Fouts
5 Cadillacs, Dallas, TX

Ms. Joan Fowler
4 Cadillacs, Dallas, TX

Mr. Joseph Fowler
12 Cadillacs, Boca Raton, FL

Mr. Ralph W. Fowler
12 Cadillacs, Cleveland, OH

Mr. Charles Fox
35 Cadillacs, Charleston, WV

Mr. Joe T. Fox
3 Cadillacs, Dayton, OH

Mrs. Lovella H. Fox
2 Cadillacs, Bloxom, VA

Mrs. Artie Lee Moss Foxx
8 Cadillacs, San Antonio, TX

Mr. Bertrand Fraga
24 Cadillacs, San Leandro, CA

Mr. James T. France
6 Cadillacs, Carrollton, TX

Keith E. & Eileen France
1 Cadillac, Havana, IL

Mr. Thomas Franciamore
2 Cadillacs, Trenton, NJ

Ms. Patricia Francis
3 Cadillacs, Cincinnati, OH

Mr. Alex Frank
3 Cadillacs, Jonesville, LA

Mr. Norman E. Frank
2 Cadillacs, Williamsville, NY

Mr. Wilbert A. Frank
1 Cadillac, Largo, FL

Valentine Frankie
6 Cadillacs, Junction City, KS

Mr. Donald Franklin
6 Cadillacs, Indianapolis, IN

Mr. James R. Franklin
6 Cadillacs, Omaha, NE

Jessie Franklin
7 Cadillacs, Memphis, TN

Mr. Caspian S. Franks
2 Cadillacs, Raleigh, NC

Mr. Anthony Franz
1 Cadillac, San Francisco, CA

Mr. Donald W. Fraser
1 Cadillac, Lansing, MI

Ms. Doris A. Fraser
2 Cadillacs, Chester, MT

Ms. Jeanne E. Fraser
6 Cadillacs, Rockford, IL

Ruth E. & Gordon A. Fraser
3 Cadillacs, Brunswick, ME

G.E. Frayser
7 Cadillacs, Abingdon, VA

Ms. Alma A. Frazier
2 Cadillacs, Salyersville, KY

Benjamin Frazier
5 Cadillacs, Savannah, GA

Mr. Clyde E. Frazier
1 Cadillac, Belton, TX

Ms. Evelyn Frazier
4 Cadillacs, Atlanta, GA

Mrs. Juanita S. Frazier
1 Cadillac, Pollock, LA

Ms. Rachel Frazier
3 Cadillacs, Lawrenceville, GA

Angee C. Frederickson
3 Cadillacs, Summerton, SC

Ms. Betty Freed
3 Cadillacs, Parkersburg, WV

Mr. Walter Freedman
3 Cadillacs, Washington, DC

Mr. C. Freeman
1 Cadillac, Nepean, ON

Mr. Dana B. Freeman
21 Cadillacs, Lebanon, TN

John A. Freeman
6 Cadillacs, Kerrville, TX

Mr. Walter L. Freeman
1 Cadillac, High Point, NC

Ms. Wanda M. Freeman
5 Cadillacs, Columbus, OH

Mr. Ordean M. Freese
2 Cadillacs, Eldora, IA

Mr. William Freischlag, Sr.
1 Cadillac, Roanoke, VA

Ms. Mary J. Fretag
2 Cadillacs, Minneapolis, MN

Mr. Andrew F. Frey
2 Cadillacs, Bay St. Lou, MS

Mr. Charles Frey
2 Cadillacs, Montoursville, PA

Mr. Roy Friedman
5 Cadillacs, Caldwell, NJ

Mr. George W. Friedrich
2 Cadillacs, Jackson, MO

Mr. P. Friend
1 Cadillac, Edmonton, AB

Mr. James M. Friery
14 Cadillacs, Oneonta, NY

Mr. Elmer L. Fristrom
4 Cadillacs, Greeley, CO

Mr. Carl E. Frith
7 Cadillacs, Palm Harbor, FL

Mr. Charles M. Fritz
12 Cadillacs, Seffner, FL

Mr. Roland C. Fritz
14 Cadillacs, Silver Spring, MD

George Froehlich
2 Cadillacs, East Quogue, NY

Mr. James E. Froelich, Jr.
6 Cadillacs, Columbus, TX

Mr. Victor P. Frohlich
1 Cadillac, Panama City, FL

Ms. Bessie P. Frost
Vidalia, GA

C.J. "Jack" Frost
2 Cadillacs, Cincinnati, OH

Mr. Harry E. Fruitrich
38 Cadillacs, Sugarloaf, PA

Mr. Melvin E. Fryer
3 Cadillacs, Carver, MA

Miss Frankie L. Fryman
40 Cadillacs, Abilene, TX

Ms. Freda Fuchs
6 Cadillacs, Holly, MI

Winkler B. Fuchs
7 Cadillacs, Martinez, GA

Mr. Richard L. Fugate
1 Cadillac, Louisville, KY

Mr. Charles A. Fulgham
Neches, TX

Ms. Mary Fulkerson
14 Cadillacs, Rolling Hills, CA

Mr. Cecil Fullen
3 Cadillacs, Dallas, TX

Mr. Walter W. Fuller
5 Cadillacs, Shreveport, LA

Mr. Kenneth H. Fullerton
1 Cadillac, Burnsville, MN

Mr. Maynard Fullington
5 Cadillacs, Palmer, NE

Mr. Charles B. Fults
3 Cadillacs, La Grange, CA

Mr. Dorsie D. Fulwiler
3 Cadillacs, Kingsport, TN

Brian & Terry Funk
1 Cadillac, McLean, IL

Mr. Osvaldo Furano
3 Cadillacs, Youngstown, OH

Mr. Frank J. Furlan
7 Cadillacs, Naples, FL

Nicholas Furnarotto
10 Cadillacs, Irvington, NY

Peter J. Fusco
1 Cadillac, Brooklyn, NY

Ralph Fusco
Edison, NJ

G

Mr. James Gabriel
20 Cadillacs, McKeesport, PA

Mr. Malcolm Gachette
2 Cadillacs, Tullahoma, TN

Mr. Mitchel E. Gadsden
3 Cadillacs, Fayetteville, NC

Mr. Daniel Gadzaliszyn
2 Cadillacs, Flushing, NY

Mr. Paul Gagner
Saint Albans, VT

Mr. Joseph K. Gailbreath
5 Cadillacs, Ruidoso, NM

Anthony J. Galdes
2 Cadillacs, Plymouth, MI

Mr. Charles Galleher
2 Cadillacs, Jonesboro, AR

Mr. William C. Gallimore
2 Cadillacs, Ellerbe, NC

Mr. Ervin Galloway
11 Cadillacs, Carlsbad, NM

Rev. Henry L. Galloway
8 Cadillacs, Houston, TX

Mr. Vince Galvin
10 Cadillacs, Seattle, WA

Mr. Joseph Gamby
12 Cadillacs, Las Vegas, NV

Mr. Rusi D. Gandhi
1 Cadillac, Montville, NJ

Mr. Rocky C. Ganino
3 Cadillacs, Stamford, CT

Mr. Alphonso Gantt
2 Cadillacs, Temple, TX

Elaine Garant
1 Cadillac, Windsor, ON

Mr. Melvin T. Garbe
1 Cadillac, Saint Paul, MN

Ms. Karen Garbeil
6 Cadillacs, Wynnewood, PA

Mr. John Garber
4 Cadillacs, Jacksonville, FL

Eleanor Garcia
4 Cadillacs, Waterloo, IL

Mr. Hector L. Garcia, Sr.
1 Cadillac, Tucson, AZ

Mr. Edward F. Gardas
1 Cadillac, Willow Spgs., IL

Mr. Johnny S. Gardner
1 Cadillac, Dayton, OH

Mmr G. Gardner, Sr.
5 Cadillacs, Detroit, MI

Mr. Walter M. Gardner
3 Cadillacs, Warrenton, NC

Capt. Winston L. Garesche
1 Cadillac, Maitland, FL

Ms. Lucille S. Garfield
6 Cadillacs, Miami, FL

Ms. Jeanne B. Garland
11 Cadillacs, Pomona, CA

Mr. Louis A. Garland
6 Cadillacs, Wheaton, IL

Mr. James M. Garlick
4 Cadillacs, Houston, TX

Mrs. Dorothy M. Garlinger
1 Cadillac, Wheelersburg, OH

Mr. Fred Garlington
3 Cadillacs, Philadelphia, PA

Ms. Alma R. Gaskin
3 Cadillacs, Jackson, MS

J. Gelinas
4 Cadillacs, Alfred, ON

Mrs. Joan T. Giammalvo
3 Cadillacs, East Moriches, NY

Dr. Donald O. Gilman
6 Cadillacs, Willmar, MN

Gladston & Callie Garner
1 Cadillac, Raleigh, NC

Mr. Neil Gaskin
3 Cadillacs, Mississauga, ON

Mr. P. Gelley
1 Cadillac, St. Catharines, ON

Mr. Albert Giannini
5 Cadillacs, Belvidere, IL

Leland J. Gilson
1 Cadillac, Minocqua, WI

Ms. Ruby D. Garner
9 Cadillacs, Brownfield, TX

Mr. Candie Gaskins
1 Roselle, NJ

Mr. Emile P. Gendreau
6 Cadillacs, Westport, MA

Mr. P. Giannone
3 Cadillacs, Edmonton, AB

Mr. Calogero Gioe
4 Cadillacs, Chalmette, LA

Richard Garofola
4 Cadillacs, Eastpointe, MI

Mrs. Flora Gates
Ventura, CA

Vinny Caddy Genna
12 Cadillacs, Holbrook, NY

Mr. Ralph L. Giant
3 Cadillacs, Aurora, CO

Mr. Harold F. Gipe
12 Cadillacs, Boca Raton, FL

Mr. James L. Garret
11 Cadillacs, Birmingham, AL

Mr. Salvator A. Gatta
13 Cadillacs, Clinton, MS

Peter Genoff
4 Cadillacs, Detroit, MI

Mr. John A. Giardino
1 Cadillac, Pueblo, CO

Jerry Girard
2 Cadillacs, Lynnwood, WA

Mr. Billie J. Garrett
5 Cadillacs, Michie, TN

Mr. Clarence A. Gaub
1 Cadillac, Silverton, OR

Mrs. Betty K. Gentry
9 Cadillacs, Advance, NC

James Giatras
10 Cadillacs, Ocean City, MD

Mrs. V. Girhiny
1 Cadillac, Burlington, ON

Guy A. Garrett
2 Cadillacs, Holiday, FL

Mr. Elbert L. Gaudet
2 Cadillacs, Thibodaux, LA

Mary Gentry
6 Cadillacs, Chesapeake, VA

Mr. Roy H. Gibbs
11 Cadillacs, Trivoli, IL

Mrs. Flora G. Gisclar
1 Cadillac, San Antonio, TX

Mr. Lamar A. Garrett
4 Cadillacs, Ft. Walton Bch., FL

Anthony J. Gaudio, Sr.
4 Cadillacs, Youngstown, OH

Mr. Charlie B. George, Jr.
4 Cadillacs, Jonesville, TX

Mr. William Giberson, Jr.
10 Cadillacs, Jacksonville, FL

Ms. Mildred S. Gittings
6 Cadillacs, Baltimore, MD

Ms. Marian A. Garrett
1 Cadillac, Bonnerdale, AR

Mrs. Fran J. Gaudio
26 Cadillacs, Naples, FL

Mr. William R. George
9 Cadillacs, Lancaster, OH

Mr. Bill Gibson
1 Cadillac, Wando, SC

Pat J. & Anna N. Giunta
9 Cadillacs, Raytown, MO

Mr. & Mrs. Marion Garrett
2 Cadillacs, Shawnee Msn., KS

Mr. Freeman Gause
4 Cadillacs, Sunset Beach, NC

Ms. Jane G. Gerard
3 Cadillacs, Waterloo, IA

Mr. & Mrs. Don Gibson
Tyler, TX

Maria Givens
3 Cadillacs, Statesville, NC

Ruth & G.P. Garrett
18 Cadillacs, Birmingham, AL

Mr. Paul E. Gauthier
8 Cadillacs, Fairfax, VA

Morris Gerber
25 Cadillacs, Highland Park, IL

Ms. Helen M. Gibson
3 Cadillacs, Ft. Walton Bch., FL

Mr. Marvin H. Gladen
5 Cadillacs, Sebring, FL

Mr. Nathaniel Garrison
6 Cadillacs, Orwell, OH

Dr. Anne R. Gayles-Felton
4 Cadillacs, Tallahassee, FL

Mr. Anthony A. Gerome
2 Cadillacs, Santa Maria, CA

Mr. Thomas E. Gifford
3 Cadillacs, Youngstown, OH

Mr. John C. Gladhill
3 Cadillacs, Middletown, MD

Mr. Reynold Garrison
9 Cadillacs, Vero Beach, FL

Ms. Dorothy Gaylord
8 Cadillacs, Detroit, MI

Mr. Adam J. Gerres
29 Cadillacs, Canton, MI

Mr. John Giganti
1 Cadillac, White Plains, NY

Mr. Robert Glassford
1 Cadillac, Oshawa, ON

Mr. Leonard H. Garton
1 Cadillac, Menomonie, WI

Mr. Milton Geason, Jr
2 Cadillacs, Oakland, CA

Mr. Harold Gerring
22 Cadillacs, Elkhart, IN

Frank J. Gigliotti
2 Cadillacs, Winter Haven, FL

Ms. Winnifred E. Glasshof
Milwaukee, WI

Mr. Ole A. Garvick
Sioux Falls, SD

Mr. Arthur Gehman
5 Cadillacs, Denver, PA

Mr. Irving Gerring, Jr.
Port St. Lucie, FL

Mr. Eugene G. Gilbert
6 Cadillacs, Milwaukee, WI

Mr. Arpad Glatz
2 Cadillacs, Glenview, IL

Enos Garvin, Sr.
3 Cadillacs, Savannah, GA

Mr. Bernard Geier
5 Cadillacs, Fairfax, VA

Mr. Fred Gettman
4 Cadillacs, Odessa, WA

Ms. Donna Gilchrist
Mazon, IL

Mr. Earle R. Glenn
3 Cadillacs, Los Angeles, CA

Mr. Ronald L. Garwick
7 Cadillacs, Morrison, IL

Ms. Pauline D. Geier
3 Cadillacs, Forestville, WI

Mr. Robert F. Geyer
9 Cadillacs, Hamilton, OH

G. Gilchrist
3 Cadillacs, Wainwright, AB

Mr. Albert Gleza
1 Cadillac, Buckhannon, WV

Ms. Sue M. Gary
2 Cadillacs, Mapleton, IL

Mr. B. Geisam
3 Cadillacs, Regina, SK

Mr. George J. Ghikas
1 Cadillac, Sheridan, WY

Dr. Vernon Gillenwater
1 Cadillac, Powder Spgs., GA

Mr. Chris M. Glogovac
Lafayette, CA

Russell Gash
1 Cadillac, Fresno, CA

Mr. Arthur C. Geldner
5 Cadillacs, Buena Park, CA

Mr. Andrew J. Giamfortone
2 Cadillacs, La Marque, TX

Ms. Virginia H. Gillum
5 Cadillacs, San Antonio, TX

Kenneth J. & Carol Glomb
7 Cadillacs, Hinsdale, IL

Ms. Betty D. Glover
3 Cadillacs, Gardendale, AL

Mr. Earnest Glover, Jr.
2 Cadillacs, Kissimmee, FL

Mr. Weyman Glover
1 Cadillac, Pelham, GA

Mr. Middie D. Glymph, Jr.
11 Cadillacs, Winston Sal., NC

Robert C. Gnagey
1 Cadillac, Derby, KS

Freya A. Gnerre
2 Cadillacs, Yonkers, NY

Mr. Henry F. Gober, Jr.
2 Cadillacs, Kingsport, TN

Ms. Lyria L. Gobert
3 Cadillacs, Marshall, TX

Mr. Willis R. Goble
1 Cadillac, Columbia City, IN

Mrs. La Cleda Godfrey
8 Cadillacs, Winnsboro, TX

Mr. Paul C. Goebel
6 Cadillacs, Golden, CO

Marlene Goertz
1 Cadillac, Sherwood Park, AB

Mr. Wendell E. Goeske
4 Cadillacs, Luverne, MN

Dorbie Goff
1 Cadillac, Shelbiana, KY

Jo Anne Goff
2 Cadillacs, Kokomo, IN

Wilfert L. Goggans
2 Cadillacs, Dallas, TX

Ms. Eleanor G. Goggin
1 Cadillac, Dunkirk, NY

Mr. Morris C. Gohrick
10 Cadillacs, McGregor, ND

Mr. Harry A. Goins
2 Cadillacs, Charlotte, NC

Mr. Joe H. Gold
2 Cadillacs, Las Cruces, NM

Mr. Hyman Goldberg
11 Cadillacs, West Orange, NJ

Mr. Jack Goldenberg
6 Cadillacs, Somerset, KY

Mr. Lon R. Goldsmith
3 Cadillacs, Jericho, NY

Mr. Alfred J. Golonka, Jr.
3 Cadillacs, North Adams, MA

Mr. Preston Gomez
7 Cadillacs, Newport Beach, CA

Ms. Carolyn M. Gomillion
23 Cadillacs, Cleveland, OH

Mr. Charles Gonsalves
6 Cadillacs, E. Providence, RI

Chess L. Gooch
3 Cadillacs, Big Spring, TX

Mr. Harold I. Gooch, Sr.
1 Cadillac, Titusville, FL

Mrs. Elizabeth Good
6 Cadillacs, Indio, CA

Charles Goodale
3 Cadillacs, Collinsville, IL

Mrs. Dorothy Goodberry
5 Cadillacs, Fountain Vly., CA

Mr. Raymond C. Goode
6 Cadillacs, Winston Sal., NC

Mr. William Goode
1 Cadillac, Greensboro, NC

Mrs. Irene Goodman
2 Cadillacs, W. Hempstead, NY

Mr. Nate Goodman
6 Cadillacs, Schaumburg, IL

Mr. Ray Goodman, Jr.
20 Cadillacs, Cleveland, OH

Mr. Frank N. Goodrich
2 Cadillacs, Lakeport, CA

Earl L. Gordon
1 Cadillac, Tallahassee, FL

H.W. Gordon
5 Cadillacs, Rincon, GA

Dr. Irvine C. Gordon
7 Cadillacs, Prairie View, TX

Ms. Marion D. Gordon
5 Cadillacs, Duluth, GA

Ralph & Lucille Gordon
2 Cadillacs, Marietta, GA

Mr. Stewart G. Gordon
3 Cadillacs, Dallas, TX

Mr. Lacy L. Gore
2 Cadillacs, Clarendon, NC

Mrs. Sylvia Gore
4 Cadillacs, Taloga, OK

Mr. John Goreski
1 Cadillac, Oshawa, ON

Mr. Felix Gorgone
15 Cadillacs, Seven Hills, OH

Mrs. Kathryn Gorman, Sr.
4 Cadillacs, McDonough, GA

Miss M. Gorringe
1 Cadillac, Coquitlam, BC

Mr. Charles Gorub
5 Cadillacs, Valparaiso, IN

Mr. Mitchell W. Gorz
6 Cadillacs, Chicago, IL

Mr. Donald I. Gossard
2 Cadillacs, Baltimore, MD

Mr. Robert H. Gostomski
Neosho, WI

Mr. Lloyd Gottlieb
15 Cadillacs, Cincinnati, OH

Mr. Donald E. Gottshall
1 Cadillac, Columbus, OH

Delores Gottwald
3 Cadillacs, Fayetteville, PA

Mr. Nicholas T. Goudes
6 Cadillacs, Charlotte, NC

Mr. Raymond R. Goudreau
3 Cadillacs, Manchester, NH

Mr. Robert P. Goulas, Jr.
1 Cadillac, San Antonio, TX

Mr. L. Edward Gouthro
4 Cadillacs, Dartmouth, NS

Ms. Edna Grabstein
5 Cadillacs, Staten Island, NY

Joseph N. & Miggy Grady
12 Cadillacs, Naples, FL

Mr. Martin Graf
2 Cadillacs, Momence, IL

Jack C. Graff
11 Cadillacs, Seward, NE

Mr. Robert D. Graff
10 Cadillacs, W. Palm Bch., FL

Mr. George Grages
3 Cadillacs, Midlothian, IL

Mr. Fred C. Gragg
3 Cadillacs, Mobile, AL

Mr. Jack D. Graham
12 Cadillacs, Conway, SC

James S. Graham
1 Cadillac, Norwood, PA

Lawrence M. Graham, D.D.S.
10 Cadillacs, Cameron, MO

Ora & Glen Graham
3 Cadillacs, Parrish, FL

Mr. Robert T. Graham, Sr.
2 Cadillacs, Indianapolis, IN

Mr. James H. Gralla
3 Cadillacs, Schaumburg, IL

Ms. Sue Grammer
1 Cadillac, Dallas, TX

Frank Grande
8 Cadillacs, Somerville, MA

Mrs. Virginia M. Granitto
5 Cadillacs, McDonald, OH

Mr. George A. Grant
1 Cadillac, Cortland, NY

Mr. James U. Grant
2 Cadillacs, Charleston, IL

Mrs. Mary Jane Grant
3 Cadillacs, Midlothian, IL

Mr. Robert M. Grant
1 Cadillac, Brandenburg, KY

Ms. Virginia M. Granthum
Perry, FL

Mr. Charles E. Graves
7 Cadillacs, Heber Springs, AR

Mr. & Mrs. John M. Graves
Tucson, AZ

Mr. Billy Gray, Jr.
12 Cadillacs, Barbourville, KY

Mr. Charles A. Gray
4 Cadillacs, Syracuse, NY

Daniel Gray
6 Cadillacs, Orlando, FL

Mr. Edward G. Gray
2 Cadillacs, Rising Sun, IN

Mrs. Helen W. Gray
3 Cadillacs, Jena, LA

Ms. Joann V. Gray
3 Cadillacs, Greenwood, SC

Mr. Leon Gray
3 Cadillacs, Malvern, AR

Mr. Thomas J. Gray, Jr.
2 Cadillacs, Lithonia, GA

Wannie Gray
3 Cadillacs, Richmond, VA

Mr. Wylie Gray
3 Cadillacs, Poplar Bluff, MO

Philip A. Greco
9 Cadillacs, New City, NY

Mr. Charles E. Green
4 Cadillacs, Ashland, KY

Mr. Emmit E. Green
Akron, OH

Jack Green
3 Cadillacs, London, ON

Mr. Jessie O. Green
4 Cadillacs, Weed, CA

Ruth Green
12 Cadillacs, Roseville, MI

Mr. Victor L. Green
3 Cadillacs, Franklinville, NY

Ms. Laurette J. Greene
3 Cadillacs, Boca Raton, FL

Mr. Ralph Greene
4 Cadillacs, Yuba City, CA

Ms. Doris A. Greenleaf
1 Cadillac, Devils Lake, ND

Gilbert L. Greenstein
15 Cadillacs, Basking Ridge, NJ

Mr. Clarence Greentree
1 Cadillac, Oshawa, ON

Fay H. & A.D. Greenwood
2 Cadillacs, Clint, TX

Mrs. Alvin Greer
8 Cadillacs, Chandler, TX

Lorenza Greer
2 Cadillacs, Lanham, MD

Mr. Thomas G. Greer
1 Cadillac, Cecil, PA

Harry Gregg
2 Cadillacs, Mississauga, ON

Ms. Sandra Grego
1 Cadillac, Blairsville, PA

Mr. Richard J. Gregorek
1 Cadillac, Anaheim, CA

Mr. Albert E. Gregory
7 Cadillacs, Joliet, IL

Mr. Clarence Gregory
Pataskala, OH

Ms. Sandra H. Greifzu
8 Cadillacs, Naples, FL

Rick Gremer
7 Cadillacs, Normal, IL

Dr. Raymond F. Grenfell
6 Cadillacs, Jackson, MS

G. Grenier
1 Cadillac, Grand-Mere, QC

Mr. James L. Grienke
3 Cadillacs, Alta, IA

Mr. William A. Grier
1 Cadillac, McDonough, GA

Mr. Arthur E. Grieves
4 Cadillacs, Berkley, MI

Clifford Griffin
6 Cadillacs, Sacramento, CA

Ms. Hattie M. Griffin
2 Cadillacs, Lexington, NC

Mr. Warren B. Griffin
12 Cadillacs, Pageland, SC

William Griffin
9 Cadillacs, Los Angeles, CA

Mr. H. Griffiths
1 Cadillac, North Battleford, SK

Mr. Paul S. Grimes
4 Cadillacs, Wasilla, AK

Mr. William B. Grimm
6 Cadillacs, Lehigh Acres, FL

Mrs. Jess R. Grisham
7 Cadillacs, Yreka, CA

Mr. Harry B. Grissom
3 Cadillacs, Spencer, NC

Mr. William T. Grist
2 Cadillacs, Charlotte, NC

Ms. Virgillia Gromen
2 Cadillacs, Lima, OH

Kenneth L. & Helen Gross
3 Cadillacs, Kirksville, MO

Mr. Leonard K. Gross
3 Cadillacs, Willoughby, OH

Mr. Robert H. Grossberg
8 Cadillacs, Hollywood, FL

Mr. Eugene A. Groves
5 Cadillacs, Carbondale, IL

Mr. Melvin V. Groves
4 Cadillacs, Reynoldsburg, OH

Mr. Billy L. Grubb
4 Cadillacs, Chesapeake, VA

Mr. William W. Gruenig, Jr.
7 Cadillacs, Palm Desert, CA

Mr. Phil Grund
7 Cadillacs, Marietta, GA

Mr. C.G. Grundy
7 Cadillacs, Pulaski, PA

Ms. Gloria M. Guarino
6 Cadillacs, Milton, MA

Miss Amy E. Gubera
1 Cadillac, Alameda, CA

Norma Gudmundson
5 Cadillacs, San Rafael, CA

Ms. Kay L. Guenther
1 Cadillac, Mission, TX

Mr. Charlie Guffey
11 Cadillacs, Scottsdale, AZ

Mr. Paul G. Guignet
13 Cadillacs, Ridgecrest, CA

Stephen John Guilford
2 Cadillacs, Cleveland, OH

Mr. Maurice M. Guilleaume
3 Cadillacs, Kingman, AZ

Mr. Elward Guillory, Sr.
1 Cadillac, Houston, TX

Dr. Yves Guillory
11 Cadillacs, New Orleans, LA

Mr. Blaine Gullett
7 Cadillacs, Portsmouth, OH

Edwin Gunderson
4 Cadillacs, Wilsonville, OR

Mrs. Helen R. Gunnels-Kieper
2 Cadillacs, San Angelo, TX

Mr. R.J. Gunson
4 Cadillacs, Winnipeg, MB

Mr. Jake Gunter
4 Cadillacs, Cleveland, OH

Woodrow Y. Guntharp
Los Angeles, CA

Michael W. Gurnick
10 Cadillacs, Lafayette, IN

Mr. William Guseman, Sr.
5 Cadillacs, Hollywood, FL

Mr. Don E. Gustavel
4 Cadillacs, Salem, SC

Mr. George Guthrie
1 Cadillac, Jasper, AL

Mr. John E. Guthrie
6 Cadillacs, Prospect, KY

Mr. Donald Gutzwiller
2 Cadillacs, Guilford, IN

Mr. Robert M. Gwaltney
4 Cadillacs, Louisville, KY

Mr. Kenneth W. Gwin
2 Cadillacs, Old Hickory, TN

H

H.P. Leasing
2 Cadillacs, Peoria, IL

Ms. Barbara T. Habig
Jasper, IN

Mr. Edgar Hache
9 Cadillacs, St.-Isidore, NB

Mr. Raymond H. Hack
5 Cadillacs, Rio Linda, CA

D.L. Hackathorn
4 Cadillacs, Moundsville, WV

Mr. Alexander J. Haddad
1 Cadillac, Willimantic, CT

Mr. James Hadge
6 Cadillacs, Burlington, MA

Brian Huguenard
26 Cadillacs, Fort Wayne, IN

Mr. H. Hafke
1 Cadillac, Kelowna, BC

Ms. Elizabeth N. Hagedorn
2 Cadillacs, Middletown, OH

Mr. Donald B. Hagen
4 Cadillacs, Tyler, TX

Aurthur W. Hahn, III
4 Cadillacs, Greenport, NY

Louis Hahn
14 Cadillacs, Sarasota, FL

Mr. D. Haig
1 Cadillac, Brighton, ON

Billie Lou Hail
2 Cadillacs, Morehead City, NC

Mr. Calvin Hailey
Bakersfield, CA

Mr. George C. Hair
5 Cadillacs, Jamesville, NY

Mr. Alfred Halasz
1 Cadillac, Bad Axe, MI

Mr. Raymond E. Hale
4 Cadillacs, Las Vegas, NV

Mr. Richard Hale
1 Cadillac, Galax, VA

Mr. Howard J. Haley
12 Cadillacs, Emerald Isle, NC

M. Halfpenny
7 Cadillacs, Cherry Hill, NJ

Bishop Milton L. Hall
9 Cadillacs, Kokomo, IN

Mr. D. Hall
1 Cadillac, Guelph, ON

Mr. Donald Hall
2 Cadillacs, Evansville, IN

Mr. Howard Hall
6 Cadillacs, Moultrie, GA

Ms. Katherine B. Hall
2 Cadillacs, N. Wilkesboro, NC

Leonard Hall
2 Cadillacs, Dauphin, MB

Ms. M. Hall
1 Cadillac, Amherstburg, ON

Mr. Mervin Hall
3 Cadillacs, Port Orchard, WA

Mr. Milford H. Hall
3 Cadillacs, Concord, NC

Mrs. Neal A. Hall
7 Cadillacs, Diamondhead, MS

Ms. S. Hall
1 Cadillac, Scarborough, ON

Mr. Sam F. Hall, Jr.
8 Cadillacs, Kingsport, TN

Mr. William Hall
8 Cadillacs, Moweaqua, IL

Ms. Martha R. Hallberg
1 Cadillac, El Paso, TX

Mr. Raymond C. Halter
1 Cadillac, Robinson, IL

Mrs. Madora H. Haltom
2 Cadillacs, Midland, TX

Mr. Charles H. Ham
7 Cadillacs, Shalimar, FL

Mr. Vernon L. Hamann
4 Cadillacs, Bradley, IL

Ms. Grace A. Hambel
1 Cadillac, Crystal River, FL

Mr. Dale E. Hamilton
3 Cadillacs, Inez, KY

Mr. Dewey L. Hamilton
8 Cadillacs, London, KY

Hazel R. Hamilton
8 Cadillacs, Abingdon, VA

Mr. Howard C. Hamilton
Crane Hill, AL

Janet L. & Billy G. Hamilton
1 Cadillac, Manito, IL

L. Hamilton
1 Cadillac, Winnipeg, MB

Mrs. Pat Hamilton
7 Cadillacs, Harker Hghts., TX

Ms. Vera W. Hamilton
1 Cadillac, San Augustine, TX

Brian D. Hamm
Tallahassee, FL

Robert Hammer
8 Cadillacs, Oak Park, IL

Mr. Walter Hammock
4 Cadillacs, Cleveland, OH

Mr. Charles Hampton
2 Cadillacs, Cincinnati, OH

Mr. Joseph R. Hampton
4 Cadillacs, Wichita, KS

Mr. D.L. Hanauer
5 Cadillacs, Avon, MN

Mr. Gordon H. Hancock
Sebree, KY

Ms. Mildred W. Hancock
17 Cadillacs, Ocala, FL

Mr. William L. Hancock
1 Cadillac, Saint Joseph, MO

Mr. William Hancock
33 Cadillacs, Knoxville, TN

Mr. & Mrs. Frank Handra
4 Cadillacs, West Harrison, IN

Mr. Ladislav Hanecak
2 Cadillacs, Thornhill, ON

Dr. Rolenzo A. Hanes
4 Cadillacs, Naples, FL

Mr. Donald E. Haney
7 Cadillacs, Cookeville, TN

Mr. Edward L. Haney
7 Cadillacs, Macomb, IL

Mr. Robert W. Hank
4 Cadillacs, Elgin, IL

Mr. Charles E. Hankins
5 Cadillacs, Lavallette, NJ

Mr. Clayton E. Hanlin
6 Cadillacs, Hamilton, IL

G. Hannah
1 Cadillac, Fonthill, ON

Mr. James H. Hannah
1 Cadillac, Mayfield, KY

George W. Hansen
1 Cadillac, Chicago, IL

Mr. Leon Hansen
1 Cadillac, New Palestine, IN

Mr. & Mrs. O.R. Hansen
13 Cadillacs, Lakewood, CA

Mr. Thomas C. Hansen
Lake Worth, FL

Mr. Ben Hansford
28 Cadillacs, Elgin, IL

Mr. Robert C. Hanson
6 Cadillacs, Monarch, MT

Mr. Rodney M. Hanson
1 Cadillac, Shreveport, LA

Verne Hanson
12 Cadillacs, Couderay, WI

Mr. William R. Hanson
4 Cadillacs, Brookfield, WI

Noboru Hanyu
5 Cadillacs, San Francisco, CA

Carol Hanzo
10 Cadillacs, Garfield, NJ

Mr. Ronald M. Haram
5 Cadillacs, Marion, OH

Mrs. Carolyn A. Harbin
2 Cadillacs, Concord, CA

G. Harbin
1 Cadillac, Kenosha, WI

Dave & Alice Harbour
1 Cadillac, Leeds, UT

Mr. James Hardaway
6 Cadillacs, Detroit, MI

Leo Hardell
1 Cadillac, Wausau, WI

Mr. Wilmer L. Hardy
4 Cadillacs, Brandywine, MD

Mr. Kevin F. Hargadon
2 Cadillacs, Walpole, MA

Mr. Paul Hargash
Saginaw, MI

Cynthia Hargens
2 Cadillacs, Laredo, TX

Mr. Carter L. Hargrave
8 Cadillacs, Louisville, KY

Mrs. Martha Hargrave
1 Cadillac, Webster City, IA

Haring Energy Company
1 Cadillac, San Antonio, TX

Mr. Charles H. Harkins
5 Cadillacs, Childersburg, AL

Mr. Lew D. Harkins
2 Cadillacs, Vicksburg, MS

Mr. George L. Harlow
3 Cadillacs, Waukegan, IL

Mr. Gerald J. Harman, Jr.
1 Cadillac, Beverly Hills, CA

Mr. William L. Harman
6 Cadillacs, Phoenix, AZ

J. Harmon
26 Cadillacs, Woodland, WA

Mr. Michael W. Harmon
9 Cadillacs, Baytown, TX

William O. & Edna Harmon
5 Cadillacs, Fort Pierce, FL

Claus Harms
8 Cadillacs, Brampton, ON

Mr. Vahram Haroian
Saint Louis, MO

Mr. Ole B. Haroldson
9 Cadillacs, Prescott, AZ

Mr. Elmer L. Harp
2 Cadillacs, Fort Myers, FL

Mr. Albert J. Harper, Jr.
2 Cadillacs, Shreveport, LA

E. Harper
6 Cadillacs, Halifax, NS

Mr. Joe S. Harper
6 Cadillacs, Haskell, TX

Mr. Alfred B. Harrell
25 Cadillacs, Orange Beach, AL

Mr. & Mrs. Donald Harries
Troy, MI

Mrs. Bernice A. Harrington
2 Cadillacs, Waterville, ME

Mr. James G. Harrington
2 Cadillacs, Cumming, GA

Ms. Annie B. Harris
1 Cadillac, Rayville, LA

Mr. Arthur L. Harris
Rahway, NJ

Felton & Annie Harris
6 Cadillacs, Kissimmee, FL

Mr. Ivan L. Harris
6 Cadillacs, Austin, TX

Mr. James O. Harris
2 Cadillacs, Niceville, FL

Mr. John A. Harris
6 Cadillacs, Shreveport, LA

Mrs. Oceal W. Harris
3 Cadillacs, Baton Rouge, LA

Ross Harris
2 Cadillacs, Amherstburg, ON

Mr. Smith H. Harris
2 Cadillacs, Arlington, TX

Mr. Walter R. Harris
8 Cadillacs, Tampa, FL

Mr. Walter Harris
5 Cadillacs, Newark, NJ

Mr. Bert Harrison
3 Cadillacs, Weslaco, TX

Mr. Don Harrison
11 Cadillacs, Conway, AR

Mr. James N. Harrison
7 Cadillacs, Niles, MI

Mr. John T. Harrison
6 Cadillacs, Williamsburg, VA

Mrs. Marion Harshbarger
9 Cadillacs, Gainesville, FL

Mr. Hugene W. Hart
2 Cadillacs, W. Des Moines, IA

Jean L. Hart
13 Cadillacs, Deerfield Bch., FL

Mr. Neilan Hart
2 Cadillacs, Columbia, MO

S. Hartlen
3 Cadillacs, U. Stewiacke, NS

Mr. Horace M. Hartman
10 Cadillacs, Johnson City, TN

Ms. Margaret K. Hartman
15 Cadillacs, Camden Wyo., DE

Ms. Elizabeth G. Hartsfield
2 Cadillacs, Mill Creek, WA

Dewey & Clarece D. Hartwell
2 Cadillacs, Salem, VA

Mr. Gene A. Harvey
5 Cadillacs, Colorado Spgs., CO

Dirk Harvuot
4 Cadillacs, Miamisburg, OH

Barbara Harwas
2 Cadillacs, E. Lehigh Acres, FL

Mr. Eldon Haselhuhn
14 Cadillacs, Findlay, OH

Mr. Wallace M. Haselton
1 Cadillac, Manchester, ME

Mr. Kent Hasemeier
9 Cadillacs, Columbus, GA

N. Hashman
New Washington, IN

Mr. Robert J. Hasner
12 Cadillacs, Yorktown, VA

Mr. Francis L. Hassett
14 Cadillacs, Fort Myers, FL

Mr. John S. Haster
11 Cadillacs, Ocala, FL

J. Hastings
2 Cadillacs, Mississauga, ON

Mr. Archie E. Hatfield
9 Cadillacs, Fortson, GA

Ms. Audrey R. Hatfield
7 Cadillacs, Knoxville, TN

Mr. Gus D. Hatfield, Jr.
6 Cadillacs, Chattanooga, TN

John Hatt, Chapeau Rentals
51 Cadillacs, Cedar Rapids, IA

Mr. Martin J. Hatzakorzian
4 Cadillacs, Hopkinsville, KY

Mr. Glen S. Haugen
1 Cadillac, Saint Paul, MN

Don E. Haupert
7 Cadillacs, Fairfield, IA

Mr. Irwin C. Haus
9 Cadillacs, Las Vegas, NV

Ms. Mary Haverty
7 Cadillacs, Pittsburgh, PA

Mr. Peter P. Haviar, Jr.
2 Cadillacs, San Diego, CA

Mr. Kenneth G. Hawks
1 Cadillac, Winston Salem, NC

Ms. Helen C. Hawley
4 Cadillacs, Monroe, LA

Mr. Daniel O. Hawthorne
2 Cadillacs, Riverside, CA

Mr. W.T. Hawthorne
3 Cadillacs, College Sta., TX

F. Hay
1 Cadillac, Roseneath, ON

Mr. Lowell H. Hay
5 Cadillacs, Ortonville, MN

Mr. Paul Haycraft
4 Cadillacs, Westchester, IL

William F. Hayden, M.D.
6 Cadillacs, Little Rock, AR

Mr. Bryce Hayes
1 Cadillac, Lompoc, CA

Mr. Doug K. Hayes
8 Cadillacs, Taylor Ridge, IL

Mrs. Mary Hayes
6 Cadillacs, Ada, OK

Mr. Royal R. Hayes
1 Cadillac, Troutman, NC

Mrs. Elizabeth B. Haynes
Chicago, IL

Mr. Paul D. Haynes
2 Cadillacs, Iowa Park, TX

Joan Hayslip
3 Cadillacs, New Lebanon, OH

Ms. Annie Lee Haywood
5 Cadillacs, Elgin, TX

Mrs. Phyllis P. Haywood
6 Cadillacs, Raleigh, NC

Mr. Bill Hazelwood
4 Cadillacs, Sun City, AZ

Mrs. Marjorie M. Hazelwood
80 Cadillacs, Richmond, VA

Mr. Arthur G. Hazen
6 Cadillacs, Oshkosh, WI

Ray W. & Helen Head
4 Cadillacs, Chico, CA

Mr. Charlton F. Headley
1 Cadillac, Millbrook, AL

Mr. James C. Heard
2 Cadillacs, Sandy, UT

Mr. & Mrs. Ralph Hearlson
1 Cadillac, Federal Way, WA

Samuel Heaton
5 Cadillacs, Indianapolis, IN

Ms. Ann Heavener
15 Cadillacs, Blacksburg, VA

Ms. Marjorie N. Hebden
17 Cadillacs, Fort Myers, FL

Mr. Roy B. Hebel
2 Cadillacs, Gainesville, FL

Ms. Carol H. Hebert
2 Cadillacs, Zachary, LA

Mr. James C. Hecht
4 Cadillacs, Southington, CT

William R. Heck
7 Cadillacs, Williamson, GA

Mr. William Hecox
1 Cadillac, Rio Rico, AZ

Ms. Doris A. Hector
13 Cadillacs, Mountainside, NJ

Mr. Paul Hedrick
3 Cadillacs, Smithville, OH

Mr. Gerald Heffern
6 Cadillacs, Diamond Bar, CA

Mr. Werner E. Hegstrom
15 Cadillacs, Saint Paul, MN

Mr. Irvin L. Heideman
2 Cadillacs, Pensacola, FL

Mr. William Heikoop
1 Cadillac, Welland, ON

Mr. John Heilig
8 Cadillacs, York, PA

Mr. Donn R. Hein
5 Cadillacs, Stevens Point, WI

Mr. & Mrs. Paul Heinrich
2 Cadillacs, Mandan, ND

Mr. Lewis & Lois Heisey
1 Cadillac, Elizabethtown, PA

Ms. Lillian H. Heitman
1 Cadillac, Salisbury, NC

Mr. Melvin Helitzer
8 Cadillacs, Athens, OH

Ronald Heller
14 Cadillacs, Miami, FL

Mr. William A. Hellmann
4 Cadillacs, Las Vegas, NV

Ms. Gloria D. Helm
3 Cadillacs, Sherman, TX

Mr. Glen H. Helverson, Sr.
3 Cadillacs, Raytown, MO

Mr. Harlan W. Helzer
2 Cadillacs, York, PA

Dick W. Hemphill
2 Cadillacs, Phoenix, AZ

Mr. Otis E. Henard
22 Cadillacs, Rogersville, TN

Mr. Murray H. Hendel
3 Cadillacs, Naples, FL

Muriel & Wayne Hendershot
6 Cadillacs, Syosset, NY

Alfred Henderson
10 Cadillacs, U. Marlboro, MD

Mr. Alva M. Henderson
8 Cadillacs, Apple Valley, CA

C. Allen & Truman Henderson
Greenwood, SC

Charley S. Henderson
4 Cadillacs, Merrillville, IN

Mr. Clarence E. Henderson
1 Cadillac, Cook, MN

Mr. Deangelo B. Henderson
3 Cadillacs, Jackson, MS

Ms. Marilyn Henderson
1 Cadillac, Genoa, OH

Mrs. Patricia Henderson
6 Cadillacs, Indianapolis, IN

Ms. Rose M. Hendle
2 Cadillacs, Naples, FL

Mr. John B. Hendon
7 Cadillacs, Lubbock, TX

Mr. James Hendrick
2 Cadillacs, Little Rock, AR

Mrs. Connie Hendricks
8 Cadillacs, Richmond, KY

Mr. Raymond T. Hengels
2 Cadillacs, Chicago, IL

Mr. Henry Henke
10 Cadillacs, Carnegie, PA

Mary T. Henley & H.R. Terry
1 Cadillac, Fairmont, NC

Ronald & Josephine Hennecke
3 Cadillacs, West Chester, OH

Mr. John F. Hennessey
2 Cadillacs, Southbury, CT

Mernia Henninger
2 Cadillacs, Arcanum, OH

Mrs. Florence Henry
10 Cadillacs, Flourtown, PA

Mrs. Louise W. Henry
15 Cadillacs, Grants Pass, OR

Sharon Holland Henry
3 Cadillacs, Flossmoor, IL

Ms. Eugenia Herbst
3 Cadillacs, Schuylerville, NY

Mr. Roland C. Herdine
1 Cadillac, Lakewood, CO

Mrs. Rebecca J. Hermann
6 Cadillacs, Akron, OH

Ms. Eileen Hermsen
3 Cadillacs, Pr. Du Chien, WI

Mr. Benito D. Hernandez
3 Cadillacs, Saginaw, MI

Gerald H. Herndon
2 Cadillacs, Keystone Hts., FL

Mr. Gerald H. Herndon
2 Cadillacs, Keystone Hts., FL

Mr. John Herod
6 Cadillacs, Nashville, TN

Mr. Walter O. Herren
1 Cadillac, Clearwater, FL

Florence Herrle
5 Cadillacs, Elyria, OH

Mr. Charles R. Herrmann
6 Cadillacs, Owatonna, MN

Mr. Howard W. Herron
1 Cadillac, San Jose, CA

Ms. Virginia G. Herron
5 Cadillacs, Orangeburg, SC

Mr. William J. Herscheid, Jr.
8 Cadillacs, Chicago, IL

Kathryn F. Hersey
6 Cadillacs, The Woodlands, TX

Mr. David B. Hershberger
5 Cadillacs, Wampum, PA

Mr. Otto Hertel, Jr.
2 Cadillacs, Beeville, TX

Mr. John & Marie Heska
38 Cadillacs, Mt. Vernon, WA

Dud Hess, Jr.
3 Cadillacs, Spring Hill, FL

Mr. Paul L. Hesson
4 Cadillacs, Westchester, IL

Mr. Carlton T. Hester
4 Cadillacs, Fairfield, CA

Ms. R.D. Hester
Matteson, IL

Tommy L. Hester
12 Cadillacs, Tuscaloosa, AL

Mr. Jack B. Hethcox
2 Cadillacs, Talladega, AL

Mr. Carl F. Hettmansberger
Oakwood, IL

Mr. Paul Hewitt
6 Cadillacs, Tulsa, OK

Mr. William R. Hewitt
7 Cadillacs, Chicago, IL

Manford Hiatt
2 Cadillacs, Creston, IA

Mr. Asa Hickman
10 Cadillacs, Chincoteague, VA

Mr. Larry M. Hickman
1 Cadillac, Kalamazoo, MI

Mr. Edward Hicks, Sr.
1 Cadillac, Birmingham, AL

Mr. Norman F. Hicks
1 Cadillac, Ozark, MO

Ms. Ernestine Hickson
5 Cadillacs, Miami, FL

Mr. Osborne Higgenbothem
10 Cadillacs, San Antonio, TX

Mrs. Betty Higginbotham
3 Cadillacs, Purcell, OK

Mr. Dexter C. Higgins
10 Cadillacs, Bakersfield, CA

C.R. Hildreth/E.N. Hildreth
7 Cadillacs, Austin, MN

Dorothy & Harold Hileman
2 Cadillacs, Homestead, PA

David Hill
7 Cadillacs, Scarborough, ON

Ms. Elizabeth H. Hill
22 Cadillacs, Ft. Lauderdale, FL

Kevin Hill
1 Cadillac, Santa Ana, CA

Mrs. Mary Hill
5 Cadillacs, Spanish Fort, AL

Mr. Thomas R. Hill
1 Cadillac, Ottawa, IL

Mr. William S. Hill
4 Cadillacs, Riviera Beach, FL

Mr. William B. Hill
4 Cadillacs, Raleigh, NC

Mr. Joe B. Hilliard
12 Cadillacs, Anderson, SC

Mr. Harry Hinch
1 Cadillac, Lethbridge, AB

Mr. William A. Hindon
Littleton, CO

Mrs. Evelyn Hine
4 Cadillacs, Springfield, IL

Miss Billie F. Hines
1 Cadillac, Shreveport, LA

Mr. George Hines
1 Cadillac, Dublin, GA

Mr. Elvis D. Hinton
1 Cadillac, Great Bend, KS

Catherine & Andrew G. Hirko
1 Cadillac, Mesa, AZ

Dorothy & Marvin Hirsch
15 Cadillacs, Brownsville, TX

Mr. James K. Hirst
1 Cadillac, Okemos, MI

Mr. Jackson P. Hise
9 Cadillacs, Port Arthur, TX

Ms. Yvonne T. Hix
8 Cadillacs, Bedford, TX

Mr. Paul Hnatiw
24 Cadillacs, Saskatoon, SK

Mazelle C. Hobbs
3 Cadillacs, Jacksonville, FL

Mr. Ed Hockensmith
8 Cadillacs, Gallatin, MO

Mr. Thomas P. Hocker
6 Cadillacs, Sherman, TX

Mrs. Marion T. Hockman
2 Cadillacs, Carroll, OH

Alfred D. Hodge, Jr.
12 Cadillacs, Dallas, TX

Mr. James A. Hodges
6 Cadillacs, Dunnellon, FL

Mr. John L. Hodges
7 Cadillacs, Encinitas, CA

Ms. Sallie P. Hodgin
15 Cadillacs, Goldsboro, NC

Charles Hodgkins
21 Cadillacs, Shrewsbury, MA

Mr. Robert Hodgson
2 Cadillacs, North York, ON

Ms. Jetty C. Hoeft
1 Cadillac, Redwing, MN

Ms. Anna G. Hoelscher
1 Cadillac, Midland, TX

Mr. Maurice Hoffman
5 Cadillacs, Newport News, VA

Mr. Nicholas R. Hoffman
5 Cadillacs, Monsey, NY

William Hoffman
13 Cadillacs, Danville, CA

Mr. Earl L. Hogan
3 Cadillacs, Naples, FL

George Hogan
12 Cadillacs, Ft. Mitchell, KY

Mr. John J. Hogan, Jr.
1 Cadillac, Kinston, NC

Thomas J. Hogge
2 Cadillacs, Yorktown, VA

Mrs. Dean Holcomb
15 Cadillacs, Atlanta, GA

Mr. Burl H. Holcombe
2 Cadillacs, Columbiana, AL

Mr. Edgar H. Holden
14 Cadillacs, Bettendorf, IA

Mr. Dwight W. Holder
2 Cadillacs, Winston Salem, NC

Mrs. Georgia Holding
7 Cadillacs, Pampa, TX

Robert & Theola Holdmeyer
5 Cadillacs, Washington, MO

Mr. Clyde B. Holland
2 Cadillacs, Madisonville, KY

B. Hollansworth
10 Cadillacs, Phoenix, AZ

Mr. Howard Holley
4 Cadillacs, Danville, VA

Mr. Leon W. Holley
9 Cadillacs, Silver Spring, MD

Ms. Wanda K. Hollick
1 Cadillac, El Paso, TX

Mrs. Betty Holliday
3 Cadillacs, Kokomo, IN

Mr. Robert M. Hollingshead
7 Cadillacs, Ormond Beach, FL

Ms. Jean F. Hollingsworth
13 Cadillacs, Charleston, SC

Ms. May Hollingsworth
3 Cadillacs, Whitney, TX

Mr. Wesley D. Hollingsworth
3 Cadillacs, Wilmington, NC

Ms. Maxine J. Hollis
Whitley City, KY

Mr. W. Kennith Hollis
5 Cadillacs, Whitestown, IN

Mr. Jack B. Holloway
3 Cadillacs, Detroit, MI

Ms. Lillian A. Hollywood
20 Cadillacs, Ft. Lauderdale, FL

Mrs. Arrie M. Holmes
St. Petersburg, FL

Mr. Arthur P. Holmes
3 Cadillacs, Houston, TX

Mrs. Janith L. Holmes
Bay City, MI

Mr. John Holmes
15 Cadillacs, Indianapolis, IN

Edward Holsapple
2 Cadillacs, Oklahoma City, OK

Mr. Dewey A. Holst
1 Cadillac, Fayette, MO

Mrs. Alice J. Holt
1 Cadillac, Columbia, SC

Mr. Ernest H. Holt
10 Cadillacs, Greenville, NC

Mr. Henry Holt, Jr.
7 Cadillacs, Elsah, IL

M. Holt
1 Cadillac, Callander, ON

Mr. Tom S. Holt
5 Cadillacs, Fort Worth, TX

Mr. Alvin G. Holtkamp
6 Cadillacs, Saint Louis, MO

Raymond Holtz
23 Cadillacs, Naples, FL

Mr. James B. Holys
3 Cadillacs, Saginaw, MI

Mr. David G. Holzbaur
3 Cadillacs, Beverly Hills, FL

Mr. Charles W. Honaker
8 Cadillacs, Tampa, FL

Mrs. Catherine H. Hoobler
3 Cadillacs, Cleveland, OH

Mr. William R. Hoole
2 Cadillacs, Naperville, IL

Mr. Hubert Hooper
2 Cadillacs, Clayton, GA

Ms. Artis Hoosier
San Augustine, TX

Mr. Richard Hormann
6 Cadillacs, Fort Wayne, IN

Mr. Roy Horn
2 Cadillacs, Paris, TN

Mr. William A. Horn
2 Cadillacs, Lawrenceville, IL

Mr. Wallace Hornberger
3 Cadillacs, Vancouver, WA

Francis Horne
Bloomfield, MI

Mrs. Rex E. Horner
2 Cadillacs, Sweetwater, TX

Mr. Sam W. Horner
20 Cadillacs, Corpus Christi, TX

C. Hornsby
1 Cadillac, Centreville, AL

Mr. Justus L. Hornsby
15 Cadillacs, Fort Worth, TX

Mr. Martin Horowitz
6 Cadillacs, Commack, NY

Mr. Carlton L. Horton
3 Cadillacs, Jacksonville, FL

Ms. Dorothy Horvath
4 Cadillacs, Longview, TX

Mr. Lawrence F. Hoskins
12 Cadillacs, Buhl, ID

Robert K. Hosley
54 Cadillacs, Lansing, MI

Dr. Aubrey L. Hotchkiss
10 Cadillacs, Fort Worth, TX

Bill Houghton
20 Cadillacs, Fort Myers, FL

Chatmon Houston, Jr.
5 Cadillacs, Leominster, MA

Ms. Kate Houston
3 Cadillacs, Roseburg, OR

Mr. Hiram M. Hovey
2 Cadillacs, Ballston Spa, NY

Booker T. Howard
5 Cadillacs, Sumter, SC

Mr. Earl Howard
2 Cadillacs, Chattaroy, WV

Ms. Maria V. Howard
1 Cadillac, Rocky Mount, NC

Mr. Marion A. Howard
4 Cadillacs, Russiaville, IN

Edna J. Howe
12 Cadillacs, Columbus, IN

Mr. Elmer S. Howell
4 Cadillacs, Geneseo, IL

Mr. Roy C. Hoxie
2 Cadillacs, Middleton, WI

P. Hrabok
1 Cadillac, Thunder Bay, ON

Leonard F. Hubbard, III
2 Cadillacs, Springfield, IL

Mr. & Mrs. Howard J. Huber
6 Cadillacs, Safety Harbor, FL

Walter Huber
1 Cadillac, St. Catharines, ON

Hjelmer & Dorothy Huberg
4 Cadillacs, Royal, IA

Mr. Delton W. Hubert
2 Cadillacs, Monument, KS

Mr. John J. Hubert
1 Cadillac, Wilbraham, MA

Mr. Howard H. Huckman
2 Cadillacs, Los Angeles, CA

Mr. Walter H. Hucks, Jr.
2 Cadillacs, Nichols, SC

Martha & Douglas Huddle
3 Cadillacs, Baytown, TX

Mr. Edgar Hudgins
1 Cadillac, Chattanooga, TN

Mrs. Lavenia Hudgins
7 Cadillacs, Fort Worth, TX

Mr. Jack W. Hudnall
5 Cadillacs, Springhill, LA

Mr. Carl E. Hudson
1 Cadillac, Eaton Park, FL

Donald L. Hudson
15 Cadillacs, Greentown, IN

Mr. Melvin W. Hudson
4 Cadillacs, Kannapolis, NC

Mr. Frederick B. Huebner
10 Cadillacs, Western Sprgs., IL

Dr. & Mrs. Arden N. Huff
1 Cadillac, Dugspur, VA

Ms. Beulah M. Huff
17 Cadillacs, Hubert, NC

Charles E. Huff, Jr.
8 Cadillacs, Columbus, GA

Mrs. Eunice D. Huffman
17 Cadillacs, Tacoma, WA

Mrs. Aline Huggins
4 Cadillacs, Birmingham, AL

Ms. Helen C. Huggins
3 Cadillacs, Amarillo, TX

Mrs. Farnese I. Hughes-Lumpkin
1 Cadillac, Savannah, GA

Mr. Alton M. Hughes
3 Cadillacs, Longview, TX

Mr. Arlin Hughes
5 Cadillacs, Riverdale, GA

Ms. Betty J. Hughes
5 Cadillacs, Borger, TX

Mr. Bradford Hughes
5 Cadillacs, Lawrenceville, GA

Ms. Dorothy M. Hughes
1 Cadillac, Chicago, IL

Mr. Edward Hughes
1 Cadillac, Glenburnie, ON

Mr. Francis L. Hughes
2 Cadillacs, Independence, MO

Ms. Helen L. Hughes
8 Cadillacs, Sarasota, FL

Ms. Phyllis K. Hughes
8 Cadillacs, Frankfort, IN

Mr. Smith Hughes
6 Cadillacs, Quinton, OK

Longino & Helen J. Hughey
11 Cadillacs, Los Angeles, CA

Mr. Earle Hughs
31 Cadillacs, Independence, MO

Willie Hull
5 Cadillacs, Chicago, IL

Ms. Sisilia H. Humeniuk
2 Cadillacs, Alliance, OH

Mr. J. Vincent Humphrey
1 Cadillac, Powassan, ON

Mr. Dudley M. Humphries
7 Cadillacs, Canyon, TX

Mrs. Mary A. Huneycutt
3 Cadillacs, Concord, NC

Ms. Josephine D. Hunsinger
11 Cadillacs, Troy, MI

Mr. Adrian Hunt
5 Cadillacs, Searcy, AR

Curtis & Annette Hunt
1 Cadillac, Elmhurst, IL

Mr. F.C. Hunt
10 Cadillacs, Houston, TX

Mr. Leandra Hunt
8 Cadillacs, Redford, MI

Mr. Lowell L. Hunt
3 Cadillacs, Las Vegas, NV

Mr. Robert Hunt
7 Cadillacs, Summit, NJ

Mr. Herbert Hunter
2 Cadillacs, San Diego, CA

Mr. Jon D. Hunter
3 Cadillacs, Tolar, TX

Mr. Ferit Hur
5 Cadillacs, Oakville, ON

Mrs. Marjo P. Hurinenko
2 Cadillacs, Manning, ND

Mrs. Virginia Hurlburt
2 Cadillacs, Yarmouth, NS

Mr. Robert H. Hurlbut
7 Cadillacs, Honeoye Falls, NY

Mr. Glen Hurt
11 Cadillacs, Sun City West, AZ

Dr. Dominick Huster
7 Cadillacs, Morris Plains, NJ

Mr. Eben Hutchinson
7 Cadillacs, Chelsea, MA

Mr. Kenton Hutchison
1 Cadillac, Mission Viejo, CA

Ms. Mary J. Hutchison
4 Cadillacs, Nacogdoches, TX

Mr. Lonnie D. Hutson
Blackville, SC

Mr. Jimmy Hutto
2 Cadillacs, Mason, TX

Mrs. D. Hutton
2 Cadillacs, Oakville, ON

Helen Hylton
Martinsville, VA

Mr. Robert Hyson
6 Cadillacs, Pasadena, MD

I

Mr. Vincent J. Iafrate
1 Cadillac, Port Huron, MI

Peter Iannarelli
4 Cadillacs, Lackawanna, NY

Mr. Nicholas Ilaria
1 Cadillac, Wayne, NJ

Mr. David Imber
12 Cadillacs, Bellmore, NY

Mr. D.D. Imhoff
1 Cadillac, Garrett, IN

Mr. Harold E. Immell
4 Cadillacs, Chillicothe, OH

George E. Imperatore
22 Cadillacs, Boca Raton, FL

Mrs. Joyce Ingram
5 Cadillacs, San Diego, CA

Verna Ingram
8 Cadillacs, Fredericton, NB

Anthony & Elizabeth Innacell
7 Cadillacs, Bridgeport, CT

Mr. Joseph P. Inserra
2 Cadillacs, Omaha, NE

Mr. Luigi Iorio
3 Cadillacs, Amsterdam, NY

Mr. Manfred Irmer
1 Cadillac, Stockholm, NJ

Ms. Evelyn Irving
4 Cadillacs, De Kalb, IL

Mr. Woodrow Irving
2 Cadillacs, Carlsbad, NM

A. Irwin
31 Cadillacs, Banff, AB

Mrs. Delores Isaac
3 Cadillacs, Pacific Grove, CA

Mr. D. Isaacs
2 Cadillacs, Longlac, ON

T. Isaacs
1 Cadillac, Kamloops, BC

Kenneth Iske
5 Cadillacs, Sun City West, AZ

Mr. Wendell W. Iverson
1 Cadillac, Salt Lake Cty., UT

David Izen
Delray Beach, FL

J

Mr. Alfonzo Jackson
5 Cadillacs, Indianapolis, IN

Mr. Andrew R. Jackson, Jr.
6 Cadillacs, Des Plaines, IL

Ms. Carriebelle Jackson
13 Cadillacs, Roswell, NM

Mr. Douglas E. Jackson
3 Cadillacs, Dallas, TX

Mr. Ernest H. Jackson
7 Cadillacs, Birmingham, AL

Mr. Henry D. Jackson
5 Cadillacs, Jackson, MS

Joseph J. Jackson
47 Cadillacs, Tallahassee, FL

Listco R. Jackson
4 Cadillacs, Louisville, TN

Louella I. Jackson
5 Cadillacs, New Smyrna
Beach, FL

Ms. Myrna S. Jackson
3 Cadillacs, Stacyville, ME

Warren Jackson
4 Cadillacs, Flint, MI

Mr. Walter C. Jacob
1 Cadillac, Sterling, VA

Bernice Jacobs
7 Cadillacs, Boynton Beach, FL

Mr. Cal Jacobs
3 Cadillacs, Zionsville, PA

Mr. Kenneth W. Jacobs
2 Cadillacs, Park Ridge, IL

Mr. Fred A. Jaeger
3 Cadillacs, Minneapolis, MN

Daniel Jaime
Chicago, IL

Mr. Joseph Jakov
Whiting, IN

Larry Jakubowski
1 Cadillac, Thunder Bay, ON

Mr. & Mrs. Arthur James
3 Cadillacs, Yuba City, CA

Mr. Daniel A. James
6 Cadillacs, Helper, UT

Dr. John B. James
25 Cadillacs, El Monte, CA

Ms. Mary James
4 Cadillacs, Mtn. Home, AR

Ms. Mearlene James
3 Cadillacs, Detroit, MI

Mr. Willie L. James
1 Cadillac, North Augusta, SC

Mr. Ralph Jameson
2 Cadillacs, Bakersfield, CA

Mr. T. Janes
22 Cadillacs, Lady Lake, FL

Mr. Paul L. Jansen, Jr.
16 Cadillacs, Oshkosh, WI

Henry Janzen
1 Cadillac, West St. Paul, MB

Mr. Jack D. Jarboe
5 Cadillacs, Indianapolis, IN

J.W. Jarrett, Jr.
6 Cadillacs, Decatur, IL

Ms. Constance Jarvis
6 Cadillacs, Chicago, IL

Malcolm Jarvis
4 Cadillacs, Plainfield, CT

Mr. Paul Jaworski
5 Cadillacs, Phoenixville, PA

Mr. Theodore Jazwienski
60 Cadillacs, Ft. Walton Bch., FL

Mrs. Elda N. Jeanmard
6 Cadillacs, Ville Platte, LA

Mr. James E. Jeffries
2 Cadillacs, Memphis, TN

Mr. Cliffton Jenkins
4 Cadillacs, Rocky Mount, NC

Edward L. Jenkins
15 Cadillacs, San Antonio, TX

Ms. Elizabeth R. Jenkins
2 Cadillacs, Simpsonville, SC

Ms. Mabel Jenkins
5 Cadillacs, Millen, GA

Mrs. Mary T. Jenkins
2 Cadillacs, Bridgeton, NC

Mr. Raymond E. Jenkins
4 Cadillacs, Hilton Head, SC

Wilfred Ross Jenkins
4 Cadillacs, Destin, FL

Ms. Elizabeth K. Jennings
3 Cadillacs, Kerrville, TX

Mrs. Florence A. Jennings
4 Cadillacs, Idabel, OK

Stan Jennings
5 Cadillacs, Gracemont, OK

Mr. Roland J. Jensen
1 Cadillac, Minneapolis, MN

Virginia Jensen
10 Cadillacs, Sequim, WA

Willard P. Jensen
14 Cadillacs, Sugar Land, TX

Mr. Donald A. Jermier
3 Cadillacs, Stamford, CT

Ladell Jernigan
3 Cadillacs, Dallas, TX

Wm. Jerone & Laura Harber
6 Cadillacs, Stone Mtn., GA

Mr. Thomas Jesse
Fort Wayne, IN

Mr. Willie J. Jessie, Jr.
13 Cadillacs, Niagara Falls, NY

Ms. Faye Jestice
1 Cadillac, Dayton, OH

Mr. Jack T. Jilek
3 Cadillacs, Antigo, WI

Mrs. Helen D. Jobi
6 Cadillacs, Brownsville, TX

Mr. Howard Johannigmeier
7 Cadillacs, Granite City, IL

Bernice G. Johns
20 Cadillacs, Daytona Bch., FL

Bernice Johns & Harvey
20 Cadillacs, Holly Hill, FL

Mrs. Helen R. Johnsen
2 Cadillacs, Beaumont, TX

Pinkie F. Johnson-Wheatfall
1 Cadillac, Omaha, NE

Ms. Anita F. Johnson
1 Cadillac, Milwaukee, WI

Mr. Arthur E. Johnson
3 Cadillacs, Boynton Beach, FL

Clarence A. Johnson
5 Cadillacs, Atlanta, GA

Claude & Evelyn Johnson, Jr.
3 Cadillacs, Shrewsbury, PA

Mrs. Ellen H. Johnson
3 Cadillacs, Detroit, MI

Mr. Elmer A. Johnson
4 Cadillacs, Muncie, IN

Ms. Frances B. Johnson
1 Cadillac, Tampa, FL

Mr. Frank E. Johnson
1 Cadillac, Charlotte, NC

Fred H. Johnson
6 Cadillacs, Virginia Bch., VA

Mr. George C. Johnson
4 Cadillacs, Wilson, NC

Mr. Gideon E. Johnson
7 Cadillacs, Canfield, OH

Mr. Harold D. Johnson
4 Cadillacs, May, TX

Mr. Henry C. Johnson
18 Cadillacs, Pineville, LA

Ms. Hildred Johnson
9 Cadillacs, Elkhart, KS

Hubert C. Johnson
1 Cadillac, Reno, NV

Jack Johnson
14 Cadillacs, Detroit, MI

Mrs. Jacqueline P. Johnson
1 Cadillac, Houston, TX

Mr. James W. Johnson
1 Cadillac, Fairbanks, AK

Mr. James L. Johnson
Grayson, KY

Mr. Joe H. Johnson
1 Cadillac, Tallassee, AL

Ms. Leah E. Johnson
1 Cadillac, Houston, TX

Mr. Lee E. Johnson
5 Cadillacs, Flint, MI

Mr. Lemuel G. Johnson, Sr.
4 Cadillacs, Zephyrhills, FL

Mr. Levi D. Johnson
1 Cadillac, Hemphill, TX

Mr. Lloyd W. Johnson
1 Cadillac, Warren, MI

Ms. Marion D. Johnson
1 Cadillac, Riverton, UT

Mr. Melville S. Johnson
2 Cadillacs, Hinton, WV

Mr. Melvin A. Johnson
3 Cadillacs, Prescott Vly., AZ

Mr. Melvin P. Johnson
11 Cadillacs, Vida, MT

Mr. Merritt A. Johnson
3 Cadillacs, Wataga, IL

Mr. Ned Johnson
5 Cadillacs, Long Beach, CA

Mr. Norman E. Johnson
2 Cadillacs, Bakersfield, CA

Mr. Odell Johnson
3 Cadillacs, Chicago, IL

Mr. Ralph G. Johnson
6 Cadillacs, Sierra Vista, AZ

Mr. Raymond T. Johnson
7 Cadillacs, Peoria, IL

Mr. Richard E. Johnson
3 Cadillacs, Tampa, FL

Mr. Robert W. Johnson
9 Cadillacs, Northridge, CA

Mr. Robert A. Johnson
31 Cadillacs, Washington, DC

Mr. Robert R. Johnson
9 Cadillacs, Glen Burnie, MD

Mr. Ronald W. Johnson
Mound, MN

Ms. Sallie M. Johnson
1 Cadillac, Baltimore, MD

Shirley Johnson
6 Cadillacs, Hopkinsville, KY

Mr. Stanley E. Johnson
1 Cadillac, Kansas City, MO

Mr. Terrance L. Johnson
Jamaica, NY

Mr. Timothy M. Johnson
5 Cadillacs, Harker Heights, TX

Mr. Vernon L. Johnson
1 Cadillac, Pocatello, ID

Mr. Wallace R. Johnson
5 Cadillacs, Fergus Falls, MN

Mr. Willard Johnson
20 Cadillacs, Santa Rosa, CA

Mr. Willis Johnson
6 Cadillacs, Donnelly, ID

Mr. William E. Johnston
1 Cadillac, Myrtle Beach, SC

Mr. Alfred Johnstone
2 Cadillacs, Beaconsfield, QC

Clegg L. Joines
2 Cadillacs, Kannapolis, NC

Firmin Jolette
1 Cadillac, Azilda, ON

Mr. Arthur E. Jolivette
17 Cadillacs, Vero Beach, FL

Mrs. Alice A. Jones
4 Cadillacs, Macon, GA

Ms. Catherine L. Jones
1 Cadillac, Opelousas, LA

Charlotte L. Jones
1 Cadillac, Salisbury, MD

Clabourne Jones
1 Cadillac, Fort Myers, FL

Debra & Earl B. Jones
1 Cadillac, Detroit, MI

Donald E. Jones
5 Cadillacs, Covina, CA

Earl R. Jones, MD
7 Cadillacs, Florence, SC

Ms. Elizabeth Jones
1 Cadillac, Oshawa, ON

Mr. Emery Jones
7 Cadillacs, Chicago, IL

Emlyn P. Jones
3 Cadillacs, Fort Worth, TX

Mr. Ernest M. Jones
Bloomington, IL

Gatton Jones
10 Cadillacs, Lexington, KY

Ms. Gertrude B. Jones
3 Cadillacs, Live Oak, FL

Glyndwr T. Jones
37 Cadillacs, Breckenridge, TX

Ms. Helen A. Jones
4 Cadillacs, Houston, TX

Mr. James E. Jones
6 Cadillacs, Alexandria, LA

Mr. Jesse O. Jones
3 Cadillacs, Morrisonville, IL

Mrs. John W. Jones, Sr.
12 Cadillacs, San Angelo, TX

Mr. Leland E. Jones
4 Cadillacs, Stephenville, TX

Leslie P. Jones
4 Cadillacs, Mesa, AZ

Ms. Melba Jones
4 Cadillacs, Atlanta, TX

Mrs. Nan Jones
4 Cadillacs, Sn. Luis Obisp., CA

Mr. Randall C. Jones
1 Cadillac, Euless, TX

Roselle & Charles Jones
3 Cadillacs, Chicago, IL

Dr. Warren Jones
4 Cadillacs, New Bern, NC

William Howard Jones
10 Cadillacs, Pinson, AL

Mr. Willie Jones
4 Cadillacs, Houston, TX

Reverend Henry V. Jordan
3 Cadillacs, Los Angeles, CA

Mr. Joseph G. Jordan
1 Cadillac, El Paso, TX

Ms. Mary N. Jordan
18 Cadillacs, Riverside, TX

Mr. Raul Jordan
1 Cadillac, El Paso, TX

Virginia & J. Frank Jordan
3 Cadillacs, Greensboro, NC

Mr. Arthur S. Joseph, Jr.
10 Cadillacs, Naples, FL

Ms. Helen F. Joshua
13 Cadillacs, San Antonio, TX

Mr. Arthur N. Joura
6 Cadillacs, Van Meter, IA

Mr. Donald Joyce
2 Cadillacs, Midlothian, VA

Mr. Jerome A. Jozak
10 Cadillacs, Lawrence, MA

Mr. Sherman O. Julian, Jr.
7 Cadillacs, Kannapolis, NC

Mr. Thomas S. Julian
12 Cadillacs, Las Vegas, NV

Mr. Henry J. Junga
2 Cadillacs, Detroit, MI

Mr. John W. Jupe
5 Cadillacs, Amarillo, TX

Mr. Calvin D. Jurgens
5 Cadillacs, Thornton, IA

Mr. Neal C. Jurney
1 Cadillac, Goldsboro, NC

Ms. Harriet Juster
1 Cadillac, Chicago, IL

K

Dr. G. Dean Kadavy
4 Cadillacs, Omaha, NE

Mr. Arnold Kaegi
10 Cadillacs, Tacoma, WA

Dr. Stanley B. Kahane
4 Cadillacs, Montgomery, AL

Mr. Ralph L. Kahler
2 Cadillacs, Cedar Rapids, IA

Mr. & Mrs. Waino Kaihlanen
2 Cadillacs, Beverly, MA

Mr. Otto C. Kaintz
1 Cadillac, Pittsburgh, PA

Mr. Donald P. Kaiser
16 Cadillacs, Portage, WI

Dr. Max Kalm
8 Cadillacs, Westfield, NJ

Mr. Isao Kameshige
7 Cadillacs, Ontario, OR

Mr. Stanley J. Kaminski
1 Cadillac, Buffalo, NY

Mr. Herman A. Kamparosyan
6 Cadillacs, Flushing, NY

Mr. Clifford R. Kamprath
10 Cadillacs, Roswell, NM

Mr. Nicholas Kanakis
11 Cadillacs, Sarasota, FL

Maurice A. Kane
5 Cadillacs, Geneseo, IL

Ms. Barbara E. Kanniard
2 Cadillacs, Winston Salem, NC

Dr. Harold G. Kantor
8 Cadillacs, Pembroke Pines, FL

Mr. Ron Kapchinsky
5 Cadillacs, Edmonton, AB

Dr. Charlotte Kaplan
10 Cadillacs, Cleveland, MS

Mr. Milton R. Kaplan
1 Cadillac, San Antonio, TX

Richard Kaplan
11 Cadillacs, Newhall, CA

Ms. Joan W. Kaplowitz
1 Cadillac, Ormond Beach, FL

Ms. Mabel S. Kapp
10 Cadillacs, Plymouth, MI

Mrs. Suzanne Kapusta
2 Cadillacs, Greensburg, PA

Mr. & Mrs. Charles Karavidas
14 Cadillacs, Arlington Hts., IL

Ronald W. Kasper
2 Cadillacs, Cocoa, FL

Mr. Max L. Kasten
5 Cadillacs, Leadville, CO

Mrs. Judith W. Kata
1 Cadillac, Youngstown, OH

Mr. Barry Katz
4 Cadillacs, Culver City, CA

Mrs. Betsy Lynn Katz
2 Cadillacs, Atlanta, GA

Mr. Larry J. Katz
8 Cadillacs, Miami, FL

Henry Kavanaugh
10 Cadillacs, Santa Fe, NM

Mr. Theodore C. Kay
1 Cadillac, Saint Paul, MN

Edward Kazanjian
2 Cadillacs, Malvern, PA

George Kazanjian
4 Cadillacs, Malvern, PA

Mr. Russell A. Kea
Rocky Mount, NC

Mr. J.D. Keating
7 Cadillacs, Hillsboro, TX

Mr. Kenneth G. Keck
1 Cadillac, Jenks, OK

Mr. Jack H. Keen
2 Cadillacs, Covington, KY

Earl L. Keenan, Jr.
5 Cadillacs, Scottsdale, AZ

Mr. Albert M. Keeney
2 Cadillacs, Belle, WV

Mr. Les Keesee
11 Cadillacs, Duncanville, TX

Mr. Sam Kehler
8 Cadillacs, El Sobrante, CA

Mr. Edward Keil
35 Cadillacs, Evansville, IN

Ms. Ruth F. Keil
1 Cadillac, Brevard, NC

Mr. Robert L. Keim
4 Cadillacs, Homeland, CA

Mr. J. Wayne Keiser
6 Cadillacs, Watsontown, PA

Vera D. Keith
2 Cadillacs, Greentown, IN

Gerhard J. Kekelik
9 Cadillacs, Fort Myers, FL

Ms. Donna Keko
3 Cadillacs, Glendale, AZ

Ms. Dolores Kelekovich
3 Cadillacs, Exeland, WI

Mr. Joseph R. Kellam, Sr.
1 Cadillac, Salisbury, MD

Ms. Lois J. Keller
1 Cadillac, Fort Gratiot, MI

Ms. Mary C. Keller
2 Cadillacs, Galena, IL

Rudolph Keller
3 Cadillacs, Ft. Lauderdale, FL

Mr. Warren Keller
Lees Summit, MO

Ms. Dorothy F. Kelley
10 Cadillacs, Richmond, TX

Mrs. James A. Kellington
4 Cadillacs, Daytona Beach, FL

Mr. Karl J. Kellison
Springfield, OH

Mr. Kenneth W. Kellner
4 Cadillacs, Davenport, IA

Ms. B.J. Kellogg
6 Cadillacs, Roswell, GA

L. Kelly
1 Cadillac, Kitchener, ON

Margaret M. Kelly
7 Cadillacs, Canfield, OH

Patrick Kelly
1 Cadillac, Champaign, IL

Mr. Robert A. Kelly
2 Cadillacs, Brooklyn, NY

Charles L. (Pete) Kelsey
3 Cadillacs, Cincinnati, OH

Mr. Dwane Kelsey
1 Cadillac, Etobicoke, ON

Mr. T.J. Kelso
3 Cadillacs, Louisville, KY

Mr. Dale L. Kemp
1 Cadillac, Sioux City, IA

F. Raymond Kemp, M.D.
12 Cadillacs, Manhat. Bch., CA

Mr. Phillip B. Kempkes
9 Cadillacs, Ocean Springs, MS

James C. Kenady
San Diego, CA

Mr. Raymond H. Kenady
24 Cadillacs, Naples, FL

Mr. J. Ward W. Kencke
Great Falls, MT

Polly S. Kendzior
9 Cadillacs, Franklin, PA

James A. & Eloise Kennedy
11 Cadillacs, Flint, MI

Ms. Kathleen E. Kennedy
3 Cadillacs, Troy, NY

Mr. Stephen P. Kennedy
3 Cadillacs, Blue Springs, MO

Mr. Willard F. Kennedy
2 Cadillacs, Huntington, NY

Mr. James R. Kennell
4 Cadillacs, Flint, MI

Walter Kenner
Clarksville, TN

Mrs. Mina C. Kent
5 Cadillacs, Beals, ME

Mr. Robert L. Kent
6 Cadillacs, Indianapolis, IN

Robert Kent
5 Cadillacs, Puyallup, WA

William Keough
2 Cadillacs, Brampton, ON

Charles & Eva Kerchusky
2 Cadillacs, Sewell, NJ

Mr. Maynard W. Kerns
6 Cadillacs, Marion, IN

Mrs. Arlyne V. Kerr
14 Cadillacs, Fort Pierce, FL

Mrs. K. Kerr
3 Cadillacs, Blairmore, AB

Mr. William J. Kersey
1 Cadillac, Inverness, FL

Ms. Luella D. Kesner
3 Cadillacs, Arvada, CO

Mr. William Ketchijian
1 Cadillac, Encino, CA

T.S. & Jogi Khanna
9 Cadillacs, Danville, CA

Mr. Clyde W. Kidd
3 Cadillacs, Maryville, TN

Mr. William Kierein
16 Cadillacs, South Bend, IN

Mr. Robert H. Kifer
6 Cadillacs, Ford City, PA

Ms. Dorothy M. Kildoo
8 Cadillacs, Butler, PA

Mr. Robert A. Kiles
15 Cadillacs, Fort Wayne, IN

J.V. & Hazel Kilgore
7 Cadillacs, Russellville, AR

Mr. Raymond Killingsworth
9 Cadillacs, Houston, TX

Mr. James Kimm
3 Cadillacs, Glenview, IL

Mr. Harrison S. Kincaid
1 Cadillac, Charlotte, NC

Mr. Thomas W. Kincaid, Jr.
1 Cadillac, Huntington, WV

Ms. Doris S. King
2 Cadillacs, Groves, TX

Mr. George S. King
3 Cadillacs, North Canton, OH

Mr. Gilbert D. King
Lake Charles, LA

H. King
32 Cadillacs, Arlington, TX

Mr. John H. King, Jr.
4 Cadillacs, Freeport, NY

Mr. John E. King
1 Cadillac, Hustontown, PA

Mr. V.F. King
7 Cadillacs, Southampton, NY

Mr. Warren G. King, Sr.
4 Cadillacs, Nashville, TN

Mr. & Mrs. Duey Kingsley
Detroit, MI

Mr. Charles R. Kinnaman
11 Cadillacs, Roselle, IL

Mrs. Jean Kinsey
1 Cadillac, Peterborough, ON

Ms. Mellie Kinslow
3 Cadillacs, Macon, GA

Mr. Philip L. Kintzele
2 Cadillacs, Mt. Pleasant, MI

Mr. Lydell C. Kiplin
2 Cadillacs, San Antonio, TX

Thera Dell Kirgan
6 Cadillacs, Tyler, TX

Sam E. Kirkland, Jr.
2 Cadillacs, Indianapolis, IN

Mrs. Lucille I. Kirkpatrick
8 Cadillacs, Sherman, TX

Mr. Frank L. Kirsopp, Jr.
2 Cadillacs, Huntsville, AL

Ms. Anna M. Kiryluk
6 Cadillacs, St. Petersburg, FL

Mr. Robert C. Kispert
13 Cadillacs, Cincinnati, OH

Mr. Lorant P. Kiss
1 Cadillac, Lake Placid, FL

Mr. William G. Kissel
2 Cadillacs, Arlington, TX

Mr. Larry Kix
8 Cadillacs, Burnsville, MN

Mr. Eugene Klainsek
7 Cadillacs, Joliet, IL

Mr. Carl F. Klatt
1 Cadillac, Ballwin, MO

Mr. Kenneth C. Klebsch
3 Cadillacs, Highmore, SD

Carlton D. Klein
7 Cadillacs, Miami, FL

Mr. Martin Klein
1 Cadillac, Ft. Lauderdale, FL

Jeffrey Kleinberg
1 Cadillac, New York, NY

Mr. Harry S. Kleindorfer
2 Cadillacs, Phoenix, AZ

Mr. Melvin C. Kleinschmidt
8 Cadillacs, Oshkosh, WI

Carl Klemencic
3 Cadillacs, Lake Orion, MI

Edward Klemm
5 Cadillacs, Bay Village, OH

Mrs. Harry D. Kleweno
2 Cadillacs, N. Las Vegas, NV

Ms. S. Klim
1 Cadillac, East Selkirk, MB

Ms. Imogene L. Kline
12 Cadillacs, Katy, TX

Mr. Daniel Kling
3 Cadillacs, Cleveland, OH

Mr. Don Klinger
2 Cadillacs, Long Beach, CA

Mr. Everett Klinger
4 Cadillacs, Allerton, IA

Santena G. & D'Jack Klingler
5 Cadillacs, Fairborn, OH

Mr. John P. Klipstine
2 Cadillacs, Valparaiso, IN

Mr. Karel C. Klos
1 Cadillac, Ponca City, OK

Mr. George P. Kluchnik
2 Cadillacs, Huntingtn. Sta., NY

Mr. Roderick Klugh
1 Cadillac, Oakland, CA

Mr. Lloyd R. Knapp
3 Cadillacs, Greenville, PA

Mr. Henry H. Knight
8 Cadillacs, Powder Spgs., GA

L. Roger Knight, M.D.
12 Cadillacs, Tyler, TX

Mr. Robert O. Knight
3 Cadillacs, East Moline, IL

Imon W. Knippers
1 Cadillac, Baton Rouge, LA

Lydia Geneva Knoll
7 Cadillacs, Tucson, AZ

William W. Knoll
7 Cadillacs, Tucson, AZ

Mr. Harold E. Knorr
6 Cadillacs, Bedford, TX

Mr. Jesse Knowles
27 Cadillacs, Lake Charles, LA

Melvin A. Knowles
2 Cadillacs, Aiken, SC

Edward Knox
2 Cadillacs, White Hse. Sta., NJ

Mr. William E. Knox
12 Cadillacs, Medford, OR

Wan-Sik Ko
1 Cadillac, Flushing, NY

Mr. Fred Koby
5 Cadillacs, Vero Beach, FL

Mr. Andrew M. Koch
6 Cadillacs, North Babylon, NY

Mr. William H. Koechel
2 Cadillacs, Chesterfield, MO

Mr. Bernard S. Koehmstedt
3 Cadillacs, Osnabrock, ND

Mr. Emil E. Koenig
11 Cadillacs, Minneapolis, MN

Dr. Harold H. Koenig
28 Cadillacs, Jensen Beach, FL

Ms. Helen E. Koenig
4 Cadillacs, Richland Ctr., WI

Mr. James B. Koger
1 Cadillac, Miami, FL

Mr. Reed M. Kohl
1 Cadillac, Lincoln, NE

Catherine C. Kohler
3 Cadillacs, Westwood, MA

Dr. Neta Kolasa
Boca Raton, FL

Mr. Frank J. Kolassa
Harper Woods, MI

Mr. Allison L. Kolbe
6 Cadillacs, Keystone Hgts., FL

Mr. Theodore W. Kolbe
1 Cadillac, Carson City, NV

Ms. Lillian Kolbusz
4 Cadillacs, Weston, CT

Ms. Lucille M. Kolk
4 Cadillacs, Naples, FL

Mr. Benjamin J. Kolkman
Grand Rapids, MI

Mr. Howard Kolp, Jr.
4 Cadillacs, West Salem, OH

Mr. Stanley E. Kolstad
2 Cadillacs, Mission, TX

Dr. Walter F. Kondratowicz
4 Cadillacs, Bloomingdale, IL

Mr. Robert C. Konieska
3 Cadillacs, Moose Lake, MN

William Konze
8 Cadillacs, Oxon Hill, MD

Dr. Raymond C. Koorenny
4 Cadillacs, Huntsville, TX

Mrs. Betty J. Kopey
6 Cadillacs, Brookfield, OH

Mr. Ronald H. Kopitzke
Shawano, WI

Henry R. Korman
4 Cadillacs, Longview, WA

Mr. Joseph Koroncey
5 Cadillacs, Carlsbad, CA

Mr. Fred B. Korte
14 Cadillacs, Mesa, AZ

Michael Koruda
3 Cadillacs, Spring Hill, FL

Mr. Frank J. Kosa, Jr.
9 Cadillacs, Warren, OH

Ms. Maxine L. Kosbau
1 Cadillac, North Platte, NE

Mrs. Constantina T. Kosmitis
Shreveport, LA

Mr. Alan Kosow
3 Cadillacs, Needham, MA

Mr. David Koss
14 Cadillacs, Guilderland, NY

Mr. John G. Kossow
4 Cadillacs, Bethesda, MD

Mr. Anthony Kotulak
10 Cadillacs, Plymouth, PA

Mr. Frank J. Kowalski
8 Cadillacs, El Paso, TX

Mr. John Kowalski
2 Cadillacs, Cherry Hill, NJ

Mr. Paul Kozachuk
1 Cadillac, N. Battleford, SK

Ms. Alice Kozma
1 Cadillac, E. Brunswick, NJ

Mr. Earl K. Kraemer
5 Cadillacs, Charleston, SC

Carl Krakat
7 Cadillacs, Livonia, MI

Mr. Joseph E. Kramer
6 Cadillacs, Ft. Myers, FL

Mr. Edward G. Krantz
22 Cadillacs, Marion, IL

John Krauss
1 Cadillac, Bonita Spgs., FL

Mr. Herman F. Kraybill
3 Cadillacs, Olney, MD

Dominic J. Kreczmer
2 Cadillacs, Baltimore, MD

Ms. Dorris I. Kreher
6 Cadillacs, Blue Mound, IL

Ronald Krentz
1 Cadillac, Simcoe, ON

Mr. Jess Krenzel
Leoti, KS

Mr. Ralph Kress
3 Cadillacs, Shreveport, LA

Yolanda Kresslein
1 Cadillac, Alexandria, VA

Mr. Thomas E. Kressly
3 Cadillacs, S. Williamsprt., PA

Ms. Virginia F. Kreutz
53 Cadillacs, St. Petersburg, FL

Mr. Louis F. Krick, Jr.
Des Moines, IA

Mr. Thomas Krill
2 Cadillacs, Tavares, FL

Narayana S. Krishnappa
1 Cadillac, Hoffman Est., IL

Mr. Bernard H. Kriska
3 Cadillacs, Bardwell, TX

Mr. Vance R. Krites
1 Cadillac, Wooster, OH

Dr. David H. Kronisch
17 Cadillacs, Federal Way, WA

Mr. James W. Kronmiller
3 Cadillacs, Crestview, FL

Mr. Robert J. Krost
3 Cadillacs, Menlo Park, CA

Mr. Walter L. Krudop
7 Cadillacs, Patchogue, NY

Mr. Donald G. Krueger
9 Cadillacs, Green Bay, WI

Mr. Fritz H. Krueger
2 Cadillacs, Lone Tree, IA

Mr. Charles Kruger
2 Cadillacs, Albuquerque, NM

Duane L. Krull
34 Cadillacs, Pasadena, CA

Mr. John F. Krupa
9 Cadillacs, Clearwater ,FL

Mr. Nicholas Krut
4 Cadillacs, Campbell, OH

Mr. Stanley Krysztofik
2 Cadillacs, Trenton, NJ

Mr. Michael J. Krzyminski
3 Cadillacs, Framingham, MA

Ms. Mary Ku
3 Cadillacs, Lewisville, TX

Dr. Thomas R. Kubacki
18 Cadillacs, Morrisville, PA

Jerry Kucala
4 Cadillacs, Saint Paul, MN

Mr. Daniel S. Kuchar
3 Cadillacs, Scranton, PA

Mr. Steven Kudelka
1 Cadillac, Chicago, IL

Mr. David Kujala
6 Cadillacs, Allen Park, MI

Mr. Aloysius A. Kukla
6 Cadillacs, Manistee, MI

Mr. Hugo O. Kumitz
2 Cadillacs, Memphis, TN

Mr. Vernon M. Kummel
51 Cadillacs, Ft. Walton Bch., FL

Mr. Michael P. Kuntz
3 Cadillacs, Jackson, MN

Mr. John Kurfiss
6 Cadillacs, Alexandria, LA

Ms. Norene Kurth
4 Cadillacs, Fort Myers, FL

Harold K. Kurtz
15 Cadillacs, Kutztown, PA

Mrs. Hedwig H. Kurz
2 Cadillacs, Louisville, KY

Ms. Mary Kusher
1 Cadillac, Johnstown, PA

Dr. Alan Kushner
7 Cadillacs, Bala Cynwyd, PA

Mr. Robert E. Kusterman
6 Cadillacs, Casey, IL

Mr. William Kuznitsof
3 Cadillacs, Bowling Green, KY

Mr. Charles J. Kveton
3 Cadillacs, Countryside, IL

Dr. Chwan Kyan
1 Cadillac, Mantua, NJ

L

Mr. Leo La Monica
17 Cadillacs, Hazleton, PA

Mr. Billy La Roche
3 Cadillacs, Duncan, OK

George T. Laboda
1 Cadillac, Lake Worth, FL

Mr. Malcolm Lacey
4 Cadillacs, Lake Placid, FL

Mr. Darwin Lackey
6 Cadillacs, Weyburn, SK

Ms. Arlene M. Lackner
4 Cadillacs, Fort Myers, FL

Leopold Lacroix
3 Cadillacs, Ottawa, ON

Franklin Ladson
2 Cadillacs, Simpsonville, SC

Mr. George D. LaDuke
7 Cadillacs, Waterford, MI

Ms. Virginia R. Lafferty
3 Cadillacs, Switz City, IN

Mr. Roger P. Laflamme
2 Cadillacs, Fort Myers, FL

Mr. Chris Lageotakes
9 Cadillacs, Oak Brook, IL

Mr. Albert Laham
11 Cadillacs, San Diego, CA

Mr. John N. Lahm
8 Cadillacs, Shannon, IL

Mrs. Judy G. Lail
3 Cadillacs, Bessemer City, NC

Mr. Raymond W. Lajoie
5 Cadillacs, Van Buren, ME

B. Lalonde
1 Cadillac, Goderich, ON

Edna Lalonde
1 Cadillac, Alexandria, ON

Mr. L. Lalonde
1 Cadillac, Gatineau, QC

Mr. Charles Lam
9 Cadillacs, Verona, VA

Anthony LaMantia
5 Cadillacs, Gloversville, NY

Ms. Anna L. Lamb
17 Cadillacs, Farmer City, IL

Mr. Artie L. Lamb
3 Cadillacs, Savannah, GA

Mr. George W. Lamb
3 Cadillacs, Hendersonvlle., NC

Mr. Joseph Lamb, Jr.
8 Cadillacs, East Berne, NY

Mr. Paul H. Lampel
6 Cadillacs, Las Vegas, NV

Ms. Marilyn S. Lamping
1 Cadillac, Menomonee Fls., WI

Mrs. Elberta M. Landenberger
8 Cadillacs, Gladwin, MI

Mr. Hershel L. Landers
Gadsden, AL

Robert Landin
6 Cadillacs, Ellison Bay, WI

Mr. Stephen H. Landolt
1 Cadillac, Oshkosh, WI

Mr. Charles Landwehr
1 Cadillac, Taft, CA

Mrs. Alice C. Lane
6 Cadillacs, Jesup, GA

Mr. Jack A. Lane
10 Cadillacs, Seminole, FL

Mr. Maurice V. Lane
1 Cadillac, Atascadero, CA

Sidney H. Lane
4 Cadillacs, Dyersburg, TN

Ms. Velma B. Lane
8 Cadillacs, San Angelo, TX

Mr. Edwin J. Lang
2 Cadillacs, Owensville, MO

Mr. Joseph Lang, Jr.
4 Cadillacs, Old Town, FL

Mr. Simeon K. Langlinais
1 Cadillac, Youngsville, LA

Mrs. Jeanne Langone
24 Cadillacs, Woodbury, NJ

Mr. Joe V. Langston
2 Cadillacs, Cape Coral, FL

Mr. W. Laperle
1 Cadillac, Cornwall, ON

Mr. Lincoln M. Larkin
9 Cadillacs, Benton Harbor, MI

Mr. Paul Larouche
3 Cadillacs, Baie-Comeau, QC

Mr. Arthur G. Larson, Sr.
18 Cadillacs, Idobe Sound, FL

Edward T. & Leona B. Larson
6 Cadillacs, Minot, ND

Eldon Larson
7 Cadillacs, Wahpeton, ND

Ms. Marjorie A. Larson
3 Cadillacs, Minneapolis, MN

Mr. Milton E. Larson
5 Cadillacs, Wheaton, MN

Mrs. Robert G. Larson
1 Cadillac, Miami, FL

Mr. Charles Laskin
6 Cadillacs, Stonewall, LA

Ms. Isabel D. Latham
4 Cadillacs, Orange Park, FL

Mr. Alfred F. Latimer, II
3 Cadillacs, Saint Charles, IL

C. Lau
1 Cadillac, Winnipeg, MB

Dominic Laubach
20 Cadillacs, Sartell, MN

Clarence V. Laubinger, Jr.
4 Cadillacs, Union, MO

Mr. W. Lauder
1 Cadillac, Edmonton, AB

Mr. William Lauder
4 Cadillacs, Anchorage, AK

Dr. Harold E. Lauer
5 Cadillacs, Lima, OH

Paul Lauermeier
1 Cadillac, Welland, ON

Mr. Darrell Laufer
3 Cadillacs, Weatherford, OK

Mr. Arde O. Laulainen
4 Cadillacs, Framingham, MA

Mr. Layton J. Laurent
17 Cadillacs, Marrero, LA

Mr. John M. Laux
1 Cadillac, Oak Park, IL

Mr. Jean-Claude Lauziere
5 Cadillacs, Drummondville, QC

Lois & Paul Lavendar
2 Cadillacs, Columbus, GA

Ms. Eula Mae Lavender
13 Cadillacs, Black Mtn., NC

G. Lavergne
1 Cadillac, Sturgeon Falls, ON

Ms. Phyllis N. Lawhon
1 Cadillac, Reno, NV

Ms. Wendy Lawrence
1 Cadillac, London, ON

Mr. Layton Laws
9 Cadillacs, Palmetto, FL

Helen & James L. Lawson
Eustis, FL

Mr. Robert E. Lawson
6 Cadillacs, Hayward, CA

Mr. William E. Lawson
1 Cadillac, Corbin, KY

Mr. Frank J. Laycock
5 Cadillacs, New London, CT

Mr. Larry H. Layton
4 Cadillacs, Acton, CA

Mrs. Earleen Leach
6 Cadillacs, Dallas, TX

Mr. William Leach
2 Cadillacs, Bellflower, CA

Harold C. Leahy
5 Cadillacs, Raton, NM

Mr. Raymond Leaming
10 Cadillacs, Liberal, KS

Velma Bradshaw Leavell
Galveston, TX

Mr. Gerald Leblang
8 Cadillacs, West Chester, PA

Mr. Hervey J. LeBoeuf
15 Cadillacs, Sun City Ctr., FL

Mr. Guy Lebow
3 Cadillacs, New York, NY

Mr. Edgar H. Lechner
6 Cadillacs, Mendota Hts., MN

Mr. Fred J. Lechner
18 Cadillacs, Hickory Hills, IL

Timothy Lednum
5 Cadillacs, Asheboro, NC

Arthur Jean LeDuc
26 Cadillacs, Inverness, FL

Beverly & John T. Lee
12 Cadillacs, Anderson, IN

Chiles B. Lee
1 Cadillac, Los Angeles, CA

James Lee
1 Cadillac, Tampa, FL

Rebekah Ann Lee
1 Cadillac, Palestine, TX

Ms. Rowena B. Lee
11 Cadillacs, St. Petersburg, FL

Frank Leeder
1 Cadillac, Little Rock, AR

Mr. Grady & Martha W. Leese
5 Cadillacs, Vicksburg, MS

Mr. Ernest J. Lefner, Jr.
3 Cadillacs, Mechanicville, NY

Mrs. Irene H. Leftwich
3 Cadillacs, Carthage, TX

Mr. George C. Lega, Jr.
8 Cadillacs, Schenectady, NY

Mr. Neal N. LeGette, Jr.
4 Cadillacs, Greensboro, NC

Mr. Albert Lehecka
4 Cadillacs, Ocean City, MD

Barbara Jeanne Lehman
1 Cadillac, Saint George, UT

Mr. & Mrs. Thomas L. Leib
2 Cadillacs, Joplin, MO

Mr. Albert J. Leibham
1 Cadillac, Sheboygan, WI

Russell N. Leidy
10 Cadillacs, Stuart, FL

Mr. Joseph Leifer
14 Cadillacs, Lincolnwood, IL

Mr. Kenneth E. Leifer
3 Cadillacs, Milwaukee, WI

Mr. Seymour Leifer
11 Cadillacs, Englewood, NJ

Mr. Leon H. Leigh
1 Cadillac, Ft. Walton Bch., FL

Mr. Joe Lekach
1 Cadillac, Ituna, SK

Mr. George E. Lellos
Elmhurst, IL

Ms. Rita O. Leming
4 Cadillacs, Milford, OH

George Lemkau
18 Cadillacs, Davenport, FL

Mr. John Lemry
3 Cadillacs, Terre Haute, IN

Mrs. Gertrude M. Lenhart
8 Cadillacs, Palm Springs, CA

Mrs. Jean B. Leoffler
7 Cadillacs, Ormond Beach, FL

Mr. Joseph P. Leonowicz
8 Cadillacs, Green Bay, WI

John Leprich
2 Cadillacs, Mississauga, ON

Carole S. Lerner
4 Cadillacs, Asheville, NC

Capt. Frank A. Lerose, III
4 Cadillacs, Woodbury, CT

Mr. Daniel J. LeRoy
16 Cadillacs, Fort Pierce, FL

Mr. Leon T. LeRoy, Jr.
6 Cadillacs, Chicago, IL

Mr. Joseph V. Lesizza
4 Cadillacs, Springfield, MO

Mr. Charles E. Leslie
1 Cadillac, Marshall, MO

Mr. Leon Lesnik, Esq.
1 Cadillac, Springfield, NJ

Mr. Martin J. Less, Sr.
2 Cadillacs, Ottawa, IL

Mr. Keith A. Lester
4 Cadillacs, Prudenville, MI

Ms. Ruth Lester
2 Cadillacs, Corpus Christi, TX

Dr. Alex Lesuk
2 Cadillacs, Delmar, NY

Mr. Lester C. Letourneau
4 Cadillacs, Daytona Beach, FL

Jack Letts
3 Cadillacs, Denver, CO

Mr. F. Leuenberger
7 Cadillacs, Gulfport, MS

Ms. Carolyn B. Levenson
1 Cadillac, Bishopville, SC

Mr. William Levenson
2 Cadillacs, Warner Robins, GA

Mr. Laurent G. Levesques
8 Cadillacs, Salem, MA

Jerome Levick
6 Cadillacs, Tamarac, FL

Daniel H. Levine
Hallandale, FL

Mr. Robert L. Levine
60 Cadillacs, Woodbridge, CT

Mr. Elbert E. Levy
2 Cadillacs, Winston Salem, NC

Mr. Robert W. Levy
3 Cadillacs, Honolulu, HI

Joseph Lewandowski
23 Cadillacs, Cherry Hill, NJ

Mr. James R. Lewin
4 Cadillacs, Front Royal, VA

Mr. Arthur Lewis
8 Cadillacs, Fresno, CA

Mr. Charles T. Lewis
6 Cadillacs, Williamsburg, VA

Ms. Geneva S. Lewis
4 Cadillacs, Hollandale, MS

Mr. John W. Lewis, Jr.
2 Cadillacs, Birmingham, AL

Joycelle C. Lewis
5 Cadillacs, Chicago, IL

Mary Rhodes Lewis
1 Cadillac, Overton, TX

Ms. Peggy Ann Lewis
5 Cadillacs, Baltimore, MD

Ms. Sandy Lewis
1 Cadillac, Philadelphia, PA

Sue A. Lewis
7 Cadillacs, Wichita Falls, TX

Mr. Ted Lewis
1 Cadillac, Shreveport, LA

Ms. Virginia F. Lewis
3 Cadillacs, St. Petersburg, FL

Mr. Willie F. Lewis, Jr.
6 Cadillacs, Detroit, MI

Jennie M. Liberto
9 Cadillacs, Tonawanda, NY

Mr. Carl C. Lick
2 Cadillacs, Montrose, CO

Eddie Liepert
2 Cadillacs, Lloydminster, SK

Gene & Erna Liermann
2 Cadillacs, Amelia, NE

Ms. Margaret I. Light
Peoria, IL

Ms. Victoria C. Lima
Santa Rosa, CA

Anthony Lindauer
5 Cadillacs, Riverside, IL

Dr. Paul A. Lindauer
1 Cadillac, Jacksonville, NC

Mr. Marvin A. Linder
1 Cadillac, Batavia, OH

Ralph Lindgren
5 Cadillacs, N. Vancouver, BC

Dr. John A. Link
15 Cadillacs, Scottsdale, AZ

Ms. Virginia A. Linley
5 Cadillacs, Anson, TX

Mr. Harry Linn
5 Cadillacs, Veedersburg, IN

Mr. Edward A. Lioen
1 Cadillac, Rock Island, IL

Lip-Man and the Lips
3 Cadillacs, Lantana, FL

Mr. Aloysius J. Lisk
3 Cadillacs, Osage Beach, MO

Mr. Jacob D. Lite
10 Cadillacs, Saint Louis, MO

Ms. Mozelle J. Little
6 Cadillacs, Easley, SC

Ruby Jean Little
12 Cadillacs, San Antonio, TX

Mr. Willie E. Little
2 Cadillacs, Radcliff, KY

Mr. James A. Littleton
10 Cadillacs, Earth, TX

Albert & Georgia Lloyd
6 Cadillacs, Clinton, MD

Mr. Louis H. Lobes
6 Cadillacs, Clinton Twp., MI

Mr. Arthur J. Lobo
5 Cadillacs, Vandalia, OH

Mr. Earl W. Lockett
1 Cadillac, El Dorado, AR

Mr. Thomas Lockett
3 Cadillacs, Camden, AR

Mr. John Lockhart
3 Cadillacs, Forrest City, AR

Mr. James H. Locklear
4 Cadillacs, Baltimore, MD

Mr. Vernon Lockwood
16 Cadillacs, Evansville, IN

Mr. Eugene J. Logan, Sr.
1 Cadillac, Wilmington, NC

Dr. G. Bruce Loganbill
5 Cadillacs, Long Beach, CA

Mr. Harold M. Lokey
2 Cadillacs, Inverness, FL

Mr. Dennis Lombardi
34 Cadillacs, Bangor, ME

Mr. William Lomicka
7 Cadillacs, Clearwater, FL

Mr. Alvin W. Long
6 Cadillacs, Boynton Beach, FL

Mr. Joe H. Long
2 Cadillacs, Kure Beach, NC

Mrs. Susan C. Long
2 Cadillacs, Pleasanton, CA

Mrs. Jackie Longdin
2 Cadillacs, Newton, IA

David & Elizabeth Longnecker
2 Cadillacs, Olympia, WA

Lemuel G. Loofbourrow
5 Cadillacs, Fort Myers, FL

Mr. Craig Loomis
8 Cadillacs, Providence, RI

Mrs. Marion R. Loper
1 Cadillac, Kermit, TX

Ms. Maria E. Lopez
3 Cadillacs, Brownsville, TX

Mr. Vincent L. Lopez
6 Cadillacs, Tuscumbia, AL

Ms. Micaela C. Lopizich
1 Cadillac, Chula Vista, CA

Ms. Philomena Lorello
4 Cadillacs, Anaconda, MT

Mr. Saverio Loria
7 Cadillacs, Sarasota, FL

Mr. Leo C. Lorigan
1 Cadillac, Cadogan, PA

Darlene & John Lorscheider
10 Cadillacs, Lake Havasu, AZ

Mr. John Loscutoff
4 Cadillacs, McCloud, CA

Mr. Stanley J. Loss
4 Cadillacs, Jarrettsville, MD

Imogene J. Lott, Sr.
3 Cadillacs, Abilene, TX

Mr. Walter B. Lotz, Jr.
8 Cadillacs, Slingerlands, NY

Mr. Frank Love
2 Cadillacs, Albuquerque, NM

Ms. Ruth Lovejoy
6 Cadillacs, Clairton, PA

Mr. Hugh H. Lovelady, Sr.
5 Cadillacs, Vienna, WV

Mr. Philip T. Lovick
5 Cadillacs, Burnsville, MN

James Lowe
2 Cadillacs, Lakeside, CA

Kenneth E. Lowe
Springville, UT

Mrs. Linda L. Lowe
4 Cadillacs, Decatur, IL

Mrs. Robin Lowe
2 Cadillacs, Alexander, NY

Mr. Thomas A. Lowe
25 Cadillacs, Satellite Bch., FL

Colonel Raymond P. Lowman
6 Cadillacs, Niceville, FL

Mr. William E. Lowther
3 Cadillacs, Haddonfield, NJ

Mr. Howard R. Loyd
2 Cadillacs, Orlando, FL

Mr. Guillermo Lozano
5 Cadillacs, San Antonio, TX

Quwen V. Lubelsky
2 Cadillacs, Isle of Palms, SC

Mr. John R. Lubert
2 Cadillacs, Warren, OH

Ms. Cleo M. Lubin
3 Cadillacs, Fort Worth, TX

Mr. Eugene J. Lucas, Jr.
1 Cadillac, Charleston, SC

Mr. M.J. Lucas
8 Cadillacs, Scranton, PA

Mr. Albert Luciano
3 Cadillacs, Downers Grove, IL

Mr. Glen H. Luckner
14 Cadillacs, Clearwater, KS

Mr. Robert Ludwig
3 Cadillacs, Scranton, PA

John Luelo
3 Cadillacs, Windsor, ON

Mr. Earl Luke
4 Cadillacs, Savannah, GA

Marie Luker
2 Cadillacs, Selma, AL

Mr. Peter Lukich
1 Cadillac, El Segundo, CA

Mr. Thomas J. Lukowicz, Sr.
1 Cadillac, Antigo, WI

Mr. Sammy Luna
2 Cadillacs, El Paso, TX

Mr. Bobby E. Lund
5 Cadillacs, Muskegon, MI

Mr. Lowell W. Lundberg
4 Cadillacs, Mesa, AZ

Mr. Clifford A. Lundquist
1 Cadillac, Saint Paul, MN

Mr. Harry Lundquist
3 Cadillacs, Idyllwild, CA

Milton Lundquist
7 Cadillacs, Rockford, IL

Mr. Harry J. Lundy
7 Cadillacs, Chickamauga, GA

Jess & William Luper, Sr.
5 Cadillacs, New Bern, NC

Ms. Frances Lupo
2 Cadillacs, Trenton, NJ

Milton Lupow
6 Cadillacs, Merrick, NY

Mr. George R. Lusink
2 Cadillacs, Melbourne, FL

Mr. Robert G. Luttrell
4 Cadillacs, Lufkin, TX

Mr. Elwood Lutz
N. Miami Beach, FL

Ms. Ruth L. Lutze
1 Cadillac, Winthrop, MA

Roy & Arlene Lybarger, Sr.
4 Cadillacs, Oakland, IA

Reverend Athel J. Lynch
8 Cadillacs, Kalkaska, MI

Mr. E. Lynch
1 Cadillac, Chatham, ON

Mr. Nathaniel W. Lynch
3 Cadillacs, Rogue River, OR

Mr. Patrick Lynch
1 Cadillac, Franklin, TN

Dr. & Mrs. Richard D. Lynch
6 Cadillacs, Palm Desert, CA

Mr. Everett L. Lynn
2 Cadillacs, Helena, MT

Ulysses G. Lyon
8 Cadillacs, Washington, DC

Mrs. Dorothy Lyons
3 Cadillacs, Pittsburgh, PA

Mr. Elder Lyons
1 Cadillac, Sulphur, LA

Ms. Marjorie Lyons
2 Cadillacs, Winnipeg, MB

Mrs. Betty R. Lyttle
7 Cadillacs, Enterprise, AL

Mr. Ned H. Lytton
Mathis, TX

M

Mrs. Bernadette Maas
4 Cadillacs, Irvine, CA

Mrs. Maxine A. Maas
3 Cadillacs, Napa, CA

Mr. Curtis W. Maaske
6 Cadillacs, Manitowoc, WI

Mr. Eric C. Maass
1 Cadillac, Sandpoint, ID

Eric & Jean Maass
3 Cadillacs, Sandprint, ID

Mr. William E. Mabe
3 Cadillacs, Beaufort, SC

Mr. Marvin G. Maberry
3 Cadillacs, Reno, NV

Mr. Jack R. Mabry
3 Cadillacs, Amity, OR

Mr. J. MacBain
3 Cadillacs, Dartmouth, NS

Colonel Hugh MacDonald
8 Cadillacs, Indianapolis, IN

Mr. Malcolm K. MacDonald
3 Cadillacs, Medfield, MA

William MacDonald
2 Cadillacs, Port Colborne, ON

Mr. Camilo P. Machin
5 Cadillacs, Laredo, TX

Ralph & Sally Macisco
12 Cadillacs, Stratford, CT

Mr. Emelian J. Mack
1 Cadillac, Racine, WI

Roland Mack, USN (Ret)
5 Cadillacs, Norfolk, VA

Mr. Thomas W. Mack
23 Cadillacs, Pittsburgh, PA

Mr. Alvin MacKenna
1 Cadillac, Bridgewater, NS

Mr. Joseph Macko
42 Cadillacs, Flint, MI

Mr. Raymond W. MacLean
1 Cadillac, Vero Beach, FL

Donald MacLeod
5 Cadillacs, Charlottetown, PE

Mr. J. MacLeod
4 Cadillacs, Bridgewater, NS

Mr. Paul S. MacMichael
2 Cadillacs, Redmond, WA

J. MacPherson
2 Cadillacs, Delta, BC

Mr. Thomas J. Madden
2 Cadillacs, Chelsea, MA

Mrs. John Maddox
4 Cadillacs, Arlington, TX

Mr. Ode Maddox
2 Cadillacs, Oden, AR

Edmond Madion
3 Cadillacs, Vista, CA

Mr. Robert A. Mady
5 Cadillacs, Saint Louis, MO

Mr. Jacob Maechtlen
3 Cadillacs, Clearwater, KS

Mr. Gerald R. Magaw
8 Cadillacs, Port St. Lucie, FL

Mr. Kenneth F. Magee
8 Cadillacs, Kenner, LA

Mr. Lawrence E. Magee
1 Cadillac, Collins, MS

Mr. Richard E. Magee
7 Cadillacs, Anderson, TX

Andrew Maggio
5 Cadillacs, Prospect Hts., IL

Ms. Kathleen M. Magliano
3 Cadillacs, Brooksville, FL

Mr. Chester O. Magnuson
1 Cadillac, Holdrege, NE

Mr. Paul L. Magruder
5 Cadillacs, Wonewoc, WI

Mr. George Mahan
1 Cadillac, Whitby, ON

Mr. Thomas M. Mahan
2 Cadillacs, Jamaica Plain, MA

Mr. A. Maheu
3 Cadillacs, Azilda, ON

Mr. Billy F. Mahler
2 Cadillacs, Wichita Falls, TX

Ms. Della Mahon
1 Cadillac, Sioux City, IA

Mr. Hardy Mahone
1 Cadillac, Ft. Lauderdale, FL

Mr. Phil J. Maillet
3 Cadillacs, Big Stone Cty., SD

Mr. Michael Maino
9 Cadillacs, Belleville, NJ

Dr. & Mrs. P. Donald Maiocco
6 Cadillacs, Havertown, PA

Mr. R. Major
1 Cadillac, Cornwall, ON

Capt. Oliver W. Majors, USNR
55 Cadillacs, Corpus Christi, TX

Mr. Z.D. Makasjian
1 Cadillac, Los Angeles, CA

Mr. Andreas Makris
1 Cadillac, Silver Spring, MD

M.E. Maksymiu
2 Cadillacs, Thornton, ON

Mr. Frank Malavotte
15 Cadillacs, Federal Way, WA

Donald Malcolm
1 Cadillac, Scarborough, ON

George Malesich
11 Cadillacs, Denver, CO

Ms. Betty Malin
2 Cadillacs, Hubbard, OH

Mr. Paul H. Mallette
12 Cadillacs, Houston, TX

Mr. Donald Mallman
1 Cadillac, San Diego, CA

Mrs. Frances B. Mallow
2 Cadillacs, Howard, OH

Mr. Charles W. Malloy
4 Cadillacs, Ashland, KY

Mr. Anthony L. Malone
13 Cadillacs, Elmira, NY

Ms. Frances M. Malson
2 Cadillacs, Plainfield, WI

R.C. Maltby
1 Cadillac, Guelph, ON

Ms. Irene Mamos
4 Cadillacs, Lynn, MA

Mr. Peter Manceri
4 Cadillacs, Marlton, NJ

Mr. Pasquale Mancino
2 Cadillacs, Englishtown, NJ

Mr. Nick Manda
1 Cadillac, Canton, OH

Mr. Joseph Mangano
4 Cadillacs, Jamesburg, NJ

Thaddeus Mangrum
4 Cadillacs, Jonesboro, AR

Mr. Anthony T. Maniace
10 Cadillacs, Columbus, OH

Mr. Donald B. Manlick
1 Cadillac, Manitowoc, WI

General Lyle Mann
6 Cadillacs, Alexandria, VA

Mr. Mario Mannarino
3 Cadillacs, Brooklyn, NY

A. Mannina
7 Cadillacs, Windsor, ON

Mr. Howard Manning, Sr.
7 Cadillacs, Carlisle, PA

Mr. Godfrey Mansfield
1 Cadillac, Calgary, AB

Mr. Dale J. Manson
1 Cadillac, Granite City, IL

Mr. James B. Manthey
6 Cadillacs, Rocky River, OH

Mrs. Jean Manuel
2 Cadillacs, Scarborough, ON

Mrs. Anne H. Marbury
3 Cadillacs, Cocoa Beach, FL

Gino Marchetti
20 Cadillacs, Hinsdale, IL

Mr. Edward J. Marcinek
2 Cadillacs, Omaha, NE

Mr. Joseph Marcucci
1 Cadillac, Murrieta, CA

Mr. Herman Marcuccio
4 Cadillacs, Amsterdam, NY

Mr. V.L. Marcum
6 Cadillacs, Fairfax, VA

Mr. Henry E. Marcus
7 Cadillacs, Huntsville, AL

Mr. Dellie A. Mardis, Jr.
2 Cadillacs, New Orleans, LA

Mr. Raymond F. Mardis
4 Cadillacs, Davenport, IA

Mr. Justo L. Mari
2 Cadillacs, Fargo, ND

Mr. R. Marin
1 Cadillac, Ottawa, ON

Mr. Joseph E. Marinacci, Sr.
3 Cadillacs, Pompano Beach, FL

Mr. Robert J. Marineau
5 Cadillacs, Macomb, MI

Mr. Dewey Mark
6 Cadillacs, Fair Oaks, TX

Mr. Robert M. Markham
1 Cadillac, Meridian, MS

Mr. Regis Marko
3 Cadillacs, E. Pittsburgh, PA

Mr. Claude D. Marks
2 Cadillacs, Wichita, KS

Joseph Marlowe
1 Cadillac, Unadilla, GA

Leonard V. Marrone, MD
35 Cadillacs, Utica, NY

Mrs. Jean H. Marrot
4 Cadillacs, Pleasanton, CA

Mr. Charles W. Marrs
15 Cadillacs, Kansas City, MO

Mr. Charles J. Marsala
2 Cadillacs, East Hampton, NY

Mr. Joseph Marsala
10 Cadillacs, River Grove, IL

Dr. Eugene L. Marsh
5 Cadillacs, Co. Bluffs, IA

Gerald H. Marsh
2 Cadillacs, El Reno, OK

Mahatta Flinn Marsh
4 Cadillacs, Marlow, OK

Mr. William E. Marsh
4 Cadillacs, Dothan, AL

Mr. Dean Marshall
8 Cadillacs, Burlington, IA

Mr. Lyman T. Marshall, Jr.
1 Cadillac, Duluth, MN

Mr. Robert P. Marshall
9 Cadillacs, San Jacinto, CA

Ms. Lorraine Martel
1 Cadillac, Suncook, NH

Mr. Frank E. Martin
4 Cadillacs, Miami, FL

Mr. Gary H. Martin
3 Cadillacs, De Queen, AR

Mr. Grant Martin
1 Cadillac, Gilbertsville, KY

James Martin
24 Cadillacs, Leeds, AL

Mr. Jimmy L. Martin, Sr.
1 Cadillac, Kelly, LA

Mrs. Josephine Martin
3 Cadillacs, Parsippany, NJ

Mr. Mortimer Martin, Jr.
1 Cadillac, Front Royal, VA

Murdelle C. Martin
3 Cadillacs, Normangee, TX

Mr. Otho W. Martin, Jr.
2 Cadillacs, Appomattox, VA

Mr. Robert T. Martin
5 Cadillacs, Greenville, MS

Mr. Vernon R. Martin
4 Cadillacs, Shawnee, OK

Willis & Mary R. Martin
6 Cadillacs, Decatur, IL

A. Martinez-Pico, MD
4 Cadillacs, San Juan, PR

Mr. Isadore J. Martini
6 Cadillacs, Itasca, IL

Clifford Harry Martinson
8 Cadillacs, Zephyrhills, FL

David Martison
3 Cadillacs, Mississauga, ON

John L. Maruna
1 Cadillac, Chicago, IL

Mr. Michael D. Marx
3 Cadillacs, Falls City, NE

Dr. Paul Marx
13 Cadillacs, Lincoln, NE

Ms. Vera Masingill
1 Cadillac, DeQuincy, LA

Mr. Ben D. Maska
7 Cadillacs, Chicago, IL

Mr. & Mrs. Burnis L. Mason
9 Cadillacs, Big Spring, TX

C.L. Mason
2 Cadillacs, French Lick, IN

Mr. Clarence E. Mason
Petersburg, VA

Mrs. Emma J. Mason
5 Cadillacs, Athens, IL

H. Jack Mason
7 Cadillacs, Lexington, KY

James S. Mason
1 Cadillac, Centerville, GA

Mr. Joseph Mason
14 Cadillacs, Albany, NY

Mr. Robert R. Mason
3 Cadillacs, Grand Jct., CO

Mr. Earl A. Masoner
3 Cadillacs, Beavercreek, OR

Mr. Joseph Massae
4 Cadillacs, Yuba City, CA

Mr. Robert Massaroni
2 Cadillacs, Schenectady, NY

Mr. Ray G. Massey
1 Cadillac, Denton, TX

Augustus Massie
2 Cadillacs, Lake Orion, MI

Mr. Russell Massie
5 Cadillacs, Carbondale, IL

Mr. William F. Masterson
1 Cadillac, El Paso, TX

Mr. James R. Matheis
4 Cadillacs, Peoria, IL

Mr. Lewis Matheny
7 Cadillacs, Byesville, OH

Mrs. Marcella K. Mathews
4 Cadillacs, Cedar Falls, IA

Ms. Jean M. Mathiak
1 Cadillac, Menomonee Fls., WI

Mr. Roger Mathieu
4 Cadillacs, Beauceville Est., QC

Mr. Johnnie W. Mathis
3 Cadillacs, Baltimore, MD

Mr. Robert N. Matison
4 Cadillacs, Lincoln, NE

Ms. Marsha L. Matlock
1 Cadillac, Arlington, TX

Robie Lee Matlock
5 Cadillacs, Clovis, NM

Mr. William B. Matlock
2 Cadillacs, Oak Harbor, WA

Maral Matte
1 Cadillac, St. Sauveur, QC

Mr. Louis C. Matter
5 Cadillacs, De Graff, MN

Mr. E. Matthes
1 Cadillac, Winnipeg, MB

Mr. Billy E. Matthews
4 Cadillacs, Donaldsonvlle, LA

Ms. Evelyn W. Matthews
4 Cadillacs, Dunn, NC

Mr. G. Matthews
1 Cadillac, Riverview, NB

Mr. Hank Matthews
25 Cadillacs, Burnaby, BC

Mr. John H. Matthews
3 Cadillacs, Coronado, CA

Mr. Philip R. Matthews
4 Cadillacs, Hixson, TN

Ms. Ruth C. Matthews
12 Cadillacs, Gibson City, IL

Mr. Wayne Matthews
5 Cadillacs, Altadena, CA

Thomas M. Mattox
1 Cadillac, Lake Charles, LA

Ms. Lucille B. Matysiak
3 Cadillacs, Shrevesport, LA

Mr. Marvin Matz
6 Cadillacs, Wichita, KS

Dr. Randall L. Mauck
3 Cadillacs, Logansport, IN

Ms. Edgar W. Maupin
Lamar, MO

Mr. Mark F. Maurer
8 Cadillacs, Monroe, LA

Mr. Paul Maurice
1 Cadillac, Edmonds, WA

Mr. Charles Mauro
10 Cadillacs, Monte Sereno, CA

Ms. J. Mauro
22 Cadillacs, Englewd. Clfs., NJ

Mr. Mike Maxa
Chesaning, MI

Ms. Katrine Maxey
22 Cadillacs, Monument, CO

Harding W. May
2 Cadillacs, Beeville, TX

Lois & Kester May
8 Cadillacs, Sedalia, MO

Marcia Faith P. May
1 Cadillac, Metairie, LA

Mr. William G. Mayer
16 Cadillacs, Scottsdale, AZ

Mr. Richard T. Mayes
2 Cadillacs, Raleigh, NC

Mr. Edgar L. Maynard
2 Cadillacs, Decatur, GA

Mrs. Mary Maynard
12 Cadillacs, Rome, GA

Mr. Johnnie E. Mayo
3 Cadillacs, Casper, WY

Ms. Margaret M. Mayo
8 Cadillacs, Caruthersvlle., MO

Ulyss Joe Mays
9 Cadillacs, Rocky Mount, NC

Ferdinand D. Mazzeo
4 Cadillacs, Buffalo, NY

Mrs. Thomasine McAfee
5 Cadillacs, Benton Harbor, MI

Mr. Bernard C. McAllister
Rochester, NY

Mr. Herbert D. McBride
5 Cadillacs, Warren, OH

Mr. Ian McBride
4 Cadillacs, Hillsborough, CA

Mr. John T. McBride
14 Cadillacs, Champaign, IL

Ms. Virginia R. McBride
2 Cadillacs, Nokomis, FL

Mr. Charles S. McCain, Sr.
11 Cadillacs, Shreveport, LA

Mr. Kenneth D. McCall
28 Cadillacs, Centralia, IL

Mrs. Lorraine McCallister
3 Cadillacs, Winter Park, FL

Mr. Edward P. McCanna
6 Cadillacs, Rockford, IL

Mr. Knox McCardell
5 Cadillacs, Chattanooga, TN

Mr. James H. McCarthy
6 Cadillacs, Detroit, MI

William T. McCarthy
1 Cadillac, N. Brookfield, MA

Mr. Harlan L. McCartney
4 Cadillacs, Paris, TN

Mr. Charles J. McCarty
2 Cadillacs, Stanberry, MO

Mr. Bobby N. McCasland
2 Cadillacs, Greenville, TX

Ms. Annie M. McClain
2 Cadillacs, Rusk, TX

Mr. Charles McClain
2 Cadillacs, Shawnee Msn., KS

Mr. Rollis G. McClain
2 Cadillacs, Evansdale, IA

Freddie & Sherrill McClendon
3 Cadillacs, Indianapolis, IN

Mr. William M. McClendon
15 Cadillacs, Muskogee, OK

Birt W. McClure
10 Cadillacs, Saint Joseph, MO

Mr. James McClure
1 Cadillac, Savannah, GA

Ms. Josphine McClure
11 Cadillacs, Fairfax, OK

Ms. Lucia McCluskey
16 Cadillacs, Tewksbury, MA

J. Rowland McClymont
3 Cadillacs, Holdrege, NE

Mr. Norris L. McCollum
4 Cadillacs, Stone Mtn., GA

Ms. Reba I. McCollum
1 Cadillac, Birmingham, AL

Jean & Bernard H. McCombs
37 Cadillacs, Oldsmar, FL

Mr. Oscar H. McCombs
4 Cadillacs, Chicago, IL

Ms. Winifred M. McConnell
11 Cadillacs, Clearwater, FL

Mr. Leonard L. McConville
Saint Paul, MN

Mr. Clyde F. McCorkle
1 Cadillac, Florence, AL

Ms. Marie A. McCormack
5 Cadillacs, Bethesda, MD

Mr. Gerald McCormick
3 Cadillacs, Fountain, MI

Terry M. & Carie McCormick
4 Cadillacs, Houston, TX

Mr. Willie McCormick
7 Cadillacs, Detroit, MI

Mr. Ray E. McCotter
New Bern, NC

Mr. Lee McCoy
10 Cadillacs, Hazard, KY

Mrs. Christine McCrary
1 Cadillac, Chillicothe, OH

Woody McCrea
5 Cadillacs, Alma, GA

Clarence McCreless
4 Cadillacs, Dallas, TX

Mrs. Edna M. McCuley
3 Cadillacs, Sacramento, CA

Mr. James L. McCully
1 Cadillac, Baltimore, MD

Mr. E. McCutcheon
3 Cadillacs, Lions Head, ON

Mr. Charles O. McDaniel
8 Cadillacs, Madison, IL

Mrs. Kathleen Y. McDaniel
4 Cadillacs, Myrtle Beach, SC

Ms. Bertha G. McDonald
3 Cadillacs, San Antonio, TX

Mr. Frank B. McDonald
2 Cadillacs, Zanesville, OH

Mr. James E. McDonald
Washington, IN

Mrs. Janice McDonald
5 Cadillacs, Kokomo, IN

Ms. Mary B. McDonald
2 Cadillacs, Simpsonville, SC

Mr. Robert McDonald
3 Cadillacs, Decatur, MS

Kathryn McDougal
5 Cadillacs, Indianapolis, IN

Mr. John E. McElfresh
1 Cadillac, Owensboro, KY

Mr. Albert J. McElroy
7 Cadillacs, Saint Louis, MO

Elvia R. McEvoy
2 Cadillacs, St. Simons Is., GA

W. Wayne McFall
8 Cadillacs, Dayton, OH

Mrs. H.M. McFarland
1 Cadillac, Middlebrg Hts., OH

Ms. Pearl V. McFarland
6 Cadillacs, Drayton, ND

Mr. Clyde McGee
18 Cadillacs, Leechburg, PA

Mr. Edward J. McGee
2 Cadillacs, Stamford, CT

Mr. Fred M. McGee
9 Cadillacs, Oblong, IL

Ms. Maisie J. McGerry
4 Cadillacs, Merritt Is., FL

Mr. Walter E. McGervey
1 Cadillac, Walnut Creek, CA

Neal K. McGill
1 Cadillac, Greeneville, TN

Ms. Wilma W. McGill
Auburn, AL

E. Robert McGinty
1 Cadillac, Stillwater, OK

Mr. William J. McGirl
1 Cadillac, Birmingham, AL

Mr. Billy F. McGowen
1 Cadillac, Winter Haven, FL

Mr. Edward W. McGrath
3 Cadillacs, N. Royalton, OH

Ms. Louise McGrew
6 Cadillacs, Tyler, TX

Colonel Charlie T. McGugan
2 Cadillacs, Aberdeen, NC

Mr. Thomas L. McGuire
6 Cadillacs, La Habra, CA

William McGuire
4 Cadillacs, Trumbull, CT

Mr. William L. McInnis
3 Cadillacs, Vicksburg, MS

Norma & Calvin McInturff
3 Cadillacs, Boyce, VA

Mr. Harold E. McIrvin
2 Cadillacs, Reno, NV

Mr. Kenneth McKamey
8 Cadillacs, Bloomington, IN

Mr. Larry H. McKelvey
2 Cadillacs, Bealeton, VA

John McKenna
2 Cadillacs, Hixson, TN

Mr. Donald R. McKenzie
4 Cadillacs, Ashland, KY

Mr. Edker C. McKenzie
3 Cadillacs, Madison, AL

Ms. Marzelle McKenzie
4 Cadillacs, Chicago, IL

Mr. Arthur J. McKeon, Jr.
2 Cadillacs, Sun City, AZ

Mr. Jones McKinley
9 Cadillacs, Huntsville, AL

Mr. James W. McKinney
1 Cadillac, Blue Springs, MO

Ms. Margaret E. McKinney
9 Cadillacs, Carmel, IN

Michael F. McKinney
1 Cadillac, Sharpsville, IN

Mr. Carl McKinnon
5 Cadillacs, Guymon, OK

Mr. Louis McKnight
5 Cadillacs, Middletown, OH

Mr. Patrick McLaughlin
1 Cadillac, Far Rockaway, NY

Mr. John McLaurin
10 Cadillacs, Columbus, GA

Mr. Chris McLean
4 Cadillacs, Colborne, ON

Mr. Marvin L. McLeod
3 Cadillacs, Warner Robins, GA

Etta & Charles W. McLevaine
6 Cadillacs, Owensboro, KY

Roger McMahan
1 Cadillac, Marion, IN

Mr. Vernon McMikle
2 Cadillacs, Boise, ID

Mr. Autry E. McMillan
6 Cadillacs, Overton, TX

Neal McMillan
8 Cadillacs, Calgary, AB

Mr. Donald J. McMillin
2 Cadillacs, La Grange, IL

Ms. Kathy McMinn
3 Cadillacs, Belton, TX

Mr. Thomas O. McMullan
8 Cadillacs, Dunnellon, FL

Mr. Raymond McMullen, Jr.
1 Cadillac, Lady Lake, FL

Arthur McMurtrie
2 Cadillacs, Corona Del Mar, CA

Mrs. Julia A. McNally
8 Cadillacs, Yuba City, CA

Mr. James A. McNamara, Jr.
3 Cadillacs, Charlotte, NC

Mr. Milo T. McNaughton
8 Cadillacs, Wilmington, NC

Howard L. McNeal
1 Cadillac, Marion, IA

Mrs. Maureen McNeil
4 Cadillacs, Marblehead, MA

Mr. Phillip McNeil
3 Cadillacs, Danville, VA

Ms. Dorothy McNew
Jacksonville, TX

Mrs. Marjorie G. McQueen
1 Cadillac, Racine, WI

Mr. & Mrs. W.H. McQuiston
13 Cadillacs, Spokane, WA

Mr. Carey P. McTaggart
3 Cadillacs, Seneca, SC

Osborne McVay
15 Cadillacs, Butler, MO

Mr. Howard McVey
4 Cadillacs, Roanoke, VA

Mr. Melvin McWhirter
45 Cadillacs, Bullard, TX

Ms. Muriel McWilliams
2 Cadillacs, Brandon, MS

Mr. Billy Meacham
5 Cadillacs, Huntsville, AL

Mr. George C. Meadows
46 Cadillacs, Cookeville, TN

Daniel Mecca
3 Cadillacs, Haines City, FL

Ms. Natalie Medlock
Phoenix, AZ

Mr. Joseph F. Meehan
10 Cadillacs, Albany, NY

Mr. Ross B. Meek
2 Cadillacs, Tyler, TX

Ms. Esther Mehalow
3 Cadillacs, Cheyenne, WY

Mr. William M. Mehrtens
Cullahan, FL

Mr. Jack L. Meier
8 Cadillacs, Fresno, CA

Blanche Meinzinger
2 Cadillacs, Stoney Creek, ON

Mrs. Lucia Melham
9 Cadillacs, Lemoyne, PA

Mr. Thomas C. Meloy
4 Cadillacs, Mount Vernon, OH

Mr. Richard Melvin
8 Cadillacs, Cincinnati, OH

Chuck W. Menard
2 Cadillacs, Evergreen Pk., IL

Mr. Ray F. Menaugh
2 Cadillacs, Alhambra, CA

Mr. Stephen Mentrikoski
2 Cadillacs, Berwick, PA

Ms. Lynne Meredith
1 Cadillac, Richmond Hill, ON

B. Merino
1 Cadillac, Virginia Beach, VA

Mr. Steve J. Merkle
3 Cadillacs, Chicago, IL

Ms. Iris E. Merrell
10 Cadillacs, Hayti, MO

Mr. Allen H. Merritt
17 Cadillacs, Wilmington, NC

Evelen L. Mesker
2 Cadillacs, Urbana, IL

Mr. John Messer
10 Cadillacs, Navasota, TX

Mr. James D. Metcalf
6 Cadillacs, St. Augustine, FL

Mr. Walter E. Metcalf, Jr.
1 Cadillac, N. Ridgeville, OH

Harry Methfessel
4 Cadillacs, Hayesville, NC

Mr. John C. Mettler
3 Cadillacs, Charleston, SC

Mr. Charles P. Metty
2 Cadillacs, Toledo, OH

Ms. Betty Metz
1 Cadillac, Pittsburgh, PA

Mrs. Ethel Metz
4 Cadillacs, Souderton, PA

Mr. Paul C. Meyd
1 Cadillac, Severn, MD

Mr. Clarence Meyer
4 Cadillacs, Fort Scott, KS

Mr. John S. Meyer
3 Cadillacs, Fort Worth, TX

Ms. Joyce L. Meyer
3 Cadillacs, Panama City, FL

Mr. Roy Meyer
Spring Park, MN

Mr. Edwin E. Meyers
3 Cadillacs, Champaign, IL

Mr. Barry Miazga
1 Cadillac, Mississauga, ON

Joseph Miceli
13 Cadillacs, Beechurst, NY

Mr. Merle D. Michael
5 Cadillacs, Johnson City, TN

Daniel Michau
4 Cadillacs, College Park, MD

Mr. Lowell G. Michels
Apple Valley, MN

Mr. Andrew Micklos
1 Cadillac, Northampton, PA

Don Middleton
7 Cadillacs, Millbrae, CA

Mr. Stanley L. Miechowicz
2 Cadillacs, Depew, NY

Mr. Leonard D. Mielke
26 Cadillacs, Punta Gorda, FL

Mr. Harry E. Mika
1 Cadillac, Grand Rapids, MI

Mr. Alex F. Miklusak
5 Cadillacs, Griffith, IN

Ms. Joan Mikos
2 Cadillacs, Linden, NJ

P.F. Mike Mikules
7 Cadillacs, Alexandria, VA

Mr. Charles A. Milazzo
8 Cadillacs, Syracuse, NY

Mrs. Dorothy L. Miles
23 Cadillacs, Girardeau, MO

Mr. George Miles
8 Cadillacs, Easton, PA

Ms. Lynn C. Miles
1 Cadillac, Bradenton, FL

Steve Miletich
10 Cadillacs, Monroe, MI

Mr. Joseph C. Militello
4 Cadillacs, Dunkirk, NY

Mr. Jack L. Millaway
36 Cadillacs, Texarkana, AR

Mr. Abe Miller
2 Cadillacs, Phoenix, AZ

Mr. Alan Miller
6 Cadillacs, Diboll, TX

Mr. Chalice E. Miller
4 Cadillacs, North Augusta, SC

Clarence L. Miller
7 Cadillacs, Houston, TX

Mr. D. Miller
2 Cadillacs, Chateauguay, QC

Mr. Daryl D. Miller
6 Cadillacs, Great Falls, MT

Mrs. Dawn B. Miller
6 Cadillacs, Brookfield, WI

Mr. George M. Miller
7 Cadillacs, Birmingham, AL

H.E. Miller
4 Cadillacs, Mt. Holly, PA

Harry L. Miller
5 Cadillacs, Spanaway, WA

Mr. James Miller
2 Cadillacs, Patoka, IN

Mr. John W. Miller, Sr.
1 Cadillac, Pepper Pike, OH

Mr. Lawson Miller
2 Cadillacs, Los Angeles, CA

Ms. Margaret M. Miller
2 Cadillacs, Fort Gratiot, MI

Ms. Mary W. Miller
7 Cadillacs, Gautier, MS

Ms. Mary B. Miller
2 Cadillacs, Memphis, TN

Mr. Russell H. Miller
1 Cadillac, Houston, TX

Mr. Russell E. Miller
4 Cadillacs, Wisc. Rapids, WI

Samuel C. Miller, Jr.
2 Cadillacs, Camp Hill, PA

V Miller
2 Cadillacs, Newmarket, ON

W. Bruce Miller
6 Cadillacs, Baltimore, MD

Mr. William M. Miller
4 Cadillacs, Tampa, FL

William Leslie Miller
5 Cadillacs, Greenville, KY

Mr. William C. Miller, Jr.
1 Cadillac, Pawleys Isl., SC

Ms. Mary S. Milliron
4 Cadillacs, Marlin, TX

Ms. Cora B. Mills
4 Cadillacs, Ayden, NC

Mr. Marvin Mills
3 Cadillacs, Lincoln, NE

Ms. Ruth J. Mills
Carl Junction, MO

Mr. Jack Milstein
4 Cadillacs, Boca Raton, FL

Fred Mincer
5 Cadillacs, Tucson, AZ

Dr. John W. Miner
35 Cadillacs, Robbinston, ME

Mr. Michael J. Miner
14 Cadillacs, Watseka, IL

Tommy M. Miner
8 Cadillacs, Lone Star, TX

William E. Miner
4 Cadillacs, Redington Bch., FL

Mr. Ronald Minks
1 Cadillac, La Porte, TX

Mr. Joseph H. Minor
11 Cadillacs, Baton Rouge, LA

Mrs. Marie D. Minorchio
11 Cadillacs, Tacoma, WA

Fermon & Helen Minshew
10 Cadillacs, Pensacola, FL

Mr. Eugene Miranda
Flushing, NY

Mrs. Joyce Miranda
6 Cadillacs, Alameda, CA

Mr. Robert Misener
7 Cadillacs, Ocala, FL

Mr. Beverly D. Mitchell
2 Cadillacs, Detroit, MI

Mr. David R. Mitchell
3 Cadillacs, Washington, PA

Mr. Harry B. Mitchell
3 Cadillacs, Lima, OH

Ms. Jewell R. Mitchell
3 Cadillacs, Knoxville, TN

Mr. Lucien B. Mitchell
2 Cadillacs, Junction City, KS

Mr. Orrin J. Mitchell
5 Cadillacs, Sun Lakes, AZ

Z. Mitha
1 Cadillac, Stoney Creek, ON

Mr. Rembert E. Mittler
4 Cadillacs, Marthasville, MO

Mr. Thomas D. Mixon
3 Cadillacs, Horseshoe Bay, TX

Ms. Billie Y. Mize
2 Cadillacs, Big Spring, TX

Wynona C. Mize
Montgomery, AL

Mr. Abraham Mizrachi
10 Cadillacs, Las Vegas, NV

Mr. William L. Modesitt
3 Cadillacs, Sherman, TX

Mr. Arthur A. Modugno
5 Cadillacs, Lakewood, NJ

Earl R. Moffatt
12 Cadillacs, Ishpeming, MI

Mr. Lino Mogorovic
2 Cadillacs, Westchester, IL

Edward Junior Mohs
2 Cadillacs, Elkhart, KS

K. Sam Moldave
9 Cadillacs, Las Vegas, NV

Ms. Dolores M. Molina
2 Cadillacs, Odessa, TX

Mr. Herman C. Molk
1 Cadillac, Oak Lawn, IL

Dennis Molony
11 Cadillacs, Fort Thomas, KY

Mr. & Mrs. John Molstad
4 Cadillacs, Colby, KS

Mr. Jack K. Molz
Dayton, OH

Mr. Charles S. Mondragon
16 Cadillacs, San Luis, CO

Mr. Georges Monette
28 Cadillacs, Hull, QC

Ms. Ruby L. Monette
1 Cadillac, New Bern, NC

Ms. Violet Money
7 Cadillacs, Elizabethtown, PA

Mr. Claudio Mongiat
2 Cadillacs, Rockford, IL

Mr. Alfred L. Moniot
12 Cadillacs, Haddonfield, NJ

Mr. Arthur R. Monroe
5 Cadillacs, Amarillo, TX

Tom Monsey
12 Cadillacs, Tunkhannock, PA

Mrs. Catherine T. Montana
1 Cadillac, Sicklerville, NJ

Mr. John Montanelli
7 Cadillacs, Forked River, NJ

Mr. James Montgomery
9 Cadillacs, Warner Robins, GA

Mr. Ted Montoya
3 Cadillacs, Santa Fe, NM

Mr. Patrick E. Montplaisir
5 Cadillacs, Dayton, OH

Donia H. Moody
10 Cadillacs, Fort Myers, FL

Dr. Bill Moon
6 Cadillacs, Dothan, AL

Mr. Joe R. Mooney
1 Cadillac, Charleston, WV

John Mooney
1 Cadillac, Verdun, QC

Mr. Earnest Moore
2 Cadillacs, Powhatan, VA

Ms. Eddie P. Moore
3 Cadillacs, Augusta, GA

Dr. Eunice W. Moore
Montgomery, AL

Franklin D. Moore
6 Cadillacs, Saint Louis, MO

Mr. Harold Moore
4 Cadillacs, Little Rock, AR

Mr. James M. Moore
3 Cadillacs, Cordova, NC

Mr. Jonathan Moore
7 Cadillacs, Rock Island, IL

Mr. Joseph D. Moore
1 Cadillac, Raleigh, NC

Ms. Loretta W. Moore
3 Cadillacs, Hearne, TX

Ms. Mary L. Moore
San Antonio, TX

Mr. Norman L. Moore
12 Cadillacs, Vista, CA

Mr. Robert D. Moore
5 Cadillacs, Arcadia, CA

Mr. Robert Moore
5 Cadillacs, Tulsa, OK

Roosevelt Moore
9 Cadillacs, Detroit, MI

Ms. Ruby Moore
1 Cadillac, Atlanta, GA

Mr. Sammie J. Moore
6 Cadillacs, Jasper, TX

Mr. Samuel L. Moore
2 Cadillacs, New Bern, NC

Shirley A. Moore
10 Cadillacs, Cedar Rapids, IA

Mr. Wilbur G. Moore
3 Cadillacs, Walton Hills, OH

Mr. William A. Moore
3 Cadillacs, Greenville, SC

Mr. Earl Moorhous
26 Cadillacs, Saint Joseph, IL

Mr. Joseph P. Moorhouse
2 Cadillacs, Benton, TN

Mrs. Billie S. Moorman
3 Cadillacs, Horseshoe Bay, TX

John & Donna M. Morano
10 Cadillacs, Port Chester, NY

Ms. Nancy Morea
2 Cadillacs, Randolph, NJ

Mr. Raymond Morehead
9 Cadillacs, Comanche, OK

Mr. Bruno Morelli
1 Cadillac, York, ON

Mr. Lesly J. Moresco
1 Cadillac, Millbrae, CA

Ms. Ada K. Morgan
4 Cadillacs, Montgomery, AL

Mr. Charles H. Morgan
7 Cadillacs, Los Angeles, CA

Ms. Dorothy Morgan
1 Cadillac, Rio Grande, OH

Mr. Frank D. Morgan
1 Cadillac, Palm Beach, FL

Mr. James Morgan
3 Cadillacs, San Antonio, TX

Ms. Jean R. Morgan
2 Cadillacs, Plano, TX

Langston Morgan
2 Cadillacs, Raleigh, NC

Ms. Laura G. Morgan
1 Cadillac, Folsom, LA

Ms. Patricia A. Morgan
3 Cadillacs, Valley Vlg., CA

Mr. Travis O. Morgan
2 Cadillacs, Premont, TX

Mr. Virgil Morningstar
4 Cadillacs, Fort Wayne, IN

Morris Morrell
15 Cadillacs, Baltimore, MD

Dorothy & Warren Morris
20 Cadillacs, Okla. City, OK

Mr. Eugene W. Morris
4 Cadillacs, Houston, TX

Mr. Mac Morris
10 Cadillacs, Arlington, VA

Mr. Ralph F. Morris, Jr.
9 Cadillacs, Hobe Sound, FL

Ms. Sandra E. Morris
2 Cadillacs, Huntington, WV

Mr. Carl B. Morrison
1 Cadillac, Owings, MD

Ms. Jacqueline D. Morrison
1 Cadillac, Maple Hill, NC

Mr. James F. Morrison
2 Cadillacs, Tucson, AZ

Mr. Richard Morrison
14 Cadillacs, Danville, PA

Mr. Robert L. Morrison
1 Cadillac, Opelousas, LA

Mr. Roger Morrison
3 Cadillacs, Battle Ground, WA

Mr. Roland J. Morrissette
5 Cadillacs, Pinellas Park, FL

Mr. Edwin G. Morrow
1 Cadillac, Panama City, FL

Mr. Lester V. Morrow
1 Cadillac, Baton Rouge, LA

Mr. John R. Morsbach
12 Cadillacs, Enid, OK

Mr. Harold P. Morscheiser
4 Cadillacs, La Salle, IL

Ms. Katie M. Morse
1 Cadillac, Savannah, GA

Mrs. Nancy A. Morse
2 Cadillacs, Kennebunkport, ME

J.W. Mortell
8 Cadillacs, Indian Wells, CA

Mr. Kenneth P. Mortensen
4 Cadillacs, Selkirk, NY

Howard Morton
6 Cadillacs, Iowa City, IA

J.P. Morton
26 Cadillacs, Los Angeles, CA

Mr. John C. Morton
8 Cadillacs, Ridge Farm, IL

Rufus Morton
6 Cadillacs, Irvington, NJ

Mr. John P. Mosca
11 Cadillacs, Deltona, FL

Pokey J. Mose
2 Cadillacs, Huntsville, AL

Mr. Clarance E. Moseley, Sr.
6 Cadillacs, Knoxville, TN

Mr. Willie R. Moser
6 Cadillacs, Bullard, TX

Mr. Robert L. Moses, Jr.
1 Cadillac, Humble, TX

E. Moshynski
1 Cadillac, Carrying Place, ON

Mr. George Mosolgo
1 Cadillac, Crossville, TN

Ms. Gracie M. Moss
7 Cadillacs, Sweetwater, TN

Mr. M. Moss
11 Cadillacs, Calgary, AB

Byron Mot
14 Cadillacs, Wauwatosa, WI

Mr. Samuel J. Motley
2 Cadillacs, Flint, MI

Mr. Edward F. Motyka
4 Cadillacs, Uniondale, NY

Mr. Roger N. Moul
14 Cadillacs, Hanover, PA

Alberta Mount
12 Cadillacs, Livingston, NJ

Patricia & Wilbert Mrazek
10 Cadillacs, Saint Cloud, FL

Mr. Wilbert F. Mrazek
10 Cadillacs, Saint Cloud, FL

Mr. Frederick C. Mueller
1 Cadillac, Albany, NY

Ms. June O. Mueri
Peoria, IL

Mr. Bill H. Muir
2 Cadillacs, Portland, OR

Mr. Ray H. Mullen
5 Cadillacs, Mesa, AZ

Mrs. Virginia R. Mullen
3 Cadillacs, Tampa, FL

Mr. Edward C. Mullendore
3 Cadillacs, Hagerstown, MD

Mr. Bert Mullens
1 Cadillac, Russellville, AR

Mr. Andrew W. Muller
9 Cadillacs, Dalzell, SC

Ms. Gertrude Y. Muller
9 Cadillacs, Phoenix, AZ

Mrs. Doris Mulligan
1 Cadillac, Kihei, HI

Mrs. Mary Mullins
1 Cadillac, Newport, AR

Mr. Elbert Mullis
7 Cadillacs, Dublin, GA

Mr. Richard W. Munson
5 Cadillacs, W. Swanzey, NH

Ms. Charlotte F. Murawski
1 Cadillac, Chicopee, MA

Valerie P. Murdoch
Redding, CA

Lorin A. & Dorothy Murdock
2 Cadillacs, Pattonville, TX

Mr. Blair Murphy
6 Cadillacs, Haddonfield, NJ

Mr. Charles K. Murphy
2 Cadillacs, San Antonio, TX

Ms. Esther B. Murphy
10 Cadillacs, Tully, NY

Mr. Gerald E. Murphy
4 Cadillacs, Sacramento, CA

Jerrold V. Murphy
3 Cadillacs, Vienna, WV

John Murphy
6 Cadillacs, Columbine Vly., CO

Mr. Preston L. Murphy, Jr.
7 Cadillacs, Waco, TX

Mr. William E. Murphy
4 Cadillacs, Decatur, IL

Ms. Wilma Murphy
3 Cadillacs, Lakeland, FL

Mr. John J. Murray
8 Cadillacs, Slidell, LA

Ms. Julia Murray
1 Cadillac, Los Angeles, CA

Mr. Richard C. Murray
1 Cadillac, Wichita Falls, TX

Ms. Sandra S. Musacchia
2 Cadillacs, Violet, LA

Mr. Howard Muske
2 Cadillacs, Brenham, TX

Mr. James Musser
3 Cadillacs, Proctorville, OH

Mr. Jerry Mustain
15 Cadillacs, Lawton, OK

Mr. Edward P. Mutto
1 Cadillac, Belleville, IL

Mr. George M. Myer
1 Cadillac, Dallas, TX

Harold Myers
4 Cadillacs, Metairie, LA

Lois & Jack M. Myers
7 Cadillacs, Philadelphia, PA

Mr. William F. Myers, CLU
8 Cadillacs, Jacksonville, FL

N

H. Norman Nafstad
1 Cadillac, Minneapolis, MN

Dale E. Nagel
2 Cadillacs, Highland, IL

Mrs. Joan Nagel
4 Cadillacs, Clifton, NJ

Mr. John Nagle
5 Cadillacs, Northwood, IA

Mr. Bruce A. Nail
3 Cadillacs, Horseheads, NY

Mr. Edward L. Najar
8 Cadillacs, Kentwood, MI

Mr. Rex D. Nall
Snyder, TX

Mr. Robert A. Nance
1 Cadillac, Miami, OK

Mr. Daniel F. Nardo
14 Cadillacs, Wilmington, DE

Evelyn Nardone
7 Cadillacs, Elizabeth, NJ

Mr. Horace R. Narmore
3 Cadillacs, Decatur, AL

Mr. William E. Nau
2 Cadillacs, Mt. Pleasant, SC

Mr. Henry Navarrete
4 Cadillacs, Portsmouth, RI

Mr. Billy J. Neal
2 Cadillacs, Homer, LA

Mr. Herbert D. Neal
10 Cadillacs, Hernando, FL

Mr. Paul G. Neal
3 Cadillacs, Pensacola, FL

Mr. George Neale
1 Cadillac, Hamilton, ON

Mr. Irvin B. Nease
2 Cadillacs, Pauma Valley, CA

Mr. John Needham
3 Cadillacs, Concord, CA

Ms. Barbara Neely
3 Cadillacs, Lampasas, TX

Mr. Weir Neff
7 Cadillacs, Buckley, WA

G. Neilson
2 Cadillacs, Edmonton, AB

Mr. Leroy C. Neilson
West Bath, ME

Mr. Clifford D. Nelson
2 Cadillacs, Negaunee, MI

Mr. Gary W. Nelson
3 Cadillacs, San Jose, CA

Mr. Jess W. Nelson
3 Cadillacs, Redding, CA

Mr. Robert C. Nelson
8 Cadillacs, Temple City, CA

Mr. Russell H. Nelson
12 Cadillacs, Burnsville, MN

Mr. William A. Nelson
5 Cadillacs, Fort Myers, FL

William F. Nelson, Jr.
4 Cadillacs, Niceville, FL

Mr. L. Nemeth
1 Cadillac, St. Catharines, ON

Dr. George C. Neserke
6 Cadillacs, Palm Bch. Gdns., FL

Mr. Jerry Nestaval
1 Cadillac, Kelso, WA

Mr. Joseph D. Nester
3 Cadillacs, Robstown, TX

Mr. Leroy A. Neuman
1 Cadillac, Homewood, IL

Mr. J. Neville
1 Cadillac, Windsor, ON

K. Neville
3 Cadillacs, Petawawa, ON

Mr. Archibald Nevitt
7 Cadillacs, Radnor, PA

Mr. William A. Newberry
1 Cadillac, Bakersfield, CA

Mr. Melvin L. Newlin
5 Cadillacs, Rockville, IN

Mr. Frank B. Newman
8 Cadillacs, Bountiful, UT

Jarvis W. Newman
Southwest Hbr., ME

Mr. Nathan Newman
9 Cadillacs, Fresno, CA

Mr. Walter Newman
2 Cadillacs, Evansville, IN

Ms. Jacqueline L. Newmons
1 Cadillac, Wildwood, FL

Mr. Al Nichols
15 Cadillacs, W. Bloom., NY

Ms. Frances H. Nichols
6 Cadillacs, Sacramento, CA

Ms. Gladys M. Nichols
1 Cadillac, Auburn, MI

Lloyd & Jane Nichols
1 Cadillac, Bellaire, OH

Colonel Charles A. Nicholson
2 Cadillacs, Hampton, VA

Mr. Harry R. Nicholson, Jr.
Baltimore, MD

Mr. John Nickoloff
5 Cadillacs, Ormond Beach, FL

Mr. George Nicolozakes
20 Cadillacs, Cambridge, OH

Arleen, Robert, Elker Nielsen
Bannockburn, IL

Mr. Carl M. Nielsen
5 Cadillacs, Detroit Lakes, MN

Mr. George W. Nielsen
15 Cadillacs, Saint Paul, MN

Mr. Mark J. Nielsen
Houston, TX

Mr. Norman Nielsen
2 Cadillacs, Carlsbad, NM

Mr. Jeffrey L. Niemes
9 Cadillacs, Cincinnati, OH

Mr. Edwin C. Niemeyer
8 Cadillacs, Arvada, CO

Ms. Gladys M. Niemi
3 Cadillacs, Horseheads, NY

Mary Nikisher
1 Cadillac, Niagara Falls, ON

Mr. Harding C. Niston
7 Cadillacs, Mount Airy, NC

Thelma Stewart Nix
5 Cadillacs, Arlington, TX

Mr. Kenneth Nixon
4 Cadillacs, Knoxville, TN

Mr. Howard E. Noack
5 Cadillacs, Washington, DC

Charles R.J. Noble
12 Cadillacs, New York, NY

Mr. Walter H. Nohl
1 Cadillac, Elgin, IL

Dr. Ralph Nold
13 Cadillacs, Suffolk, VA

Ms. Laura F. Noller
1 Cadillac, Fulton, MS

Ervin J. Norful
3 Cadillacs, Saint Louis, MO

Dr. Edward I. Norman
7 Cadillacs, Jacksonville, FL

Mr. Mackey J. Norman
2 Cadillacs, Rock Hill, SC

Mr. Lowell Norris
4 Cadillacs, Taylorsville, MS

Northwood Products
Cheboygan, MI

Mrs. Carol M. Norton
2 Cadillacs, McVeytown, PA

Mr. James V. Norwood
5 Cadillacs, Rossville, GA

Frank J. Notariano
4 Cadillacs, Chicago, IL

Ms. Evelyn R. Notestone
Lancaster, OH

Mr. Chester J. Nowak, Jr.
1 Cadillac, Chicago, IL

Mr. Dennis Nowlin
2 Cadillacs, Manteca, CA

Mr. Frank J. Nuccilli
3 Cadillacs, Clearwater, FL

Ms. Lillian L. Nuccitelli
1 Cadillac, Fishkill, NY

Virginia Nugent
2 Cadillacs, Ocean Isl. Bch., NC

Mr. Cayetano Nunez
1 Cadillac, Jamaica, NY

Mr. Wilhelm F. Nurnberg
1 Cadillac, Washington, MO

Mr. & Mrs. Eddie D. Nutter
9 Cadillacs, Charleston, WV

Mr. W. Nye
3 Cadillacs, Montreal-Ouest, QC

Mr. John H. Nyquist
4 Cadillacs, Kansas City, MO

O

Mr. James J. O'Brien
7 Cadillacs, Mtn.. Home, AR

Joanne O'Brien
2 Cadillacs, Hunt. Beach, CA

Ms. Geraldine A. O'Connor
1 Cadillac, Holden, MA

John & Joyce O'Connor
2 Cadillacs, Brookfield, WI

Mr. James V. O'Grady
10 Cadillacs, Clinton Twp., MI

Mr. Jay E. O'Hara
43 Cadillacs, Livonia, MI

Mr. Robert O'Hare
1 Cadillac, Plainfield, IN

Norman O'Keeffe
15 Cadillacs, New Rochelle, NY

Mr. Gerald F. O'Leary
3 Cadillacs, Watertown, NY

Mr. Shannon P. O'Malley
19 Cadillacs, Winner, SD

Milton O'Quinn
8 Cadillacs, W. Bloomfield, MI

Mr. William M. O'Rourke
3 Cadillacs, Ormond Beach, FL

Thomas J. O'Toole
4 Cadillacs, Willoughby, OH

Willie Oates
2 Cadillacs, Little Rock, AR

Mr. William Obryan
2 Cadillacs, Englewood, CO

Mr. John F. Occhiuzzo
2 Cadillacs, Naples, FL

Ms. Judy A. Odell
3 Cadillacs, Mattoon, IL

Mr. John P. Oden, Jr.
8 Cadillacs, Allen, TX

Mr. James R. Odom
4 Cadillacs, Corsicana, TX

Mr. Dwight Odum
6 Cadillacs, Norfolk, VA

Mr. Philip Oetking
11 Cadillacs, Rockwall, TX

Mr. Robert F. Ogden
14 Cadillacs, Rochester, NY

Mr. Richard C. Ogle
1 Cadillac, Ferndale, MI

Mr. Harry H. Ohannessian
3 Cadillacs, Stony Brook, NY

Mr. Jack T. Ohaver
2 Cadillacs, Columbus, OH

Maynard L. Ohlson
4 Cadillacs, Portage, WI

Phil H. Olauson
5 Cadillacs, Hartsville, SC

Ms. Gayle L. Oldre
1 Cadillac, Nisswa, MN

Mr. William Oliva
12 Cadillacs, Olympia, WA

Mr. Gilbert Oliver
3 Cadillacs, Maceo, KY

Murry & Eyre Oliver
Hopewell, VA

Mr. Phillip M. Ollic
1 Cadillac, Columbus, OH

Mr. Thomas H. Olmstead
7 Cadillacs, Waterloo, NY

Mr. Roy M. Olsen
6 Cadillacs, Clearwater, FL

Mr. Chester L. Olson
3 Cadillacs, Galesburg, IL

Donald Olson
20 Cadillacs, W. Bloomfield, MI

Joseph & Lee Olson
2 Cadillacs, Glenview, IL

Mr. Robert B. Olson
2 Cadillacs, Los Angeles, CA

Robert H. Olson
2 Cadillacs, Vero Beach, FL

Mr. N. Olynyk
5 Cadillacs, Killarney, MB

Mr. Neil J. Ondracek
3 Cadillacs, Bolingbrook, IL

Mrs. Carol L. Oolman
1 Cadillac, Orange City, IA

Mr. Donald R. Oot
1 Cadillac, Kirkville, NY

Mr. Robert E. Opitz
2 Cadillacs, Hamilton, MT

Mr. Eugene H. Opperman
2 Cadillacs, South Holland, IL

Mr. Walter J. Oppermann
1 Cadillac, Neenah, WI

Mr. Jack Oremus
4 Cadillacs, Bridgeview, IL

Dr. John Orlando
3 Cadillacs, Chicago, IL

Mr. Herman Orrell
1 Cadillac, Clemmons, NC

Mr. Frank L. Orsak
1 Cadillac, Lees Summit, MO

Mrs. Lydia A. Orstad
1 Cadillac, Minneapolis, MN

Mr. Daniel H. Osman
2 Cadillacs, Canton, OH

Mr. Wilfrid L. Oster
3 Cadillacs, Saint Paul, MN

Mr. Raymond G. Ostrom
6 Cadillacs, Minneapolis, MN

Billiviee Otterson
4 Cadillacs, Merced, CA

Mr. Gary H. Otto
2 Cadillacs, Inver Grove, MN

Danny Ouimet
11 Cadillacs, Carrollton, TX

Mrs. Jean P. Ouimette
2 Cadillacs, Hazelhurst, WI

Mr. Robert Outlaw, Jr.
16 Cadillacs, Portsmouth, VA

L.W. Overly
8 Cadillacs, Ligonier, PA

Mr. Thomas D. Overy
2 Cadillacs, San Pedro, CA

Mr. James E. Owen
1 Cadillac, Salisbury, NC

Robert Owen
Winter Haven, FL

Mr. Elmer G. Owens
6 Cadillacs, Myrtle Beach, SC

Mr. James L. Owens, Jr.
2 Cadillacs, U. Marlboro, MD

Ms. Elsie A. Oxley
Bakersfield, CA

Mr. John V. Oyen
4 Cadillacs, Minneapolis, MN

P

Edwin P'Pool
Nashville, TN

Connie Rachal & John E. Pace
11 Cadillacs, Dallas, TX

Mr. Stan W. Paciorek
3 Cadillacs, Clinton, OK

Myron O. & Bette Paddock
3 Cadillacs, Edmond, OK

Joseph L. Padgett
14 Cadillacs, New Sm. Bch., FL

Mr. Wilbur Padgett
8 Cadillacs, Aliquippa, PA

Eldridge & Dorothy Page
8 Cadillacs, Paso Robles, CA

Mrs. Goldie P. Page
3 Cadillacs, Poquoson, VA

Wayne E. Page
6 Cadillacs, Clayton, MO

Graham Paige
3 Cadillacs, Green Bay, WI

Mr. Robert E. Painter
11 Cadillacs, Palm Harbor, FL

Joseph Palermo
1 Cadillac, Philadelphia, PA

J. Paley
6 Cadillacs, Edmonton, AB

Ceophus "Cee" Palmer
3 Cadillacs, Oakland, CA

Mr. James B. Palmer
2 Cadillacs, Dallas, TX

Mr. Vito M. Palmisano
3 Cadillacs, Omaha, NE

Charles Palomino
1 Cadillac, Etobicoke, ON

Mr. Frank J. Pandolfo
3 Cadillacs, W. Yarmouth, MA

Mr. Frank J. Pane
3 Cadillacs, Omaha, NE

Mr. Hugo A. Panissidi
4 Cadillacs, Boca Raton, FL

Mr. Norbert A. Panning
1 Cadillac, Orlando, FL

Ms. Dorothy J. Papa
5 Cadillacs, San Antonio, TX

L. Papenguth
37 Cadillacs, Stuart, FL

Mr. Elmer Papes
1 Cadillac, Oak Lawn, IL

Mr. Gordon R. Papke
7 Cadillacs, Indianapolis, IN

Mr. Premo Pappafaya
9 Cadillacs, Greensburg, PA

Mr. George P. Pappas
18 Cadillacs, Bethesda, MD

Mr. Remus W. Parchman
4 Cadillacs, Lake Forest, CA

Dr. W. Harold Parham
4 Cadillacs, Jacksonville, FL

E. Paul Parisi
4 Cadillacs, Warren, PA

Mr. Ernest K. Parke
2 Cadillacs, Colton, CA

Mr. Gene W. Parker
5 Cadillacs, Meeker, CO

Mr. Howard A. Parker, Jr.
4 Cadillacs, Naples, FL

Mr. John J. Parker
5 Cadillacs, Rochester, NY

Mr. Lavene L. Parker
12 Cadillacs, Sarasota, FL

Philip J. Parker
4 Cadillacs, Auburn, MA

S.C. & H.S. Parker
4 Cadillacs, Santa Fe, NM

Mr. Samuel B. Parker
2 Cadillacs, Signal Mtn., TN

Mr. Stanton E. Parker
1 Cadillac, Warren, OH

Mr. Woodrow W. Parker
9 Cadillacs, Apison, TN

Parks Investments Inc
2 Cadillacs, Oxford, MS

Howard A. Parks
1 Cadillac, Gulfport, FL

James Parks
5 Cadillacs, Fayetteville, WV

Ms. Katheryn Parks
2 Cadillacs, Louisville, KY

Nelson J. Parks, III
3 Cadillacs, Lakewood, OH

Mr. William Parks
8 Cadillacs, Hopwood, PA

Mr. Robert Parnell
1 Cadillac, Waco, TX

Mr. Marc D. Parois
1 Cadillac, Austin, TX

Mr. Milton Parrish
4 Cadillacs, Madison, FL

R.A. Parrish
Richmond, VA

Mrs. Ruth M. Parrish
4 Cadillacs, Hermitage, TN

Ms. Marion R. Parsons
1 Cadillac, Bishop, CA

Mr. Walter S. Parsons
15 Cadillacs, Pompano Bch., FL

Mr. T. Pascoe
1 Cadillac, Mississauga, ON

Mr. John W. Paskey
2 Cadillacs, Louisville, KY

Mr. Peter Paskiewich
4 Cadillacs, East Orleans, MA

Mr. George G. Passmore
2 Cadillacs, Ilwaco, WA

Mr. John Patente
10 Cadillacs, Bridgewater, NJ

Oscar & Josephine Pater
3 Cadillacs, Pompano Bch., FL

William Patram
9 Cadillacs, Fairfax, VA

Mrs. Josephine P. Patranella
1 Cadillac, Bryan, TX

Mr. John J. Patskan
4 Cadillacs, Lk. Havasu Cty., AZ

Ms. Colleen A. Patten
7 Cadillacs, Midland, MI

Dr. Charles C. Patterson
2 Cadillacs, Huntsville, AL

Mr. Robert M. Patterson
5 Cadillacs, Ida Grove, IA

Mr. Robert F. Patterson
2 Cadillacs, Houston, TX

Mr. Roy D. Patterson
San Antonio, TX

Mr. William E. Patterson
2 Cadillacs, Ottumwa, IA

Ms. Betty A. Paul
2 Cadillacs, Youngstown, OH

Mr. Gustavo J. Paul, Jr.
1 Cadillac, La Jolla, CA

Lillian Paul
4 Cadillacs, New Rochelle, NY

Eldon Paull
6 Cadillacs, Swan River, MB

Mr. Max J. Paulson
2 Cadillacs, Tucson, AZ

Mr. Wilbur Paulson
2 Cadillacs, Maple Valley, WA

Mr. J.R. Paunicka
1 Cadillac, Portage, IN

Mr. Warren H. Pautz
1 Cadillac, Lady Lake, FL

Mr. Frank J. Pavlik
12 Cadillacs, Prescott Vly., AZ

Mr. Alex Pavluk
9 Cadillacs, St. Petersburg, FL

Mr. L. Harold Paxton
3 Cadillacs, Richmond, VA

Dr. & Ms. H.M. Payan
6 Cadillacs, Gibsonia, PA

Pearlie M. Payton
2 Cadillacs, Kinston, NC

Ms. Lily C. Payuyo
3 Cadillacs, Columbus, OH

Ms. Clyde L. Peacock
1 Cadillac, Lynn Haven, FL

Mr. Harry D. Peake
12 Cadillacs, Greensboro, NC

Mr. John W. Pearce
6 Cadillacs, Peoria, IL

Mr. James Pearman
4 Cadillacs, Virginia Bch., VA

Ms. Nancy V. Pearson
5 Cadillacs, S. San Fran., CA

Mr. Robert L. Pearson
4 Cadillacs, Wichita, KS

Mr. Robin T. Pearson
1 Cadillac, Saint Louis, MO

Mr. Sampson Pearson
9 Cadillacs, Philadelphia, PA

Mr. John Peat
1 Cadillac, Lethbridge, AB

Ms. Dora M. Peele
2 Cadillacs, Ahoskie, NC

Ms. Ann M. Peelman
1 Cadillac, Cortland, OH

Phillip U. Peeples
1 Cadillac, Cedaredge, CO

Leon Pelissero
2 Cadillacs, Mississauga, ON

Mr. Thomas E. Pellaux
6 Cadillacs, Powell, TN

Mr. Albert J. Pellegrino
4 Cadillacs, Naples, FL

Mr. Antonio R. Pellegrino
2 Cadillacs, Spring Hill, FL

Ms. Linda T. Pelletier
3 Cadillacs, Madawaska, ME

Mr. Harley G. Pellman
2 Cadillacs, Elkhorn, WI

Ms. Lilliam J. Pellom
7 Cadillacs, Fayetteville, NC

Janice Pemberton
6 Cadillacs, Detroit, MI

Mr. Robert C. Peniston
1 Cadillac, Lexington, VA

Mr. George H. Pennell
3 Cadillacs, Fair Play, SC

Vivian & R.C. Pennington
2 Cadillacs, Albuquerque, NM

Mr. Gene Pensiero
6 Cadillacs, Sn. Bernrdno., CA

Teddy Peoples
3 Cadillacs, Aloha, OR

Ms. Vincenza Pepe
10 Cadillacs, Revere, MA

Mrs. Mildred R. Pepper
10 Cadillacs, St. Petersburg, FL

Mr. Corbette J. Percle
1 Cadillac, Labadieville, LA

Mrs. Gladys W. Perdue
2 Cadillacs, Rocky Mount, VA

Mr. Lester W. Perdue
2 Cadillacs, Ararat, VA

Ermilo J. Perez
1 Cadillac, San Antonio, TX

Mr. Carlo M. Perfetto
22 Cadillacs, Hamburg, NY

William J. & Nicolina Peri
2 Cadillacs, Bonita Springs, FL

Mr. Donato Perillo
4 Cadillacs, Delray Beach, FL

Ms. Stella Perino
2 Cadillacs, Denver, CO

Billy S. Perkins
1 Cadillac, Vidor, TX

Mrs. Emiliana E. Pernell
1 Cadillac, Chicago, IL

Mr. William S. Perper
5 Cadillacs, New York, NY

Mr. Claude A. Perry
4 Cadillacs, Brookhaven, MS

Mr. Duane Perry
6 Cadillacs, Williamsburg, VA

Mr. Edward Perry
1 Cadillac, Milton, ON

Hoyatt E. Perry
3 Cadillacs, St. Petersburg, FL

Mr. Mendel H. Perry
Harlingen, TX

Mr. Donald Perser
6 Cadillacs, Northbrook, IL

Mr. Ben Pertcheck
1 Cadillac, St. Petersburg, FL

Kenneth Perzanowski
3 Cadillacs, Torrington, CT

Mr. Michael Pesta
7 Cadillacs, West Wyoming, PA

Ms. Bettye F. Peteet
3 Cadillacs, Harleton, TX

Troy & Colleen Peterman
3 Cadillacs, Satellite Bch., FL

Mr. Carl Peters
3 Cadillacs, Brookfield, WI

Ms. Elouise Peters
7 Cadillacs, Lubbock, TX

Mr. Peter W. Petersen
15 Cadillacs, Mt. Prospect, IL

Mr. Robert E. Petersen
3 Cadillacs, Ft. Lauderdale, FL

B. Palmer Peterson
30 Cadillacs, Salem, OR

Ms. Barbara L. Peterson
3 Cadillacs, Silverdale, WA

Mrs. Edna E. Peterson
3 Cadillacs, Albany, GA

Mr. G.E. Peterson
4 Cadillacs, Elida, NM

Mr. Henry Peterson
2 Cadillacs, Chicago, IL

Mr. John L. Peterson
5 Cadillacs, Sacramento, CA

Ms. Kathryn T. Peterson
2 Cadillacs, Hubbard, OH

Mr. Leonard A. Peterson
19 Cadillacs, Sun City West, AZ

Ms. Nancy L. Peterson
2 Cadillacs, Plover, WI

Randy M. Peterson
2 Cadillacs, Santa Rosa, CA

Mr. James J. Pethis
7 Cadillacs, Savannah, GA

Mrs. Carol Petrarca
2 Cadillacs, Smithtown, NY

Tony Petrone
8 Cadillacs, Woodstock, NY

George Pettit
7 Cadillacs, Bridgeton, NJ

Mr. William E. Pettit
6 Cadillacs, Springfield, MO

Gene & Maryann Petty
2 Cadillacs, Alta Loma, CA

Ms. Eleanor E. Pezewski
3 Cadillacs, Milwaukee, WI

Mr. Jim Pfaff
5 Cadillacs, Chillicothe, MO

Dr. Hiram Pharr
7 Cadillacs, Winlock, WA

Mr. Robert B. Phelps
1 Cadillac, Kingsley, IA

Mr. & Mrs. Johnny C. Phifer
5 Cadillacs, Charlotte, NC

Kirk Philip
1 Cadillac, Nepean, ON

Ms. Annie T. Phillips
1 Cadillac, Chattanooga, TN

Ms. Charles Phillips
1 Cadillac, Chelsea, OK

Dano Phillips, Sr.
Williamsburg, VA

Mrs. Geraldine Phillips
2 Cadillacs, Meridian, MS

Glenda S. Phillips
3 Cadillacs, Jonesboro, AR

Mrs. Helen F. Phillips
2 Cadillacs, Bristol, TN

Mr. Jack E. Phillips
6 Cadillacs, Spartanburg, SC

Mr. James L. Phillips
3 Cadillacs, Sarasota, FL

Mr. Randy Phillips
14 Cadillacs, San Angelo, TX

Mr. Thomas Phillips
10 Cadillacs, Columbus, OH

Mr. William M. Phillips
2 Cadillacs, Leland, NC

Mr. G. Pidduck
1 Cadillac, Cameron, ON

Mr. Julian Pidutti
8 Cadillacs, Greensburg, PA

Mr. Ronald S. Pierce
2 Cadillacs, Mount Juliet, TN

Kay H. Pierson
St. Simons Island, GA

Mr. Finley W. Pifer
4 Cadillacs, Sullivan, IL

Mr. Lorne Pinch
1 Cadillac, Elgin, ON

Mr. James Pinckney
3 Cadillacs, Charleston, SC

Mr. James H. Pines
3 Cadillacs, Sun City, AZ

Mr. Donald Ping
3 Cadillacs, Stockton, CA

Morris A. & Cornelia Pinkett
6 Cadillacs, Tyaskin, MD

Mr. Bruno J. Pinkos
1 Cadillac, Mt. Prospect, IL

Richard Pinola
6 Cadillacs, Browns Mills, NJ

Mr. George L. Pinzel
7 Cadillacs, Vernon Rockvl., CT

Mr. Frederick S. Piotrowski
12 Cadillacs, Kawkawlin, MI

Mr. James Pirkle
5 Cadillacs, Washington, IN

Ms. Barbara Pirtle
20 Cadillacs, Sullivan, IN

Mr. Pasquale Pisano
4 Cadillacs, Elmwood Park, IL

Mr. Gary H. Pisel
6 Cadillacs, Glendale, AZ

Mrs. Marguerite Pittard
4 Cadillacs, Sugar Grove, VA

Glen Pittman
3 Cadillacs, San Antonio, TX

Samuel Pittman
5 Cadillacs, Marianna, FL

Ms. Juanita Pitts
1 Cadillac, Rome, GA

Mr. William Pizzute
1 Cadillac, Dumont, NJ

Mr. Harold Planer
4 Cadillacs, Gastonia, NC

Mr. David J. Platek
1 Cadillac, Pittsburgh, PA

Mr. Richard A. Platke
4 Cadillacs, Louisville, KY

Mr. Roland V. Playford
1 Cadillac, Jonesville, MI

Ms. Marine Pleasant
Flint, MI

Mr. Raymond P. Plinske
3 Cadillacs, Deer River, MN

Ms. Vivian Ploog
2 Cadillacs, Marshfield, WI

A. Plumb
1 Cadillac, Belleville, ON

Mr. J. Russell Plylar
4 Cadillacs, Winston Salem, NC

Mr. Walter Poesse
4 Cadillacs, Bloomington, IN

H. Pohl
3 Cadillacs, Tamarac, FL

Mr. Omer Pointer
2 Cadillacs, Snyder, TX

Mr. Joseph Pokojni, Sr.
7 Cadillacs, Easton, PA

Mr. Harold E. Polaski
2 Cadillacs, Mesa, AZ

William A. Polaski
6 Cadillacs, Monongahela, PA

Ms. Dorothy A. Polczynski
1 Cadillac, Mukwonago, WI

William L. Poling
12 Cadillacs, Hawthorn Wds., IL

Mr. Jefferson Polk
3 Cadillacs, Tulsa, OK

Mr. Jon R. Pollei
2 Cadillacs, Saint George, UT

Mr. John N. Polydouris
2 Cadillacs, Albany, NY

Mrs. Yolanda Polzer
1 Cadillac, Hamilton, ON

Mr. John Polzin
1 Cadillac, Clintonville, WI

Mr. Sam Pomeranz
4 Cadillacs, Fayetteville, NY

Mr. Wallace W. Pomplun
3 Cadillacs, Daytona Beach, FL

Henry P. Ponstein
5 Cadillacs, Chalmette, LA

Mrs. Mamie Poole
12 Cadillacs, Groom, TX

James L. & Ann Pope
26 Cadillacs, Baton Rouge, LA

Mr. Albert Poprik
10 Cadillacs, Cape Coral, FL

Mr. James F. Porcello
11 Cadillacs, Clermont, FL

Mr. Jimmie L. Porche
8 Cadillacs, Saint Louis, MO

Ms. Lucille S. Poroli
3 Cadillacs, Crete, IL

Mr. Harry M. Porter
2 Cadillacs, Independence, MO

Mr. J. Porter
1 Cadillac, Mobile, AL

Mr. Michael Porter
1 Cadillac, Virginia Bch., VA

Mr. Sherman L. Porter
34 Cadillacs, Bartlesville, OK

Chaumonde R. Porterfield
6 Cadillacs, Visalia, CA

Mr. Robert J. Poruba
13 Cadillacs, Princeton, IL

Mr. Walter O. Poser
10 Cadillacs, Sun City West, AZ

Ms. Faye R. Posey
8 Cadillacs, Mount Olive, MS

Mr. Richard F. Posinski
3 Cadillacs, Baltimore, MD

Mr. Amos H. Postell
1 Cadillac, Nashville, TN

Mrs. Leona C. Posthuma
10 Cadillacs, Beaver Dam, WI

N. Potechin
1 Cadillac, Ottawa, ON

Mr. Mitchell L. Pouncy
2 Cadillacs, Baton Rouge, LA

Jerry Powell
8 Cadillacs, Tyler, TX

Mr. Emmett D. Poynor
2 Cadillacs, Amarillo, TX

Ms. Dorothy Poznanski
4 Cadillacs, Wilsonville, OR

Mr. Camilo P. Prada
5 Cadillacs, Laredo, TX

Edward Preece
22 Cadillacs, Livonia, MI

Ms. Ila I. Preisser
5 Cadillacs, Denver, CO

Mr. Frank G. Prescott
10 Cadillacs, Germantown, TN

Mr. Gene Pressnell
Harlan, KY

Mr. Forrest Preston
2 Cadillacs, Hemet, CA

Mr. Robert A. Preston
1 Cadillac, Panama City, FL

W. Preston
3 Cadillacs, Georgetown, ON

Mrs. Max D. Pretorius
18 Cadillacs, Kaufman, TX

Mr. Robert W. Prettyman
5 Cadillacs, Glade Valley, NC

Mr. Harold W. Prevett
3 Cadillacs, Paragould, AR

Earl & Bonnie Pribble
8 Cadillacs, Pryor, OK

Mr. Houston L. Price
1 Cadillac, Pampa, TX

James Price
8 Cadillacs, San Jose, CA

Mr. Morris W. Price
1 Cadillac, Denver, CO

Ms. Dorothy W. Priddy
2 Cadillacs, Clemmons, NC

Mr. Arnold Priebe
5 Cadillacs, Pinellas Park, FL

Mr. Donald W. Priebe
5 Cadillacs, Balaton, MN

Mr. Thomas L. Priest
2 Cadillacs, Kokomo, MS

Mr. Joseph A. Prieto
1 Cadillac, Whittier, CA

Mr. William G. Priglmeier
4 Cadillacs, Sauk Rapids, MN

Mr. Billy R. Prim
16 Cadillacs, Ft. Wal. Bch., FL

Mr. Paul E. Princl
1 Cadillac, Mishicot, WI

Conrad Prins
18 Cadillacs, Sanborn, IA

Mr. August Printz
4 Cadillacs, Gravelbourg, SK

Mr. Blanchard L. Pritchard
3 Cadillacs, Dallas, TX

Mr. Larry G. Pritchard
2 Cadillacs, Zanesville, OH

Mr. Anthony J. Privoznik
2 Cadillacs, Bridgeview, IL

Julian Proctor, Jr.
2 Cadillacs, Tallahassee, FL

M. Julian Proctor
1 Cadillac, Tallahassee, FL

Martin Proctor
2 Cadillacs, Tallahassee, FL

W. Theo Proctor, Jr.
3 Cadillacs, Tallahassee, FL

Mr. Bernard Profitt
7 Cadillacs, Totowa, NJ

Mr. Charles R. Prokop, Jr.
1 Cadillac, Cleveland, OH

Mr. Anton Pros
13 Cadillacs, Wheaton, IL

LCDR Stanley E. Prothero
8 Cadillacs, Leesburg, FL

Mr. W. Protz
1 Cadillac, Yorkton, SK

Mr. Blaise R. Provost
2 Cadillacs, Port Neches, TX

Mrs. Marjorie E. Prudhomme
29 Cadillacs, Saginaw, MI

Mr. Clarence Pruitt
3 Cadillacs, Hampton, VA

Somnath Prusty
Chestnut Hill, MA

Mr. Wilbur F. Ptak
9 Cadillacs, Clearwater, FL

Mr. Alex Puchala
4 Cadillacs, Yorkton, SK

LaVira & Everett E. Puckett
4 Cadillacs, Fairfield, IL

Mrs. Robert G. Pugh
4 Cadillacs, Shreveport, LA

Mr. Ferris W. Purcell
7 Cadillacs, Dayton, OH

Mr. Joseph R. Purdy
3 Cadillacs, Washington, DC

Mr. William Putman
8 Cadillacs, Columbus, GA

Tilly Putnam
4 Cadillacs, Tipton, OK

Louise Putney
1 Cadillac, Tallahassee, FL

Mr. Ronald J. Puttkammer
2 Cadillacs, Madison, WI

Q

Mrs. Kathleen M. Quadrato
1 Cadillac, Torrance, CA

G. Quaile
3 Cadillacs, Nepean, ON

Mr. Francis X. Quain, Jr.
3 Cadillacs, Pleasantville, NY

Ed Quarry & Jack Dolan
7 Cadillacs, Springfield, IL

Richard & Cecilia Quint
6 Cadillacs, Garden City, KS

Mr. Orville Quirt
1 Cadillac, North Bay, ON

R

Mr. Edward Rabas
9 Cadillacs, Oconto Falls, WI

Mr. Ulric J. Racine
5 Cadillacs, Ocala, FL

Mr. William Radomske
1 Cadillac, Oliver, BC

Mr. Nick Raeber
2 Cadillacs, Highland, IL

Mr. Charles O. Ragan
2 Cadillacs, Signal Mtn., TN

Mr. Michael G. Ragan
7 Cadillacs, New Bern, NC

Mr. Don Ragsdale
1 Cadillac, Conroe, TX

Mr. John P. Ragusa
1 Cadillac, Valhalla, NY

Mr. David F. Rahbain
4 Cadillacs, Webster City, IA

Ms. Betty M. Rahn
6 Cadillacs, Brevard, NC

Mr. Albert E. Rain
1 Cadillac, Winter Park, FL

Mr. Albert J. Raineri
5 Cadillacs, Piedmont, CA

Ms. Bell Raines
3 Cadillacs, Lubbock, TX

Billy & Delores Rainey
5 Cadillacs, Greenville, SC

Mr. John Rainey
7 Cadillacs, Florence, SC

Mr. Oliver V. Rainey
3 Cadillacs, Franklin, TN

Ralph A. Mattiola Co
13 Cadillacs, Norristown, PA

Mr. James H. Ramay
7 Cadillacs, Sun City West, AZ

Ms. Martha A. Ramey
3 Cadillacs, Goldsboro, NC

Mr. Jack M. Ramos
8 Cadillacs, Fresno, CA

Mr. Herman Ramsey
1 Cadillac, Smyrna, GA

Norma Jean Ramsey
3 Cadillacs, Monroe, LA

Mr. Steven Rand
4 Cadillacs, Morganville, NJ

Mr. Melvin Randle
5 Cadillacs, Louisville, KY

Mr. L.M. Randolph
1 Cadillac, Tuskegee Inst., AL

Mr. Robert E. Randolph
1 Cadillac, E. Saint Louis, IL

Mr. Billy J. Raney
13 Cadillacs, Dalhart, TX

Robert & Emma Rangel
6 Cadillacs, Baytown, TX

Mr. George C. Ranney
1 Cadillac, Chicago Heights, IL

Ms. Sue Raphie
14 Cadillacs, Bossier City, LA

Ms. Carolyn M. Rarick
2 Cadillacs, East Leroy, MI

Mr. Willie Rascoe
2 Cadillacs, Chesapeake, VA

Mr. C.B. Rash
3 Cadillacs, Elizabethtown, IL

Mr. Robert Rasley
10 Cadillacs, North Liberty, IA

Laverne & Brenda Rasmussen
15 Cadillacs, Pinole, CA

Mr. Robert A. Rasmussen
3 Cadillacs, Oconto, WI

Mr. Andrew M. Ratcliff, Sr.
3 Cadillacs, Natchez, MS

Mr. James E. Rather
13 Cadillacs, Scottsdale, AZ

Carol E. Ratliff
16 Cadillacs, Kewanee, IL

Mr. George Ratliff, Jr.
3 Cadillacs, Jesup, GA

Mr. Walter Ratliff
4 Cadillacs, Fortuna, CA

Mr. John Ratto
3 Cadillacs, San Francisco, CA

Mr. Leon Ratzker
2 Cadillacs, Albany, NY

Col Henry Rauch, USAF (Ret)
4 Cadillacs, Cherry Hill, NJ

Mr. John M. Raulinaitis
5 Cadillacs, Cambridge, MA

Mr. Bert M. Rausch
20 Cadillacs, Saint Paul, MN

Ms. Virginia K. Rawl
3 Cadillacs, St. Petersburg, FL

Mrs. Martha C. Rawls
17 Cadillacs, Harlingen, TX

Mr. Joseph Ray, Jr.
3 Cadillacs, Millboro, VA

Ms. Karen R. Ray
5 Cadillacs, St. Petersburg, FL

Mr. Robert R. Ray
4 Cadillacs, Maitland, FL

Mr. Saverio S. Ray
4 Cadillacs, Gladstone, MO

Hetty Rayburn-Martini
Gulfport, MS

Mr. George Raynolds
1 Cadillac, Chesterfield, VA

Mr. Kenneth N. Read
5 Cadillacs, Wells, VT

J. Ready
2 Cadillacs, Brandon, MB

Mr. Melvin E. Ready
3 Cadillacs, Mukilteo, WA

Mr. Bob S. Reams
1 Cadillac, Flint, MI

Mrs. Vodithe L. Reavis
5 Cadillacs, Vandalia, IL

Mr. Ascencion M. Reavley
35 Cadillacs, Clearwater, FL

Anthony Recchia
4 Cadillacs, West Haven, CT

Mrs. Doris Recer-Ensley
3 Cadillacs, Lawton, OK

Mr. Ervin L. Recer
2 Cadillacs, Mandeville, LA

Mr. Ervin J. Rechtzigel
7 Cadillacs, Rosemount, MN

Mr. James D. Record
6 Cadillacs, Greenville, TX

Mr. Stanley Reczka
1 Cadillac, Linden, NJ

Mr. Ronald E. Reder
4 Cadillacs, Houston, TX

Mr. Garland Redford
5 Cadillacs, Crewe, VA

Clyde A. Redmon
3 Cadillacs, Vicksburg, MS

Mr. Ronald K. Redmon
2 Cadillacs, Co. Bluffs, IA

Mr. G. Redmond
1 Cadillac, Metcalfe, ON

Mr. Robert M. Reece
4 Cadillacs, Cherry Hill, NJ

Donald W. Reed
3 Cadillacs, Hutchinson, KS

Mr. Evan W. Reed, Sr.
4 Cadillacs, Rock Falls, IL

H. Reed
1 Cadillac, Odessa, ON

Mr. John H. Reed
8 Cadillacs, Washington, DC

Mr. Nathaniel J. Reed, Jr.
2 Cadillacs, Las Vegas, NV

Mr. S. Reed
1 Cadillac, Orangeville, ON

Ms. Viola Reed
6 Cadillacs, Terre Haute, IN

Edd Doris Reeves
3 Cadillacs, Lacey, WA

Mr. William Regitz
6 Cadillacs, Portland, OR

Mr. Jack F. Rehagen
2 Cadillacs, Saint Ann, MO

Mr. Jerome M. Rehr
5 Cadillacs, Boca Raton, FL

Mr. Bill Reid
3 Cadillacs, Whitehorse, YT

Mr. Dan W. Reid
5 Cadillacs, Hickory, NC

Mrs. E.P. Reid
1 Cadillac, Americus, GA

Kenneth Reid
1 Cadillac, Winchester, ON

Mr. William F. Reid
3 Cadillacs, Meridian, MS

Mr. Alfred D. Reilly
2 Cadillacs, Fullerton, CA

Mrs. Ann L. Reine
4 Cadillacs, Baton Rouge, LA

Mr. William Reinert
4 Cadillacs, Mission Hills, CA

Mr. Russell A. Reinke
2 Cadillacs, Chicago, IL

Mr. James C. Reis
7 Cadillacs, Lake Ozark, MO

William Renfro
1 Cadillac, Shepherdsvlle, KY

John T. Renfroe
5 Cadillacs, Salinas, CA

Ms. Lois V. Renick
8 Cadillacs, Bowling Green, KY

Renite Company
8 Cadillacs, Columbus, OH

Mr. Gilbert N. Renner
30 Cadillacs, Anderson, IN

Mr. Robin G. Renner
1 Cadillac, Midlothian, IL

Mr. William M. Rennick
1 Cadillac, Homosassa, FL

Mr. Billy C. Rentschler
5 Cadillacs, Mexico, MO

Mr. Louis M. Reny
3 Cadillacs, Chicopee, MA

Mr. Richard H. Reome
4 Cadillacs, Plattsburgh, NY

Mrs. Frank L. Reppler
10 Cadillacs, Ft. Lauderdale, FL

Mr. Stanley Resimont
2 Cadillacs, Ozark, AR

Mrs. Irene M. Restifo
10 Cadillacs, Erie, PA

Mr. Jesse P. Reyes
6 Cadillacs, Harker Heights, TX

Mr. Fred H. Reymore
2 Cadillacs, Erie, PA

George & Katherine Reynolds
12 Cadillacs, Cape Coral, FL

Mr. James A. Reynolds
2 Cadillacs, Lafayette, LA

Mrs. Jean Cosh Reynolds
Omaha, NE

Kenneth C. Reynolds
3 Cadillacs, Ottumwa, IA

Margaret & Gerald Reynolds
6 Cadillacs, Boynton Beach, FL

Ms. Maxine Reynolds
6 Cadillacs, Las Vegas, NV

Norris L. Reynolds
8 Cadillacs, O'Fallon, IL

Mr. William E. Reynolds
1 Cadillac, Fresno, CA

Wanda Meacham Rhea
4 Cadillacs, Graham, TX

Mr. Soo W. Rhee
1 Cadillac, Las Vegas, NV

Mr. Clifford Rhoads
5 Cadillacs, Munday, TX

James & Doris J. Rhoda
8 Cadillacs, Wausau, WI

Mr. Max B. Rhoe
2 Cadillacs, Hedgesville, WV

Mr. Herb F. Rhorbacker
7 Cadillacs, Columbus, OH

Mr. Sterling W. Rhoten
7 Cadillacs, Baltimore, MD

Mr. Harvey G. Rhyne
7 Cadillacs, Kerrville, TX

Ms. Carolyn F. Ricardelli
6 Cadillacs, Chelmsford, MA

Mr. Edwin N. Rice
5 Cadillacs, Medina, OH

Mr. Ronald E. Rice
6 Cadillacs, Greenville, NC

Ms. Charolette Richard
15 Cadillacs, Las Vegas, NV

Mr. Roy Richard, Sr.
Crowley, LA

Mr. Septime S. Richard
40 Cadillacs, Dothan, AL

Mrs. Clara D. Richards
4 Cadillacs, Jackson, MS

Ms. June E. Richards
3 Cadillacs, Myrtle Beach, SC

Mrs. Leonard R. Richards
2 Cadillacs, Vista, CA

Mrs. Nola B. Richards
2 Cadillacs, Vista, CA

Richardson
3 Cadillacs, Bobcaygeon, ON

John Richardson
2 Cadillacs, Bonita Spgs., FL

Mr. Merlin Richardson
5 Cadillacs, Anguilla, MS

Mr. Richard A. Richardson
2 Cadillacs, North Olmsted, OH

Mr. William B. Richardson
5 Cadillacs, Parkersburg, WV

Mr. Ellsworth J. Richcreek
4 Cadillacs, Coshocton, OH

Jean & Lois Richer
1 Cadillac, Temecula, CA

Mr. Leonard L. Richey, Sr.
3 Cadillacs, Sterling Hts., MI

Mr. Orin A. Richey
1 Cadillac, Chesapeake, VA

Mr. Raymond Richey
2 Cadillacs, Pleasant Plns., IL

W. Richey
8 Cadillacs, Smiths Falls, ON

Mr. Orson M. Richins
9 Cadillacs, Salt Lake Cty., UT

Mr. Jerry Richlak
7 Cadillacs, Chesterland, OH

Mr. Bill D. Richmond
16 Cadillacs, Minneapolis, MN

Mr. John W. Rick
8 Cadillacs, Saint Louis, MO

Mr. Richard W. Ricker
1 Cadillac, Franklin, TN

Mr. Charles T. Rickert
13 Cadillacs, Statesville, NC

Mr. William J. Rickert
2 Cadillacs, Waterloo, IA

Mr. William B. Ricks
7 Cadillacs, Jacksonville, IL

Mr. W.J. Riddiford
1 Cadillac, North York, ON

Mr. George & Juanita Riddle
2 Cadillacs, Bull Shoals, AR

Mr. Harold E. Riddle
2 Cadillacs, Kingsport, TN

Mr. John Ridgley
1 Cadillac, Columbus, GA

Ms. Ruth Ridgway
7 Cadillacs, Clearfield, PA

Mr. W. James Ridout, Jr.
4 Cadillacs, Bracey, VA

William A. Rieber
8 Cadillacs, Wyncote, PA

Mr. Harland Riedl
Onalaska, WA

Mrs. Julia Rienzo
West Palm Bch., FL

Mr. Gordon J. Ries
20 Cadillacs, Henry, IL

Mr. Rolland A. Ries
3 Cadillacs, Fort Meyers, FL

Karl F. Riesterer
5 Cadillacs, Ocala, FL

Mr. Samuel E. Riggan
13 Cadillacs, Tacoma, WA

Mr. Dennis Riggin
4 Cadillacs, Devils Lake, ND

Mr. Patrick F. Rigney
14 Cadillacs, Staten Island, NY

Mr. Claude R. Rigsby
3 Cadillacs, Chandler, TX

Sally E. Rihbany
3 Cadillacs, West Roxbury, MA

Raymond E. Rilea
1 Cadillac, Salisbury, NC

Mr. Daniel F. Riley
10 Cadillacs, E. Greenbush, NY

Mr. John C. Riley
44 Cadillacs, Kansas City, MO

Mr. Robert G. Riley
8 Cadillacs, Quincy, IL

Thelma & Paul Riley
2 Cadillacs, Bradenton, FL

Hoyn Rim
1 Cadillac, Oakton, VA

Mr. Ronald R. Rimko
4 Cadillacs, Hilton Head, SC

Lucille A. Rinehart
7 Cadillacs, Urbana, OH

Karns M. Ringland
1 Cadillac, Stuart, IA

Mr. Jeremiah P. Riordan
1 Cadillac, Bear, DE

Ms. Joan B. Risberg
1 Cadillac, Saint Louis, MO

Mr. Harold A. Rising
Thompsons Stn., TN

Mrs. Onnolee D. Risley
5 Cadillacs, Akron, NY

Mrs. B. Rivard
1 Cadillac, Tilbury, ON

Mr. Nicholas O. Rivellini
1 Cadillac, Las Vegas, NV

Mr. Andrew Rivers, Jr.
3 Cadillacs, Fort Wayne, IN

Mr. Ernest Rizzuto
1 Cadillac, Northampton, PA

Mr. Albert Roach
1 Cadillac, Waxhaw, NC

Rose Mary Roach
5 Cadillacs, Ooltewah, TN

Capt. Marlen C. Robb
3 Cadillacs, Washington, NC

Mr. David F. Robbins
2 Cadillacs, Venice, FL

Mrs. Evelyn E. Robbins
1 Cadillac, Boca Raton, FL

Mr. John Robbins
3 Cadillacs, Brandon, MS

Mr. Lester Robbins
5 Cadillacs, Fredonia, KS

Dr. F. Allen Roberds
4 Cadillacs, Fayetteville, AR

Mr. D. Roberts
10 Cadillacs, St. Albert, AB

Donald Roberts
7 Cadillacs, Naples, FL

Mr. Edward Y. Roberts
4 Cadillacs, Banning, CA

Mr. Fleetwood Roberts, Jr.
3 Cadillacs, Bowie, MD

Florence Roberts
6 Cadillacs, Valparaiso, FL

Gale G. Roberts
20 Cadillacs, Florissant, MO

Mr. Howard Roberts
3 Cadillacs, Pittsburgh, PA

J.B. Roberts
2 Cadillacs, Carson, CA

Mr. James H. Roberts
6 Cadillacs, Somerset, KY

Mr. Keith R. Roberts
1 Cadillac, Valparaiso, FL

Mr. Marvin R. Roberts
4 Cadillacs, Poway, CA

Mr. Randall P. Roberts
6 Cadillacs, Valparaiso, FL

Dr. Roy R. Roberts
12 Cadillacs, Plainview, TX

Ms. Sandra G. Roberts
6 Cadillacs, Astor, FL

Ms. Sybil M. Roberts
1 Cadillac, Dallas, TX

Mr. Willard V. Roberts
3 Cadillacs, Salem, OR

Carleen D. Robertson
2 Cadillacs, Buchanan, TN

Mr. Cecil E. Robertson
22 Cadillacs, Zachary, LA

Mr. Forst L. Robertson
9 Cadillacs, Key Largo, FL

Mr. Marnen E. Robertson
1 Cadillac, Camarillo, CA

Mr. Robert H. Robertson, Jr.
2 Cadillacs, Pocomoke City, MD

Mr. Charles R. Robinson
2 Cadillacs, Columbia, SC

D. Robinson
3 Cadillacs, Sarnia, ON

Mr. Dean Robinson
7 Cadillacs, Marion, VA

E.L. Robinson
4 Cadillacs, Randallstown, MD

Ms. Elisha Robinson, Jr.
4 Cadillacs, Chicago, IL

Mr. Frank J. Robinson
6 Cadillacs, Moline, IL

Mr. James L. Robinson
10 Cadillacs, Baltimore, MD

Ms. Margaret D. Robinson
2 Cadillacs, Conway, SC

Mrs. Margaret Robinson
2 Cadillacs, Sutherland, VA

Michael Robinson
4 Cadillacs, Detroit, MI

Ms. Mildred E. Robinson
Eastover, SC

Mrs. Nannie L. Robinson
13 Cadillacs, Cayce, SC

Mr. Ryland Robinson, Jr.
3 Cadillacs, Pine Bluff, AR

Mr. Stansell B. Robinson
4 Cadillacs, Prattville, AL

Mr. Bennie J. Robison
5 Cadillacs, Huntsville, AL

Mr. James A. Robison
6 Cadillacs, Sandusky, OH

Jean Robitaille
2 Cadillacs, Quebec, QC

J. Robson
3 Cadillacs, Deleau, MB

Mr. Reynaldo S. Rocha
5 Cadillacs, San Antonio, TX

Mr. Raymond Rock
1 Cadillac, Salina, KS

Edward Rockwell, Jr.
6 Cadillacs, Tamarac, FL

Ms. Marjorie Rodd
10 Cadillacs, Elizabeth, NJ

Hugh Rodden
1 Cadillac, Saskatoon, SK

Ms. Charlotte Rodecker
6 Cadillacs, Bishop, CA

Ms. Julia V. Rodenburg
5 Cadillacs, Missouri Vly., IA

Mr. Patrick Rodrigue
7 Cadillacs, Augusta, ME

Mr. Art Rodriguez
5 Cadillacs, Mason City, IA

Mr. John Rodriguez
2 Cadillacs, Columbia, SC

Ms. Shirley L. Rodrique
8 Cadillacs, Vacherie, LA

Mr. Walter J. Roe
6 Cadillacs, Dearborn, MI

Mr. Jack F. Roeder
1 Cadillac, Chesterfield, MO

Mr. Richard Roehll
5 Cadillacs, Columbus, OH

Edna Chambers Roemer
6 Cadillacs, Hopkinsville, KY

Mr. Wayne R. Roepke
4 Cadillacs, Manitowoc, WI

Mr. Martin J. Roetto
1 Cadillac, Pierce City, MO

Mr. Cleo C. Rogers
Winfield, KS

Mr. Irvin P. Rogers
3 Cadillacs, Whitesville, KY

Mr. J. Rogers
3 Cadillacs, Bristol, TN

Mr. Jack Rogers
10 Cadillacs, Lebanon, MO

Mr. John Rogers
6 Cadillacs, Fresno, CA

Ms. Leora M. Rogers
1 Cadillac, Edgerton, WI

Mrs. Mary L. Rogers
3 Cadillacs, Arlington, TX

Mr. Robert W. Rogers, III
2 Cadillacs, Moncks Corner, SC

Victor Rogers
2 Cadillacs, Victorville, CA

Mr. Ernest A. Rohana
1 Cadillac, Baltimore, MD

Mr. Warren M. Rohsenow
7 Cadillacs, Falmouth, ME

Ms. Mary D. Roller
9 Cadillacs, Jacksonville, NC

Anthony M. Romano, M.D.
1 Cadillac, Co. Bluffs, IA

Mr. Nathan Romano
2 Cadillacs, Ramsey, NJ

Salvatore Romano
15 Cadillacs, Schaumburg, IL

Mr. & Mrs. Jewel H. Romans
1 Cadillac, Elizabeth, IN

Mrs. Margaret Rondina
4 Cadillacs, West Haven, CT

Bruna L. Rongone
1 Cadillac, Youngstown, OH

Mr. Ben M. Rooke
3 Cadillacs, Montgomery, AL

Mr. Sidney G. Rooney
6 Cadillacs, Sturgeon Bay, WI

Mr. Abb L. Roquemore, Jr.
11 Cadillacs, Palestine, TX

Richard Rorschach
2 Cadillacs, Kilgore, TX

Mr. Louis G. Rosa
2 Cadillacs, Syracuse, NY

Alice Marrama Rosario
4 Cadillacs, Windsor Locks, CT

Ms. Geneva R. Rose
1 Cadillac, Madisonville, KY

Howard Rose, Jr.
5 Cadillacs, Washington, DC

James M. & Eva J. Rose
1 Cadillac, Henderson, KY

Molly Rose
1 Cadillac, Calgary, AB

Mr. Robert Rose
10 Cadillacs, Glenview, IL

Mr. M. Rosen
6 Cadillacs, Houston, TX

Dr. Marvin O. Rosen
4 Cadillacs, W. Bloomfield, MI

Ms. Rose Rosen
9 Cadillacs, Rcho. Santa Fe, CA

Mrs. Shirlye E. Rosen
3 Cadillacs, Miami, FL

Mr. Louis & Rose Rosenberg
1 Cadillac, Sn. Bernardino, CA

Mr. Edward F. Rosenhauer
5 Cadillacs, Diamondhead, MS

Mr. Jack Rosenthal
3 Cadillacs, Pompano Bch., FL

Mr. Joseph R. Roskuski
4 Cadillacs, Bonita Spgs., FL

Joseph & Nancy Roskuski
4 Cadillacs, Bonita Springs, FL

Mr. Benjamin A. Rosner
11 Cadillacs, Phoenix, AZ

Mr. Ralph P. Rosnick
43 Cadillacs, Omaha, NE

C. Ross
1 Cadillac, Calgary, AB

Mrs. Carolyn G. Ross
3 Cadillacs, Alhambra, CA

Mr. Hezekiah Ross
2 Cadillacs, Richmond, VA

Mr. Thomas A. Ross
2 Cadillacs, Venice, FL

Ms. Veronica F. Ross
Browns Mills, NJ

Mr. William Ross
1 Cadillac, Manotick, ON

Frederick B. Rossiter
2 Cadillacs, Boca Raton, FL

Mr. George A. Roth
9 Cadillacs, Springfield, IL

Mr. Martin C. Roth
3 Cadillacs, Pollock, LA

Mr. Paul Roth, Sr.
2 Cadillacs, Pittsburgh, PA

Mr. Robert C. Rothermel
7 Cadillacs, Huntsville, AL

Mr. Matthew Rotkovich
15 Cadillacs, Sarasota, FL

Reba W. Rouanzion
1 Cadillac, Hendersonville, NC

Mr. William Rouch
3 Cadillacs, Pt. Charlotte, FL

Ms. Ann G. Roughton
5 Cadillacs, Dothan, AL

John Roulston
1 Cadillac, Etobicoke, ON

Mr. William S. Roush, Jr.
5 Cadillacs, Saint Albans, WV

Mr. John R. Rowan
7 Cadillacs, Montgomery, AL

Mr. Joseph F. Rowan
5 Cadillacs, Indiantown, FL

Ms. Gertrude V. Rowe
3 Cadillacs, Zanesville, OH

Mr. Sherman Rowe
1 Cadillac, Decatur, GA

Mr. & Mrs. James O. Rowland
2 Cadillacs, Lincolnton, GA

Mr. Harry Rowlett
3 Cadillacs, Jonesville, VA

Calvin Rowley
4 Cadillacs, Scottsdale, AZ

Mr. Dennis B. Roxworthy
1 Cadillac, Elgin, IL

Ms. Doris L. Roy
3 Cadillacs, Houston, TX

Mr. Gilbert G. Roy
3 Cadillacs, Waterford, NY

Mr. James A. Roy, Jr.
3 Cadillacs, Clinton, MD

Mr. Clifford Royer
6 Cadillacs, Granville, OH

Mrs. John H. Royer
5 Cadillacs, Chagrin Falls, OH

Mr. Edwin H. Royle
12 Cadillacs, Shreveport, LA

Mr. William Ruark
4 Cadillacs, Bellevue, WA

Mr. Ray L. Rubenstein
10 Cadillacs, Cincinnati, OH

Harry Ruby
1 Cadillac, Winnipeg, MB

Mr. Roger Rucker
6 Cadillacs, Lexington, SC

Mr. Eugene A. Ruckstaetter
4 Cadillacs, Sanibel, FL

Robert Ruddy
1 Cadillac, Saint Paul, MN

Mrs. Eleanor L. Ruggles
2 Cadillacs, Findlay, OH

Wynnelle Rumble
5 Cadillacs, Carrollton, GA

Mr. Donald L. Rumiano
1 Cadillac, Painted Post, NY

Mrs. Inez B. Runager
17 Cadillacs, Decatur, AL

Mr. Carl M. Rupp
1 Cadillac, Torrington, WY

Mr. William Rurycz
Parma, OH

Mr. Steve Rusnov
3 Cadillacs, Cleveland, OH

Mr. Austin H. Russell
4 Cadillacs, Oxford, MS

Dr. Charles E. Russell
1 Cadillac, Vacaville, CA

Mr. Charles C. Russell
3 Cadillacs, Kansas City, MO

David O. Russell
1 Cadillac, Roanoke, TX

Mr. Gordon L. Russell
2 Cadillacs, Columbus, GA

Mr. John Russell
12 Cadillacs, Indianapolis, IN

Laverne Russell
1 Cadillac, Welland, ON

Mrs. Lena Russell
4 Cadillacs, Sumner, WA

Ms. Loretta J. Russell
1 Cadillac, Houston, TX

Mr. Richard J. Russell
4 Cadillacs, Salt Lake Cty., UT

Mrs. Vera Jo H. Russell
20 Cadillacs, Houston, TX

Ms. Virginia M. Russell
3 Cadillacs, Jaxville Bch., FL

Mr. Nicholas C. Russin
5 Cadillacs, Kingsport, TN

Mr. Robert L. Russo
1 Cadillac, Staten Island, NY

Mr. G. Rust
3 Cadillacs, Shaunavon, SK

Mr. Ruth
3 Cadillacs, Bon Accord, AB

Ms. Bettie A. Ruth
6 Cadillacs, Marion, OH

Ms. Christine Rutherford
2 Cadillacs, Atlanta, TX

Mrs. Naomi Rutherford
10 Cadillacs, Bristol, TN

Mr. Dana Ruthers
3 Cadillacs, Lexington, KY

Mr. Charles W. Rutledge
2 Cadillacs, Payson, AZ

Mr. Richard Ryall
3 Cadillacs, Livingston, NJ

Mr. Anatol Rychalski
1 Cadillac, Pittsburgh, PA

Mr. Gordon D. Ryckman
5 Cadillacs, Gold Canyon, AZ

Mr. Harold L. Ryder
12 Cadillacs, Jacob, IL

Mr. Maurice G. Ryon
1 Cadillac, Johnson City, TN

S

Mr. Philip A. Sabatino
Albany, NY

Ero Saccone
7 Cadillacs, Salinas, CA

Mr. Melvin L. Sachs
12 Cadillacs, Minneapolis, MN

Mr. Howard T. Sackett
1 Cadillac, Bradenton, FL

Ms. Aileen Sadler
2 Cadillacs, Troup, TX

Mr. Wolford Sadovsky
9 Cadillacs, San Antonio, TX

Mr. Paul Safreed
6 Cadillacs, Ellwood City, PA

Mr. Thomas E. Sage
5 Cadillacs, Waukegan, IL

Mr. Paul A. Saimond
4 Cadillacs, Watervliet, NY

Mr. Thomas J. Sain
5 Cadillacs, Roanoke, VA

Dr. Augustus W. Sainsbury
7 Cadillacs, Fort Myers, FL

Mr. Sam Sakellaris, Sr.
20 Cadillacs, Danville, VA

Charles & Eleanor Sakris
3 Cadillacs, Springfield, IL

Morris N. Saks
1 Cadillac, Baltimore, MD

Mr. Michael Sakso
3 Cadillacs, Sebring, FL

Michael S. Salah, Sr.
3 Cadillacs, Rochester, NY

Mr. Maurice Salamy
3 Cadillacs, Orlando, FL

Mr. Muhammad Salaymeh
8 Cadillacs, Westminster, CA

Clorinda M. Salciccioli
2 Cadillacs, Tampa, FL

Mr. William Sales
2 Cadillacs, Kihei, HI

Dr. Robert Salisbury
4 Cadillacs, Whisper Pines, NC

Eleanor M. Salivonchikl
8 Cadillacs, Plainview, NY

Ms. Martha L. Salkin
4 Cadillacs, Pmbk. Pines, FL

Wayne Sallee
1 Cadillac, Independence, MO

Mr. Robert Sallie
7 Cadillacs, New Brighton, PA

Mr. Melvin J. Sammann
3 Cadillacs, Dallas, TX

Mrs. Lorraine Sammons
4 Cadillacs, Columbus, OH

Mr. Merrick S. Samms, Jr.
5 Cadillacs, Jacksonville, FL

Ms. Teresa Sample
12 Cadillacs, Sulphur, LA

Ms. Julia K. Sampson
15 Cadillacs, Saint Paul, MN

Ruthella F. Samuel
4 Cadillacs, Houston, TX

Mr. & Mrs. C. Sanatore
11 Cadillacs, Fort Myers, FL

Mrs. Billy Ray Sanborn
2 Cadillacs, N. Tonawanda, NY

Mrs. Dorothy Sanders
3 Cadillacs, Ulmer, SC

Mrs. I.N. Sanders
11 Cadillacs, Roswell, NM

Mr. Russell L. Sanderson
Derby, KS

Ms. Jean A. Sanesi
4 Cadillacs, Salem, OR

K. Sangha
1 Cadillac, Vancouver, BC

Mr. Arthur Sangiuliano
4 Cadillacs, Cranford, NJ

Ms. June C. Santoro
2 Cadillacs, Methuen, MA

Mr. Joseph F. Santos
4 Cadillacs, San Jose, CA

Mr. James Sapp
2 Cadillacs, Columbus, GA

Mr. Carl H. Sapper, Jr.
24 Cadillacs, Independence, MO

Mr. Raymond J. Sargent
12 Cadillacs, Harrison, MI

Dyan P. Sarnecky
1 Cadillac, Keego Harbor, MI

Joseph Sarnecky
1 Cadillac, Leonard, MI

Ms. Nellie D. Sarner
3 Cadillacs, Houston, TX

Glenn & Dorothy Sash
1 Cadillac, San Antonio, TX

Mr. John Sass, Jr.
1 Cadillac, Little Falls, NJ

Ms. Virginia Sass
Plainfield, NJ

June Sasser
4 Cadillacs, Savannah, GA

Mr. William B. Satterwhite
2 Cadillacs, Mayfield, KY

Mr. Gerald F. Sauer
2 Cadillacs, Monticello, IL

Mr. Irvin Saunders
2 Cadillacs, Baltimore, MD

Mr. Kenneth V. Saunders, Sr.
4 Cadillacs, Bishop, CA

Mr. Ralph W. Sauper
8 Cadillacs, Naperville, IL

Danny Sava
3 Cadillacs, Pt. Charlotte, FL

William J. Savara
8 Cadillacs, Grand Rapids, MI

Mr. Arnold Savitt
5 Cadillacs, Beechhurst, NY

Mr. Gerald J. Savoie
1 Cadillac, Waterford, MI

Mrs. Irene L. Savoie
2 Cadillacs, Crandon, WI

Mr. David L. Sawyer
5 Cadillacs, Las Vegas, NV

Mr. Joel M. Sawyer
2 Cadillacs, Sapulpa, OK

Theodore E. Sazzmann
7 Cadillacs, Sherman Oaks, CA

Mr. Dominic Scacci
5 Cadillacs, Bloomingdale, IL

Mr. Alfred E. Scarborough
1 Cadillac, Ellenton, FL

Ms. Elaine B. Schaal
7 Cadillacs, Hopkins, MN

William C. Schadrack, Jr.
8 Cadillacs, Memphis, TN

Robert & Augustine Schaefer
6 Cadillacs, Columbia, IL

Mr. Harold Schafer
5 Cadillacs, La Crosse, IN

Ms. Margery L. Schafer
1 Cadillac, Pompano Beach, FL

Mrs. Shirley M. Schaible
4 Cadillacs, East Lansing, MI

Victor E. Schall
2 Cadillacs, Elderton, PA

Mr. Allan Schappert
6 Cadillacs, Diamond Spgs., CA

Mrs. Marolyn E. Scheffel
6 Cadillacs, Parker, CO

Ms. Helen L. Scheffler
9 Cadillacs, Saint Marys, OH

Mr. D. Scheidt
2 Cadillacs, Luseland, SK

Mr. Joseph Schein
3 Cadillacs, Walnut Creek, CA

Leonard Scheitzerhof
40 Cadillacs, Cupertino, CA

Mr. J. Schell
1 Cadillac, Kelowna, BC

Mr. Paul D. Scherrer
1 Cadillac, Poplar Bluff, MO

D. Schettler
1 Cadillac, St. Adolphe, MB

Mr. Frank H. Scheuring
6 Cadillacs, Hoyt Lakes, MN

Mr. Mathew J. Schiehsl
5 Cadillacs, Palm Coast, FL

Mr. John W. Schienda
1 Cadillac, Bellefontaine, OH

Ms. Barbara A. Schild
1 Cadillac, Bensenville, IL

Mr. Michael J. Schill
25 Cadillacs, Cleveland, OH

John Schilling
3 Cadillacs, Bay Shore, NY

Mr. Robert E. Schilling
8 Cadillacs, Haysville, KS

Mr. Harris Schimmel
8 Cadillacs, Hallandale, FL

T. Schirmuhly
5 Cadillacs, Fairport, NY

Ms. Joann Schlagbaum
7 Cadillacs, Lima, OH

Mr. Lloyd R. Schlecht
7 Cadillacs, Paradise, CA

Mr. Marvin Schleinz
2 Cadillacs, Neenah, WI

Mr. C. Graydon Schlichter
23 Cadillacs, Shippensburg, PA

Mr. Kenneth E. Schlottman
1 Cadillac, Boyceville, WI

James A. Schmidt
6 Cadillacs, Gainesville, FL

John R. Schmidt & Dick Illian
12 Cadillacs, Saint Edward, NE

Mr. John Schmidt
6 Cadillacs, Marmora, NJ

Mr. Robert A. Schmidt
5 Cadillacs, San Antonio, TX

Mr. Jack Schmitt
1 Cadillac, Nokomis, FL

Mr. Richard M. Schmitz
2 Cadillacs, Sauk Centre, MN

Mr. Leo A. Schmoyer
1 Cadillac, Crystal, MN

Jack Schneider
1 Cadillac, Northbrook, IL

Mr. Jerrold K. Schneider
7 Cadillacs, Hudson, OH

Ms. Muriel G. Schneider
7 Cadillacs, Sarasota, FL

Mr. Randolph Schneider
2 Cadillacs, Elsa, TX

Mr. Bernard Schnoor
4 Cadillacs, Silver City, IA

Mr. Ernest C. Schocke
3 Cadillacs, Milwaukee, WI

Mr. Norman Schoemann
3 Cadillacs, Mtn. Home, AR

Mr. John H. Schoene
6 Cadillacs, Dublin, OH

Mrs. Louise Schoenfeld
5 Cadillacs, Portage, PA

Mr. Stephen L. Scholl
13 Cadillacs, Michigan City, IN

Ms. Beatrice A. Scholz
3 Cadillacs, Hastings, MN

Dr. J. Ronald R. Schoolcraft
4 Cadillacs, Jacksonville, FL

Ms. Maxine R. Schortman
3 Cadillacs, Broad Brook, CT

Mr. Carl & Wilma Schroeder
2 Cadillacs, Crawfordsvlle, IN

Mr. Harold A. Schroeder
6 Cadillacs, Lexington, MI

Ms. Margaret M. Schroeder
1 Cadillac, Ocala, FL

Mr. August Schroeyens
2 Cadillacs, London, ON

Mr. Donald D. Schropp
3 Cadillacs, McPherson, KS

Ms. Ginette M. Schroth
1 Cadillac, Charlotte, NC

Mrs. Betty J. Schubert
7 Cadillacs, Glenpool, OK

Mr. Charles J. Schuler
3 Cadillacs, Eureka Spgs., AR

Milton L. Schuler
8 Cadillacs, Cape Coral, FL

Mr. Arthur F. Schultz
5 Cadillacs, Oak Park, IL

Mr. Gilbert A. Schultz
2 Cadillacs, Minneapolis, MN

J.A. Schultz, Jr.
37 Cadillacs, Mercer, WI

Mr. Jerome A. Schultz, Sr.
37 Cadillacs, Mercer, WI

Mr. Leon W. Schurr
2 Cadillacs, Fort Collins, CO

Mr. John Schuster
7 Cadillacs, Scranton, PA

Mr. Charles Schwab
5 Cadillacs, Shawnee Msn., KS

Ms. Clara A. Schwandt
15 Cadillacs, Clinton, MI

Bill Schwartz
3 Cadillacs, Sheboygan, WI

Mr. Conrad P. Schwartz
8 Cadillacs, Belleville, MI

Mr. Leonard Schwartz
6 Cadillacs, Hensel, ND

Mr. Franklin Schwartzott
2 Cadillacs, Yukon, OK

Mr. Henry Schwarz
8 Cadillacs, Alexandria, VA

R. Schweid
1 Cadillac, Clifton, NJ

Mr. Ben A. Schwellenbach
Neillsville, WI

Dr. Phillip B. Schworer
12 Cadillacs, Ft. Mitchell, KY

Mr. Angelo Scialabba
4 Cadillacs, Naples, FL

Mr. Aaron Scott
8 Cadillacs, Baltimore, MD

Mr. Alfred D. Scott
6 Cadillacs, Flint, MI

Mr. Augustus L. Scott
2 Cadillacs, Naples, FL

Mr. Clyde T. Scott
1 Cadillac, Memphis, TN

Mr. Dewey L. Scott
3 Cadillacs, Orange, TX

Holly Mae Simons Scott
2 Cadillacs, Columbia, SC

Mr. Michael D. Scott
2 Cadillacs, Houston, TX

Ms. Phyllis Scott
3 Cadillacs, Bellmawr, NJ

Mr. Ramon R. Scott
1 Cadillac, Lancing, TN

Mr. Russell J. Scott
5 Cadillacs, Richmond, IN

Walter Scott & Jane Blomeley
4 Cadillacs, Sullivan, IL

Richard J. & Elaine Scrivens
3 Cadillacs, Live Oak, CA

Mr. Robert O. Scruggs
3 Cadillacs, Powderly, TX

Mr. R. Seaborne
1 Cadillac, St. Catharines, ON

Mr. Joseph Seabrook
3 Cadillacs, Pittsford, NY

James Seah
7 Cadillacs, Cincinnati, OH

Mr. E. Gordon Seale
9 Cadillacs, Oxford, MI

Ms. Julia D. Seale
1 Cadillac, Tuscaloosa, AL

Mrs. Mary Beard Seale
3 Cadillacs, Birmingham, AL

Howard & Winona Seaman
2 Cadillacs, Parkersburg, WV

Mr. Bill Searcy
1 Cadillac, Independence, KS

Mr. Owen A. Searl
5 Cadillacs, Ripon, WI

Mr. Leo Searles
5 Cadillacs, Worcester, NY

Ms. Irene Sears
3 Cadillacs, Saint Albans, VT

George & Martha Setcavage
1 Cadillac, Marco Island, FL

Ms. Esma J. Shankle
1 Cadillac, Jasper, TX

Mr. James B. Sheffer, Jr.
4 Cadillacs, Sun City Ctr., FL

Ms. Joyce G. Shipp
5 Cadillacs, Spring, TX

John Sebo
34 Cadillacs, Pittsford, NY

Chun Yeung Seto
3 Cadillacs, Greenwood, MS

Mr. Jack L. Shanks
5 Cadillacs, Galena, IL

Mr. Dale A. Shelley
14 Cadillacs, Little Falls, MN

Mr. Alvin Shnider
1 Cadillac, Toledo, OH

Bobby & Mary Sechrest
3 Cadillacs, Lexington, NC

Mrs. Edythe A. Setzer
Salisbury, NC

Mr. Grover T. Shannon
14 Cadillacs, Tyler, TX

Mr. Allen G. Shelton
7 Cadillacs, Clay, KY

Mr. Charles Shockley
1 Cadillac, Tyler, TX

Mr. James H. Secor, III
3 Cadillacs, Midland, MI

Mrs. Frances C. Setzer
8 Cadillacs, Marion, NC

Robert F. Sharapata
3 Cadillacs, Naples, FL

Ms. Jacqueline Shelton
6 Cadillacs, Southfield, MI

Marie M. Shoemaker
7 Cadillacs, North Platte, NE

Mr. Richard Secor
28 Cadillacs, Toledo, OH

Mr. Palmer E. Severance
1 Cadillac, Nampa, ID

Mr. Robert F. Sharapata
3 Cadillacs, Palatine, IL

Mr. John Martin Shelton
2 Cadillacs, Winston Salem, NC

Mr. Stephen Shoemaker
4 Cadillacs, Moscow, PA

Ms. Nancy L. Seggebruch
Geneseo, IL

Vera J. & Robert G. Severns
4 Cadillacs, Mattoon, IL

Ms. Ruby W. Sharber
4 Cadillacs, Camden, NC

Mr. & Mrs. Judson G. Shelton
2 Cadillacs, Los Osos, CA

Dr. Robert W. Shoenthal
7 Cadillacs, Elgin, IL

Mr. Warren Seichrist
1 Cadillac, Cincinnati, OH

Mr. & Mrs. Lex Severson
3 Cadillacs, Memphis, TN

Jerry Sharp
3 Cadillacs, Bradenton, FL

Mr. Lloyd T. Shelton
1 Cadillac, Depew, NY

G. Joette Shoffer
4 Cadillacs, Indiana, PA

Mr. Russell Seidel
3 Cadillacs, Rochester, NY

Mr. Gene T. Sexton
2 Cadillacs, Spring City, TN

Ms. Joan K. Sharp
3 Cadillacs, Ithaca, NY

Mr. Martin J. Shemanski
2 Cadillacs, Hemet, CA

Mr. Richard Sholes
14 Cadillacs, Cranston, RI

Mr. Norman K. Selby
11 Cadillacs, Kansas City, MO

Mrs. Francis Seyler
3 Cadillacs, Brampton, ON

Ottes M. Sharp
15 Cadillacs, Mesa, AZ

Mr. Noble N. Shepherd, Jr.
2 Cadillacs, St. Augustine, FL

Mr. Clifford M. Short
3 Cadillacs, Winchester, OR

Mr. Robert T. Selby
2 Cadillacs, Henry, IL

Mr. Nicholas J. Sfakianos
1 Cadillac, Timonium, MD

Mrs. Ruth J. Sharp
1 Cadillac, Sugar Grove, OH

Howard Sherline
1 Cadillac, W. Bloomfield, MI

Mr. Frederick R. Short
27 Cadillacs, Atlantic Bch., FL

Mr. Melvin J. Sellers
2 Cadillacs, El Paso, TX

Mr. Phillip Shadi
8 Cadillacs, Toledo, OH

Mr. William Sharpe
1 Cadillac, N. Las Vegas, NV

Mrs. Renee C. Sherline
6 Cadillacs, Pompano Beach, FL

Ms. Mary A. Shotwell
Dover, OH

Ms. Theresa Ann Sellers
Montgomery, AL

Mr. Leo N. Shady
2 Cadillacs, Orange, CA

Mr. E. Sharper
4 Cadillacs, Sicklerville, NJ

Orrien Sherrer
14 Cadillacs, East Point, GA

Mr. Walter Showers
2 Cadillacs, Marion, OH

Mr. Patsy Sena
1 Cadillac, Nutley, NJ

Mr. Clarence R. Shafer
5 Cadillacs, Gardnerville, NV

Mr. Jewel F. Shaver
2 Cadillacs, Stamps, AR

Mr. Richard L. Sherriff
2 Cadillacs, Brownsville, OR

Dr. Albert W. Shub
2 Cadillacs, Swampscott, MA

Mr. Rodger E. Seney
8 Cadillacs, Deltona, FL

Mr. Edward I. Shaffer
1 Cadillac, Dayton, OH

Clara Sanderson Shaw
7 Cadillacs, Lakeland, FL

Mr. Fred L. Sherrill, Jr.
2 Cadillacs, Conover, NC

Mr. Robert A. Shultis
5 Cadillacs, Olivebridge, NY

Mr. John H. Seng
7 Cadillacs, Bridgeport, NE

Walter G. Shaffer
6 Cadillacs, Bowie, MD

Mr. Keith Shaw
5 Cadillacs, St. Eleanor's, PE

Ms. Sara T. Sherrill
9 Cadillacs, Sanford, NC

Dallas C. Shults, Jr.
6 Cadillacs, Lexington, SC

June F. Seng
3 Cadillacs, Grand Forks, ND

Mr. S. Shahrebani
1 Cadillac, Richmond Hill, ON

Mr. Richard M. Shaw
5 Cadillacs, Lima, OH

Mr. Theron E. Shields
6 Cadillacs, Little River, SC

Mr. Herbert Shultz
5 Cadillacs, Crown Point, IN

Ralph E. Sentz
5 Cadillacs, Cumberland, PA

Mrs. Estelle Shane
1 Cadillac, North York, ON

Mr. Robert A. Shaw
2 Cadillacs, Medford, OR

Thomas I. Shields
9 Cadillacs, Waynesboro, VA

Ms. Patricia Shultz
3 Cadillacs, Thayer, MO

Mr. John W. Serig
8 Cadillacs, Wheeling, WV

Mrs. Sho C. Shang
2 Cadillacs, Kingsport, TN

Mrs. Juanita Sheegog
3 Cadillacs, Hazard, KY

William & Ruth Shipman
6 Cadillacs, Jacksonville, FL

Joe J. & Lubys M. Shumate
1 Cadillac, Timberlake, NC

Mr. Rafael Serrata
3 Cadillacs, Bronx, NY

Mr. Duane C. Shankel
12 Cadillacs, Ellenton FL

Yolanda & Eugene Sheehan
4 Cadillacs, Annandale, VA

Mr. Dennis Shipp
2 Cadillacs, Mobile, AL

Dr. Edward Shumofsky
9 Cadillacs, New Rochelle, NY

Mr. Glenn M. Shumway
2 Cadillacs, Luthvle. Timon, MD

Mr. Winfred C. Shuping
1 Cadillac, Salisbury, NC

Ms. Lula N. Shurtleff
2 Cadillacs, Marion, LA

Mrs. E.S. Shy
1 Cadillac, Alpine, NJ

Ms. Mae M. Sibert
5 Cadillacs, London, KY

Mr. Olson Sidney
19 Cadillacs, Miami, FL

Mr. Jacob Siegal
3 Cadillacs, Pompano Bch., FL

Mr. C.E. Sieja
1 Cadillac, Midland, MI

Mr. Paul Sigel
23 Cadillacs, Delray Beach, FL

Mr. James E. Sightler
3 Cadillacs, Winter Park, FL

Wayne Sigmen
5 Cadillacs, Scottsdale, AZ

Dr. Joseph Silber
2 Cadillacs, Tenafly, NJ

Mr. Irving Silberberg
3 Cadillacs, Miami, FL

Mr. Charles T. Silk
4 Cadillacs, Ruskin, FL

Mr. Tony Silvain
3 Cadillacs, Virginia City, NV

Edward Silverman
7 Cadillacs, Savannah, GA

Mr. Mario Silvestri
6 Cadillacs, Elmwood Park, IL

Mr. Daniel Simatovich
1 Cadillac, Moline, IL

Mr. Anthony Simeo
2 Cadillacs, Cinnaminson, NJ

Mr. Robert Simminger
1 Cadillac, Clearwater, FL

A.B. & Lorraine Simmons
3 Cadillacs, Tallahassee, FL

Cephus Simmons, Sr.
3 Cadillacs, Bhom, AL

Mr. James W. Simmons
7 Cadillacs, Collierville, TN

Mr. Bernard Simon
4 Cadillacs, Dunedin, FL

Cheryl A. Simon
2 Cadillacs, Englewood, OH

Mr. Matthew Simon
2 Cadillacs, New Orleans, LA

Mr. J. William W. Simons
4 Cadillacs, Elmhurst, IL

Mr. B. Simpson
1 Cadillac, Brighton, ON

Mr. Donald R. Simpson
7 Cadillacs, Lodi, NY

Ms. Dorothy G. Simpson
2 Cadillacs, Tyler, TX

Mr. Red Simpson
3 Cadillacs, Brady, TX

Mr. Leslie A. Sims
2 Cadillacs, Kalamazoo, MI

Mr. Carl A. Sinclair
10 Cadillacs, Williamsville, NY

Mr. Milton Sinclair
12 Cadillacs, Williamsville, NY

Ms. Irene L. Singletary
1 Cadillac, Aurora, CO

Dr. George W. Singleton
1 Cadillac, Selma, AL

Ms. Juanita W. Singleton
2 Cadillacs, Westland, MI

James J. & Ruth Sink
5 Cadillacs, Queensbury, NY

Bernard J. & Erika Sinkora
2 Cadillacs, Schenectady, NY

Mr. George G. Sinpoli
7 Cadillacs, Fresno, CA

Mr. Albert G. Sipka
4 Cadillacs, Warren, OH

Bob Sircy
10 Cadillacs, Savannah, TN

Ms. Barbara A. Sirota
6 Cadillacs, Great Neck, NY

Mr. William H. Sisco
6 Cadillacs, Huntsville, AL

Mr. Marlon M. Sitasz
1 Cadillac, Chicago, IL

Mr. M. Sitzer
1 Cadillac, North York, ON

Mrs. Edward Sixt
1 Cadillac, Orlando, FL

Mr. John A. Sjostrom
Wichita Falls, TX

Mr. L. Skelly
6 Cadillacs, North York, ON

Gordon D. Skeoch, M.D.
12 Cadillacs, San Diego, CA

Copeland H. Skinner
1 Cadillac, Lumberton, NC

Mr. Jim Skinner
8 Cadillacs, Des Moines, IA

Mr. William R. Skinner
7 Cadillacs, Lake Wales, FL

Mrs. Anna Sklarov
15 Cadillacs, Miami, FL

Mr. Kenneth E. Skogman
1 Cadillac, Bellevue, WA

Mr. Robert E. Slabe
5 Cadillacs, Pittsburgh, PA

Mr. John A. Slade, Jr.
1 Cadillac, De Kalb, TX

Mr. Robert L. Slagle
9 Cadillacs, Springfield, IL

Ms. Ruth Slate
3 Cadillacs, South Boston, VA

Mrs. Elizabeth J. Slater
11 Cadillacs, Lecanto, FL

Mr. Phillip L. Slater
6 Cadillacs, Gaithersburg, MD

Ms. Mildred P. Slaton
4 Cadillacs, Orange, TX

Donald Slaughter
8 Cadillacs, Dunnellon, FL

Mr. Herbert Slayton
18 Cadillacs, Benton, IL

Mr. Raymond Sledge
6 Cadillacs, Homestead, PA

Senator P. Nevin Sledge
2 Cadillacs, Cleveland, MS

Mr. Arthur F. Slick
5 Cadillacs, Mt. Pleasant, SC

Mr. Loren N. Slinkard
1 Cadillac, Cape Girardeau, MO

Mr. Ralph A. Sloan
7 Cadillacs, Lilburn, GA

Mr. William Sloman
8 Cadillacs, Norcross, GA

Mr. Albert W. Slopik
3 Cadillacs, Easton, PA

Troy B. Sluder, Jr.
3 Cadillacs, Chapel Hill, NC

A.H. Small
2 Cadillacs, Kalispell, MT

Ms. Florrie C. Smallwood
7 Cadillacs, Palmetto, FL

Mr. Fredrick Smalwood
2 Cadillacs, Bainbridge, GA

Evelyn L. Smart
1 Cadillac, East Peoria, IL

Mrs. Marjorie Smart
Heber Springs, AR

Mr. William J. Smetana
2 Cadillacs, Downers Grove, IL

Mr. Joseph W. Smialek
8 Cadillacs, Ft. Washington, MD

Mr. Lloyd E. Smiley
3 Cadillacs, Heber Springs, AR

Mr. Peter J. Smilgin
10 Cadillacs, Amsterdam, NY

Ms. Arlis J. Smith
3 Cadillacs, Jasper, TX

Mr. Barney Smith
1 Cadillac, Talbott, TN

Mr. C. Smith
1 Cadillac, Chilliwack, BC

Mr. Carl C. Smith, Jr.
1 Cadillac, Marysville, OH

Mr. Charles Smith
1 Cadillac, E. Saint Louis, IL

Mr. Charles L. Smith
5 Cadillacs, Charleston, SC

Mr. Charles Smith, Jr.
7 Cadillacs, Houston, TX

Clinas William Smith
4 Cadillacs, Bristol, VA

Earl L. & Clara Smith
4 Cadillacs, Alpharetta, GA

Mr. Eldon W. Smith
2 Cadillacs, Myrtle Beach, SC

Mrs. Elma Smith
1 Cadillac, Spring Lake, NC

Mr. Elmer V. Smith
4 Cadillacs, Fallston, MD

Ms. Elsie G. Smith
2 Cadillacs, Los Angeles, CA

Ms. Elsie M. Smith
5 Cadillacs, East Bend, NC

Mr. Eugene I. Smith
1 Cadillac, Two Rivers, WI

F. Neil Smith
9 Cadillacs, Henderson, NV

Fincher Smith
2 Cadillacs, Tallahassee, FL

Mr. Floyd E. Smith
2 Cadillacs, Tucson, AZ

Gary M. Smith
1 Cadillac, Danville, IN

Mr. George Smith
4 Cadillacs, New Haven, IN

Ms. Gertrude E. Smith
3 Cadillacs, Kingston, NH

Mr. Glenn Smith
2 Cadillacs, Littcarr, KY

Mr. Harold L. Smith
2 Cadillacs, Saint Louis, MO

Henry F. Smith
6 Cadillacs, Tallahassee, FL

J. Veleen Smith
3 Cadillacs, Tallahassee, FL

Mr. Jack Smith
3 Cadillacs, Waynesboro, GA

Mr. Jake Smith
4 Cadillacs, Snyder, TX

Mr. Jere F. Smith
4 Cadillacs, Fairbanks, AK

Mr. John W. Smith
2 Cadillacs, Salisbury, MD

John A. Smith, Sr.
10 Cadillacs, Severna Park, MD

Mr. Joseph A. Smith
6 Cadillacs, Nisswa, MN

Kenneth & Nancy Smith
6 Cadillacs, Monrovia, CA

Mr. Lee A. Smith
12 Cadillacs, Chula Vista, CA

Mr. Lewis W. Smith
4 Cadillacs, Detroit, MI

Ms. Lynn D. Smith
Knoxville, TN

Mr. Mack R. Smith
2 Cadillacs, Fordyce, AR

Ms. Madeline W. Smith
16 Cadillacs, Largo, FL

Mamie E. Smith
4 Cadillacs, Newport News, VA

Mr. Max S. Smith
12 Cadillacs, Allen Park, MI

Okla Homer Smith
Fort Smith, AR

Mr. Othel O. Smith
7 Cadillacs, Goldthwaite, TX

Mr. Owen Smith
2 Cadillacs, Hanover, ON

R.T. Smith
14 Cadillacs, Fort Smith, AR

Mr. Raymond E. Smith
1 Cadillac, Gainesville, TX

Mr. Robert T. Smith
2 Cadillacs, Sun City West, AZ

Mr. Robert C. Smith
2 Cadillacs, La Grange, IL

Mr. Robert E. Smith
4 Cadillacs, Jefferson Cty, MO

Mr. Robert Smith
2 Cadillacs, Portsmouth, VA

Ronald Smith
1 Cadillac, Hudson Bay, SK

Mr. Roy M. Smith
4 Cadillacs, San Antonio, TX

Ruby Smith
5 Cadillacs, Detroit, MI

Russell G. Smith
20 Cadillacs, Pembrk. Pines, FL

Mr. Russell G. Smith, Jr.
1 Cadillac, Pembrk. Pines, FL

Mr. Seth E. Smith
5 Cadillacs, Carthage, TX

Tinnie M. Smith
1 Cadillac, Flint, MI

W. Smith
1 Cadillac, Sarnia, ON

Mr. Walter M. Smith
6 Cadillacs, Avon Park, FL

Rev. Warnell Smith
3 Cadillacs, Greenville, MS

Mr. William E. Smith
10 Cadillacs, Lady Lake, FL

Mr. William E. Smith
4 Cadillacs, Lebanon, TN

Mr. Willie L. Smith
8 Cadillacs, Leavenworth, KS

Mr. Woodson Smith, Jr.
6 Cadillacs, Marble Falls, TX

Mr. Max Smolar
12 Cadillacs, Pittsburgh, PA

Ms. Yvonne Smolukas
1 Cadillac, Du Bois, PA

Mr. Clyde Snair
1 Cadillac, Lunenburg, NS

Mr. William H. Snee
4 Cadillacs, Port Arthur, TX

Bryant S. & Leah C. Sneed
4 Cadillacs, Lakeworth, FL

Ben Sniderman
14 Cadillacs, Columbus, OH

Mr. James P. Snodgrass
2 Cadillacs, Coleman, TX

Mr. Eldon Snowbarger
1 Cadillac, Burlington, CO

Mr. Donald E. Snyder
4 Cadillacs, Ft. Myers Bch., FL

Mr. John Snyder
4 Cadillacs, Merced, CA

Mr. Raymond E. Snyder
4 Cadillacs, Cicero, NY

Mr. Edward F. Sobczak
10 Cadillacs, Deerfield, IL

Ms. Maxine B. Soffer
20 Cadillacs, Hallandale, FL

Lettitia Sofranac
12 Cadillacs, Stone Mtn., GA

Mr. Alexander Sokal
1 Cadillac, Winnipeg, MB

Ms. Barbara K. Sokol
1 Cadillac, Columbus, OH

Mr. L. Soleway
3 Cadillacs, Vancouver, BC

Emily Soloman
7 Cadillacs, Stockton, CA

Ms. Rosemarie M. Soltis
17 Cadillacs, Pittsburgh, PA

Mr. R. Somody
3 Cadillacs, Ottawa, ON

Dr. Roger H. Sondag
18 Cadillacs, Minneapolis, MN

Mrs. M. Songer
7 Cadillacs, Jonesboro, AR

Mary Soprovich
1 Cadillac, Powell River, BC

Mr. Robert Soptic
6 Cadillacs, Kansas City, KS

Mr. James A. Sorensen
6 Cadillacs, Ringsted, IA

Mrs. Marlena Sotirake
4 Cadillacs, Baden, PA

Matthew Richard Sousa
3 Cadillacs, Palm Springs, CA

Mr. Emory N. Sova
7 Cadillacs, Tavares, FL

Mr. Dennie Sowder
2 Cadillacs, Lawrenceville, GA

Garland & Margareta Sowers
2 Cadillacs, Radford, VA

Ms. Vera M. Spadaro
12 Cadillacs, Daleville, AL

C. Edward Spahr
8 Cadillacs, Akron, OH

Ms. Anna E. Spangler
Titusville, FL

Merle & Maxine Spangler
2 Cadillacs, O'Neill, NE

Mr. Eugene Spani
W. Frankfort, IL

Dr. David B. & Mimi Sparber
2 Cadillacs, Memphis, TN

Mr. Leo Sparkia
2 Cadillacs, South Bend, IN

Ms. Avis W. Sparks
3 Cadillacs, Big Creek, KY

Helen L. Sparks
3 Cadillacs, Ft. Myers, FL

Mr. James C. Sparks, Sr.
7 Cadillacs, Lake City, FL

Mr. Roland W. Sparks
3 Cadillacs, Nacogdoches, TX

Mr. Frank W. Spatz
3 Cadillacs, Mt. Prospect, IL

Linda Spaulding
2 Cadillacs, Bargersville, IN

Mr. William E. Spavin
1 Cadillac, Davenport, IA

Mrs. Dorothy P. Spearman
3 Cadillacs, Henderson, NC

Mr. Otto E. Specht
4 Cadillacs, Pampa, TX

Mr. Ralph O. Speck
8 Cadillacs, Dunlap, TN

Ms. Janice Spector
3 Cadillacs, West Orange, NJ

Mr. Joe Speer
3 Cadillacs, Sunnyvale, CA

Mrs. Helen L. Speicher
10 Cadillacs, Indianapolis, IN

Mr. Charlie Spencer
2 Cadillacs, Buckingham, VA

Mr. Ernest O. Spencer
2 Cadillacs, Gloversville, NY

Ms. Velma R. Spicer
1 Cadillac, Middletown, OH

Mr. William A. Spicer
3 Cadillacs, Erin, TN

Mr. Bernard Spiegel
11 Cadillacs, Elkins Park, PA

Mr. Jack Spiegel
2 Cadillacs, Delray Beach, FL

Mr. Patrick Spinella
6 Cadillacs, Vallejo, CA

Mr. Merle Spinks
5 Cadillacs, Lakewood, CA

Dominick & Marge Spiotti
4 Cadillacs, Orlando, FL

Mr. John Spitler
7 Cadillacs, Brighton, MI

Mr. Phil W. Spitler
20 Cadillacs, Montoursville, PA

Mr. William M. Spotts
Jackson, MS

Russell Sprague
5 Cadillacs, Moncton, NB

Mr. Charles L. Spratt
2 Cadillacs, Summersville, WV

Mr. Frank D. Sprinkle
3 Cadillacs, Murray, KY

Mr. Edward F. Sprowl
1 Cadillac, Dayton, OH

Ms. Magda I. Squillacioti
2 Cadillacs, Merrick, NY

Wanda Srygley-Masley
16 Cadillacs, Fort Smith, AR

Mr. Roland St. Amant
17 Cadillacs, Enfield, CT

Edouard St. Gelais
1 Cadillac, Charlesbourg, QC

Mrs. Rita Stabile
9 Cadillacs, Placida, FL

Mr. Alfred F. Stacey
19 Cadillacs, St. Petersburg, FL

Ms. Martha H. Stack
3 Cadillacs, Wilmington, NC

Mr. James Stacker
5 Cadillacs, E. Saint Louis, IL

Mr. Ronald W. Stadt
4 Cadillacs, Carbondale, IL

Mr. Joseph G. Staffone
3 Cadillacs, Timonium, MD

Mr. Oscar P. Stafford
Woodstock, GA

Charles & Josephine Stagnitto
17 Cadillacs, Rochester, NY

Mr. Donald R. Stahl
1 Cadillac, Bettsville, OH

Mr. Herbert E. Stalcup
2 Cadillacs, Bloomfield, IN

Freda H. Stalls
Carbondale, IL

Mr. Lawrence Stampf
l4 Cadillacs, Jackson, CA

Mrs. Lena E. Stanek
5 Cadillacs, Easthampton, MA

Mr. John J. Stankaitis
4 Cadillacs, Orange Park, FL

Mr. Walter S. Stanley
1 Cadillac, Mount Olive, NC

Mr. Edward N. Stanton
2 Cadillacs, Las Vegas, NV

William P. Stanton
5 Cadillacs, Murrells Inlet, SC

Mr. George W. Staples
1 Cadillac, Fort Worth, TX

Jerald Stapp
4 Cadillacs, Centerville, OH

Mr. Donald R. Stark
8 Cadillacs, Cape Coral, FL

Mr. William C. Starkey
5 Cadillacs, Ingleside, IL

Mr. Weldon G. Starrett
4 Cadillacs, Henderson, NC

Nick Stasiuk
4 Cadillacs, Lloydminster, AB

Mrs. Erma R. Staton
4 Cadillacs, Brownwood, TX

William Stavisky
2 Cadillacs, Old Forge, PA

Mr. John A. Stavros
6 Cadillacs, Seattle, WA

Mr. Felix P. Stawicki
4 Cadillacs, St. James City, FL

Mr. Nicholas R. Steder
1 Cadillac, Villa Park, IL

Mr. Wayne Steed
6 Cadillacs, Dayton, OH

Ms. Janet B. Steele
40 Cadillacs, Hartford, CT

Ms. Terri L. Steele
5 Cadillacs, San Antonio, TX

Mr. Douglas L. Steelman
4 Cadillacs, Visalia, CA

Mr. Reeves M. Steelman
1 Cadillac, Winchester, TN

Mr. August Steffen
1 Cadillac, Burke, SD

Mr. Kenneth Stein
12 Cadillacs, Old Westbury, NY

Mr. Gunther T. Steinberg
2 Cadillacs, Newton, IA

Mr. Samuel M. Steinberg
3 Cadillacs, Hyattsville, MD

Mr. Seymour Steinberg
4 Cadillacs, Batavia, NY

Mr. John G. Steinle
3 Cadillacs, Fort Pierce, FL

Frank D. Stella
15 Cadillacs, Detroit, MI

Mrs. Geneva K. Stelle
8 Cadillacs, Normal, IL

Richard & Shirley Stelmach
7 Cadillacs, Clintenville, WI

Mr. Mickey Stepanic
12 Cadillacs, Kensington, OH

Catherine Stephens
4 Cadillacs, Baton Rouge, LA

Mr. Clarence Stephens
12 Cadillacs, Espyville, PA

Mr. Frank C. Stephens
1 Cadillac, Ocala, FL

Mrs. Margaret H. Stephens
2 Cadillacs, North Garden, VA

Mr. Wilford Stephenson
2 Cadillacs, Columbus, GA

Mr. David Stern
3 Cadillacs, Omaha, NE

Mr. William A. Stern, Sr.
2 Cadillacs, Ontario, CA

Mr. Robert Sternberger
9 Cadillacs, Indianapolis, IN

Mr. Arthur Steuber, Jr.
9 Cadillacs, Jersey City, NJ

Mr. Dale W. Stevens
Elmhurst, IL

Ms. Doris Y. Stevens
10 Cadillacs, Pls. Verdes, CA

Mr. Dorris W. Stevens
5 Cadillacs, Swartz, LA

James E. Stevens
4 Cadillacs, Hamer, SC

Mr. John T. Stevens
5 Cadillacs, Santa Rosa, CA

Mr. Joseph Stevens
5 Cadillacs, Columbia, MO

Mr. Robert C. Stevens
4 Cadillacs, Grants Pass, OR

Mr. Robert J. Stevens
4 Cadillacs, Tyler, TX

Ms. Sarah M. Stevens
2 Cadillacs, Borger, TX

Mr. Loren F. Stevenson
1 Cadillac, Clinton, IA

Mr. Claude S. Stewart
6 Cadillacs, Linthicum Hts., MD

Estell & Barbara Stewart
1 Cadillac, Carmi, IL

Harold & Geneva Stewart
5 Cadillacs, Frankfort, IN

Mr. Jack C. Stewart
9 Cadillacs, Strongsville, OH

Ronald Stewart
1 Cadillac, Carrying Place, ON

Ron & Suzanne Stickel
20 Cadillacs, Naples, FL

Mr. Henry S. Stiff
4 Cadillacs, Byron, MI

Mr. George J. Stile
10 Cadillacs, Ft. Lauderdale, FL

Mr. Eugene R. Still
12 Cadillacs, Kingsport, TN

Ms. Marion Still
2 Cadillacs, Powder Spgs., GA

Juanita Stinchcomb
3 Cadillacs, Conley, GA

Mr. Donald P. Stine
1 Cadillac, Turlock, CA

Dr. Walter D. Stinson
1 Cadillac, Atlanta, GA

Ms. Maxine R. Stites
10 Cadillacs, Bradenton, FL

Mr. Leslie W. Stitt
6 Cadillacs, Deerfield Beach, FL

Harry Stivers
9 Cadillacs, Las Vegas, NV

Mr. Leo E. Stiwald
3 Cadillacs, Lady Lake, FL

Mr. George J. Stobie
6 Cadillacs, Johns Island, SC

Mr. Blaine Stock
10 Cadillacs, Ambler, PA

Mr. Roger W. Stock
1 Cadillac, Manitowoc, WI

Mr. Wendell B. Stockdale
9 Cadillacs, Lancaster, PA

Mr. Stefan J. Stockton
4 Cadillacs, Batavia, NY

Mr. Carl S. Stodolak
1 Cadillac, Standish, MI

Mr. Baylous W. Stokes
4 Cadillacs, Pascagoula, MS

John & Glendora A. Stokes
7 Cadillacs, Chicago, IL

Elizabeth Stone-Watson
3 Cadillacs, Jacksonville, FL

Mr. Edwin A. Stone
2 Cadillacs, Marathon, FL

Rodger E. Stone
7 Cadillacs, Bloomingdale, IL

Robert C. Story
14 Cadillacs, Cincinnati, OH

Mr. Warren A. Stouffer
3 Cadillacs, Shreveport, LA

Ms. Rosalie Stout
18 Cadillacs, Fort Scott, KS

Mr. Stanley B. Stout
9 Cadillacs, John Day, OR

William Stoutenborough
9 Cadillacs, Forsyth, IL

Mr. Charles J. Strader
1 Cadillac, Warren, OH

Mr. James Strader
10 Cadillacs, Ridgeway, VA

Lennie B. Straham
Flint, MI

Mr. Gerald E. Strahl
3 Cadillacs, Miami, FL

Mr. Herbert A. Strain, Jr.
14 Cadillacs, Ballwin, MO

Ms. Mary Strale
7 Cadillacs, Port St. Lucie, FL

Mr. Peter Strange
5 Cadillacs, Danbury, CT

Mr. Richard Strange
1 Cadillac, Macon, GA

Mrs. Betty M. Strasser
2 Cadillacs, Akron, OH

Mr. John Strasshofer
4 Cadillacs, San Pedro, CA

Ms. Bernice A. Stratton
3 Cadillacs, Las Vegas, NV

Mr. Donald E. Stratton
2 Cadillacs, Clio, MI

Marvin & Kathleen Strauss
13 Cadillacs, Palm Beach, FL

Mr. J. Frank Strawn, Sr.
20 Cadillacs, Charlotte, NC

Olsie C. & Faye W. Strawn
2 Cadillacs, Victoria, TX

Mr. Jerry R. Strayer
4 Cadillacs, Columbus, OH

Rex A. Streets
3 Cadillacs, Billings, MT

Reverend Hopie Strickland, Jr.
3 Cadillacs, Atlanta, GA

Mr. Charles Strickler
4 Cadillacs, Staunton, VA

Richard Stroka
11 Cadillacs, Pittsburgh, PA

Mrs. Marjorie Stromenger
2 Cadillacs, El Paso, TX

D. Stroud
1 Cadillac, Columbus, GA

Mr. James E. Stroud
1 Cadillac, Amarillo, TX

Mr. Gerald S. Strum
1 Cadillac, San Antonio, TX

Aaron & Beatrice Struthers
1 Cadillac, Brattleboro, VT

Ms. Neva M. Stuckey
5 Cadillacs, Centerville, OH

Doyle E. Stumpff
91 Cadillacs, Belleville, PA

Ms. Glenda L. Sturdy
2 Cadillacs, Cleveland, TX

Ms. Viola H. Stys
1 Cadillac, Clinton Twp., MI

Mr. John F. Sublousky
4 Cadillacs, San Antonio, TX

Mr. Stephen F. Such
2 Cadillacs, Fort Pierce, FL

Mr. Leo J. Suess
3 Cadillacs, Manitowoc, WI

Lee & Jody Sulander
8 Cadillacs, Naples, FL

Ms. Dorothy J. Sullivan
5 Cadillacs, Fort Worth, TX

Mr. Gregory R. Sullivan
4 Cadillacs, Phoenix, AZ

Ollie Mae Sullivan
7 Cadillacs, Durant, OK

Mr. Robert A. Sullivan
1 Cadillac, Palm Bay, FL

Dr. & Mrs. William Sullivan
4 Cadillacs, Huntsville, AL

Saul & Alice Sumergrade
4 Cadillacs, New York, NY

Mr. Julius M. Summerour
18 Cadillacs, Detroit, MI

Gordon P. Summers
2 Cadillacs, Lake City, FL

H. Woodrow Summers
8 Cadillacs, Springfield, OH

Mr. Karl D. Summers
6 Cadillacs, Britt, MN

Mr. Hersey Sumner
2 Cadillacs, Columbus, GA

C.W. Sunday
10 Cadillacs, Lafayette, LA

Mr. Leo Sunseri
5 Cadillacs, San Jose, CA

Edgars J. & Oshida Supstiks
2 Cadillacs, Des Moines, IA

Mr. John Surber
8 Cadillacs, Anderson, IN

Mr. James A. Surles
9 Cadillacs, Kinston, NC

Ms. Cora Susin
9 Cadillacs, Bloomfield, MI

Mr. G. Sutherland
3 Cadillacs, Thunder Bay, ON

Edith H. Sutterfield
2 Cadillacs, Pocatello, ID

Mrs. Jean B. Sutton
4 Cadillacs, Mount Olive, NC

Mr. Robert Sutton
1 Cadillac, Napanee, ON

Mr. McElvin E. Swah
5 Cadillacs, Whites Creek, TN

Mr. Paul W. Swaim
1 Cadillac, Jonesville, NC

Mr. Albert H. Swann
5 Cadillacs, Newark, OH

Mr. John S. Swanton
1 Cadillac, Cincinnati, OH

Mr. Isadore Swartz
2 Cadillacs, Deltona, FL

Ms. Daisy L. Swearingen
2 Cadillacs, Panama City, FL

David M. Sweetwood
Essex Fells, NJ

Mr. & Mrs. Leo E. Swick, Jr.
31 Cadillacs, Gainesville, TX

Mr. Nathan E. Swindall
5 Cadillacs, Bradenton Bch., FL

Mr. James R. Swisher
5 Cadillacs, Burnsville, MN

Mr. George A. Switalski
5 Cadillacs, Berwyn, IL

Ms. Wilma Swofford
1 Cadillac, Atwood, IL

Mr. Robert K. Swope
1 Cadillac, Zanesville, OH

Mr. Leroy Syck
4 Cadillacs, Pikeville, KY

Jorita H. Symington
5 Cadillacs, Dallas, TX

Mr. Robert W. Symonds
5 Cadillacs, Newfane, NY

John Syverson
5 Cadillacs, Harrison, NY

Nimfa Apanel Szarka
2 Cadillacs, Lakewood, NJ

Mr. Joseph S. Szczotka
1 Cadillac, Utica, MI

Mr. Edward W. Szepelak
5 Cadillacs, Joliet, IL

Mr. Stephen G. Szymanski, Jr.
4 Cadillacs, Fort Myers, FL

T

Mr. Robert D. Taake
7 Cadillacs, Fort Smith, AR

Mr. S. Tachit
2 Cadillacs, Hines Creek, AB

Mr. James W. Tackett
3 Cadillacs, Muskogee, OK

S. Taetz
1 Cadillac, Delta, BC

Mrs. Nora A. Tafoya
1 Cadillac, Las Vegas, NM

Mr. Wiley B. Tait
11 Cadillacs, Atmore, AL

Mr. Roland B. Talbot
3 Cadillacs, Thibodaux, LA

Mr. Earl H. Talley
2 Cadillacs, Arab, AL

Mr. Marcus Talley
3 Cadillacs, Washington, DC

Mr. Alton J. Tallman
9 Cadillacs, Munising, MI

Mr. Ben Tamney
1 Cadillac, Midland, TX

Mr. Leonard L. Tango
1 Cadillac, Casselberry, FL

Mr. Roy T. Tanoue
2 Cadillacs, Arcadia, CA

Clare Walter Taplin
1 Cadillac, Bracebridge, ON

Mr. Clifton P. Tapo, Jr.
3 Cadillacs, Mount Morris, MI

Ms. Joan M. Tarbox
3 Cadillacs, Austin, TX

Nicholas Tardi
5 Cadillacs, Mount-Royal, QC

S. Tatar
1 Cadillac, Nanaimo, BC

Mr. Lowell E. Tate
7 Cadillacs, Wynantskill, NY

Ms. Reta N. Tate
16 Cadillacs, Picayune, MS

Mr. Wayne P. Tate
2 Cadillacs, Hixson, TN

William Tate
Depew, NY

Mr. Morris Taub
3 Cadillacs, San Pedro, CA

A. Doyle Taubert
2 Cadillacs, Baxter, TN

Jerry Tauger
2 Cadillacs, Santa Monica, CA

Mr. Alfred E. Taylor
1 Cadillac, Stafford, KS

Arelene Taylor
6 Cadillacs, Orlando, FL

Mrs. Betty J. Taylor
1 Cadillac, Fort Worth, TX

Mr. Bill B. Taylor
17 Cadillacs, Charleston, WV

Mr. Charles H. Taylor
4 Cadillacs, Harrison, AR

Mr. Elzie D. Taylor
9 Cadillacs, Wytheville, VA

Mrs. Margaret Taylor
Portsmouth, VA

Mrs. Mimi Taylor
2 Cadillacs, Huntington, NY

Ms. Muriel W. Taylor
1 Cadillac, Ft. Lauderdale, FL

Mrs. Nancy Taylor
4 Cadillacs, Atlanta, GA

Paul Taylor
1 Cadillac, North York, ON

Mr. Robert S. Taylor
2 Cadillacs, Louisville, KY

Mrs. Marcella Tebo
6 Cadillacs, Menominee, MI

Mr. Warren M. Tellefsen
11 Cadillacs, Tarpon Spgs., FL

Mr. Chester E. Tellock
1 Cadillac, Wittenberg, WI

Mr. Bertram H. Temple
6 Cadillacs, Leesburg, FL

Mr. Joseph A. Teresi
1 Cadillac, Middlebrg Hts., OH

Mr. Theodore T. Terpolilli
3 Cadillacs, Beverly Hills, FL

Mr. Lee R. Terrell
7 Cadillacs, Ft. Walton Bch., FL

Ms. Minnie L. Terrell
4 Cadillacs, Dayton, OH

Ms. Joyce M. Terrillion
3 Cadillacs, Canton, NY

Ann W. Terry
1 Cadillac, Halifax, VA

Mr. Clifford E. Terry
5 Cadillacs, Clayton, CA

Mr. Floyd G. Terry
6 Cadillacs, Ocala, FL

Ms. Patsy C. Terry
2 Cadillacs, Lampasas, TX

Mr. Val Terschluse
8 Cadillacs, Saint Louis, MO

Dr. Albert Terzian, MD
1 Cadillac, Wilmington, NC

Mr. Jeffery L. Teske
1 Cadillac, Shavertown, PA

Wilbur L. & Geri Tessman
2 Cadillacs, Champlin, MN

Mr. William D. Testory
10 Cadillacs, Longview, IL

Mr. Robert L. Testwuide
Sheboygan, WI

Leon Tetreault
11 Cadillacs, Montgomery, AL

Tony Tetuan
3 Cadillacs, W. Palm Beach, FL

Mr. Alfred J. Tetzlaff
12 Cadillacs, Woodbury, MN

Mr. Madowacharya M. Tewari
3 Cadillacs, Casselberry, FL

Mr. Roger L. Thackery
2 Cadillacs, Eastaboga, AL

Mr. Chester A. Thames
4 Cadillacs, Kenedy, TX

Mr. George Theeb
3 Cadillacs, Torrington, CT

Mrs. Katy L. Theirfelder
6 Cadillacs, Houston, TX

Mr. Donald R. Therasse
3 Cadillacs, Miami, FL

Candide Theriault
3 Cadillacs, Kedgwick, NB

Diana K. & Tom Thiel
9 Cadillacs, Upper Sandsky., OH

Mr. George T. Thodoropoulos
12 Cadillacs, Winnetka, IL

Mr. Charles Thomas
2 Cadillacs, Washington, DC

Mr. Charlie M. Thomas
5 Cadillacs, San Antonio, TX

Mr. Earl A. Thomas
3 Cadillacs, Hot Springs, AR

Erman Thomas
2 Cadillacs, Edmonton, AB

Ms. Eva Thomas
7 Cadillacs, Saint Louis, MO

Mr. Harry Thomas
7 Cadillacs, Gordonville, PA

Ms. Helen S. Thomas
6 Cadillacs, Slaughter, LA

Mr. James E. Thomas
1 Cadillac, Oregon, OH

Mr. James Thomas
4 Cadillacs, Redmond, WA

Mr. Jerald L. Thomas
9 Cadillacs, Saint Louis, MI

Mr. John Thomas
2 Cadillacs, Columbus, GA

Mr. & Mrs. R.D. Thomas
7 Cadillacs, Tonkawa, OK

Mr. David G. Thomason
4 Cadillacs, Des Moines, IA

Ms. Alma R. Thompson
1 Cadillac, San Angelo, TX

Ms. Barbara Thompson
1 Cadillac, Madison, WI

Mr. Benjamin F. Thompson
1 Cadillac, Muscle Shoals, AL

Mr. Caleb Thompson
5 Cadillacs, Sonora, CA

Mr. Carl J. Thompson
5 Cadillacs, Baton Rouge, LA

Mr. Clarence Thompson
3 Cadillacs, Ogden, KS

Elizabeth Thompson
1 Cadillac, Arlington Hts., IL

Lillian E. Thompson
2 Cadillacs, Swainsboro, GA

Mr. Michael L. Thompson
3 Cadillacs, Ormond Beach, FL

Mr. Ralph T. Thompson
2 Cadillacs, Saint Paul, MN

Ms. Sally M. Thompson
6 Cadillacs, Oshkosh, WI

Mr. Thomas M. Thompson
3 Cadillacs, Oxnard, CA

Mr. Wilbur W. Thompson
3 Cadillacs, Sun City, AZ

Mr. William Thompson
1 Cadillac, Clarendon Hls., IL

Mr. William Thompson
5 Cadillacs, Tacoma, WA

Wilson Edward Thompson
7 Cadillacs, Long Beach, CA

Mr. Glenn N. Thorgrimson
2 Cadillacs, Minneapolis, MN

Mr. Arthur J. Thornthwaite
6 Cadillacs, Moulton, AL

Mr. Charles M. Thornton
Waterboro, ME

Mr. Homer L. Thornton
7 Cadillacs, Zwolle, LA

Mr. Verne F. Thornton
9 Cadillacs, Wichita, KS

Mr. Mitchel A. Thrasher, Jr.
3 Cadillacs, Walnut Grove, AL

Mrs. Nancy Thumm
8 Cadillacs, Richboro, PA

Mr. Gerald R. Thurman
4 Cadillacs, Jacksonville, TX

John Thwaites
2 Cadillacs, Jackson, NJ

Mr. Dale A. Thwaits
11 Cadillacs, Bristol, IN

Mrs. Nadine E. Thyfault
6 Cadillacs, Lolo, MT

Mr. J.L. Tibbs
5 Cadillacs, Tulsa, OK

Mr. James M. Tibbs
2 Cadillacs, Mesa, AZ

Mr. Charles L. Tice
6 Cadillacs, St. Augustine, FL

Amos C. Ticehurst
7 Cadillacs, White River Jct., VT

Ronald Tidmarsh
15 Cadillacs, Old Lyme, CT

Mr. James G. Tidwell
Nashville, TN

Ms. Ramona L. Tidwell
6 Cadillacs, Joplin, MO

Mr. Samuel Tiller
4 Cadillacs, Burlington, NJ

J.B. & Clyde C. Tillery, Jr.
2 Cadillacs, Porterville, CA

Mr. Bobby B. Tilley
1 Cadillac, Blowing Rock, NC

Mr. Andre Tillman, Jr.
3 Cadillacs, Bogart, GA

Norman D. Tillman
Albany, NY

Mary Ellen E. Tillmon
3 Cadillacs, Waterford Wks., NJ

Mr. Donald O. Tilton
Portland, ME

W.W. Timbes
9 Cadillacs, Tupelo, MS

J. Timko
1 Cadillac, Burlington, ON

Mr. Joseph A. Tinsley
3 Cadillacs, Marble Hill, MO

Paul & Susan Tinsley
8 Cadillacs, Baton Rouge, LA

Mr. Edward J. Tippen
3 Cadillacs, Kennett, MO

Mr. Alvin E. Tisch
4 Cadillacs, Grandview, MO

Al M. Tisdale
5 Cadillacs, Oberlin, OH

Mr. Clayton M. Tittsworth
15 Cadillacs, Brandon, FL

Izella Todd
9 Cadillacs, Detroit, MI

Mr. John Todd
28 Cadillacs, San Diego, CA

Mr. A. Toews
1 Cadillac, Saskatoon, SK

Betty S. Tolbert-Smith
5 Cadillacs, Carrollton, GA

Mr. Frederic W. Tolbert
8 Cadillacs, Thousand Oaks, CA

Preston & Roberta Tolliver
5 Cadillacs, Washington, DC

Fred H. & Doris Tolzien
Morton Grove, IL

Mr. Robert M. Tolzien
2 Cadillacs, Glenview, IL

Mr. George J. Tomidy
14 Cadillacs, Sanford, NC

Mrs. Mary Toms
2 Cadillacs, Toms River, NJ

Mr. Jeffrey D. Tonne
4 Cadillacs, Fairmont, MN

Mr. Harold M. Topletz
12 Cadillacs, Dallas, TX

Ms. Shirley L. Torkelson
2 Cadillacs, Henning, MN

Michael S. Torrence
Morganton, NC

Mr. William A. Tosh
2 Cadillacs, Fort Worth, TX

Mr. Albert T. Totka
7 Cadillacs, Perth Amboy, NJ

Mr. Donald L. Toupin
6 Cadillacs, N. Smithfield, RI

Mr. Lyman D. Tout
8 Cadillacs, Fort McCoy, FL

Mrs. Mildred Townes
7 Cadillacs, Petersburg, VA

Rev. & Mrs. Jerry Townsend
3 Cadillacs, Kannapolis, NC

Mr. Lewis Townsend
3 Cadillacs, Manila, AR

Mrs. Debra Traichevich
1 Cadillac, St. Thomas, ON

Mr. George N. Trakas
3 Cadillacs, Garden City, NY

Ms. Lois Traktman
Brooklyn, NY

Mrs. Euphemia R. Trame
2 Cadillacs, N. Fort Meyers, FL

Mr. Fredrick A. Trascher, Jr.
2 Cadillacs, Houston, TX

Diane Trask
2 Cadillacs, Boca Raton, FL

Mr. Harvey J. Trask
2 Cadillacs, Upton, MA

Ms. Geraldine R. Traugott
5 Cadillacs, San Antonio, TX

Mr. Frank J. Traversi
31 Cadillacs, Austin, TX

D. Travis
1 Cadillac, Calgary, AB

Howard Travis
3 Cadillacs, New York, NY

Elaine & Navarre Traylor, Sr.
4 Cadillacs, Independence, LA

Ms. Marion C. Treger
10 Cadillacs, Bradenton, FL

Mr. Alfred V. Trenne
4 Cadillacs, Fergus Falls, MN

Ms. Margaret Treviso
7 Cadillacs, Kings Mtn., NC

Mrs. Mary B. Trice
4 Cadillacs, Pontiac, MI

Mr. Gerald R. Trieschmann
1 Cadillac, Ballwin, MO

Mr. Arnold C. Trimble
4 Cadillacs, Nicholasville, KY

Anthony Trinca
7 Cadillacs, Columbus, OH

Mr. Ira C. Triplett, Jr.
7 Cadillacs, Lenoir, NC

Rupert A. Triplitt
1 Cadillac, Columbus, GA

Mr. Marvin W. Tripp
1 Cadillac, Hemphill, TX

Mr. Oscar P. Tripp
1 Cadillac, Piedmont, SC

Mr. N. Trochatos
1 Cadillac, Saint-Laurent, QC

Mr. John W. Troffa
5 Cadillacs, Glen Cove, NY

Stavroula Trohatos
1 Cadillac, Saint-Laurent, QC

Mrs. Irving J. Trombley
8 Cadillacs, St. Petersburg, FL

Mr. Alfred C. Trossen
7 Cadillacs, Portland, OR

Ermon Trotter
3 Cadillacs, Saint Louis, MO

Mr. George Trout
3 Cadillacs, Lawton, OK

Colonel Baldwin L. Troutman
2 Cadillacs, Newnan, GA

Mr. Harry L. Troutman
5 Cadillacs, La Jolla, CA

Mr. Roy P. Trowbridge
25 Cadillacs, Menominee, MI

Ms. June Truman
3 Cadillacs, Portsmouth, OH

William E. Trumpler
3 Cadillacs, St. Pete. Bch., FL

Mr. Clyde Trusch
1 Cadillac, Lively, VA

Mr. James F. Trusley
5 Cadillacs, Zephyrhills, FL

Mr. Ted E. Tschappler
4 Cadillacs, Chamois, MO

Mr. Minoru Tsubota
1 Cadillac, Mercer Island, WA

Charlotte & Robert E. Tubbs
3 Cadillacs, Lake Worth, FL

Mr. Charles Tucker
4 Cadillacs, Newport News, VA

Grace M. Tucker
8 Cadillacs, Amissville, VA

Mr. Henry J. Tucker
3 Cadillacs, Klamath Falls, OR

Jane E. Tucker
2 Cadillacs, Emporia, VA

Mr. Shelton M. Tucker
3 Cadillacs, Ocean Island, NC

Mr. William Tudor, Jr.
2 Cadillacs, Monrovia, IN

Myrtle Tufford
4 Cadillacs, Beamsville, ON

Mr. Robert T. Tuite
Toledo, OH

Mr. Richard Tung
1 Cadillac, Amarillo, TX

Gene Tunney
1 Cadillac, Calgary, AB

Mr. Nicholas Tuorto
2 Cadillacs, Toms River, NJ

Mr. John E. Turgeon
2 Cadillacs, Chicopee, MA

Mr. Steve Turlis
6 Cadillacs, Tacoma, WA

R. Turner
1 Cadillac, Orleans, ON

Mr. Roy E. Turner
10 Cadillacs, Ft. Lauderdale, FL

Mr. Rupert Turner
4 Cadillacs, Johnsonville, SC

W.D. Turner
16 Cadillacs, Columbia, TN

Mr. Keith M. Turnham
16 Cadillacs, San Diego, CA

Mr. Daniel L. Tursell
6 Cadillacs, St. Clair Shrs., MI

Ms. Allie R. Twete
1 Cadillac, Selby, SD

Mr. Robert J. Twohig
1 Cadillac, Oak Lawn, IL

Mr. Joseph J. Tylka
1 Cadillac, Stevens Point, WI

Mr. Leonard R. Tyndall
3 Cadillacs, Linden, NJ

Mr. William M. Tyner
3 Cadillacs, Longview, TX

U

Mr. Gerald L. Udelhofen
5 Cadillacs, Dubuque, IA

Mr. Eugene H. Uhler
15 Cadillacs, Naples, FL

Mr. William A. Ullmark
12 Cadillacs, Summerfield, FL

Mrs. Dolores Ulrich
3 Cadillacs, Lake, MI

Ms. Martha A. Ulrich
10 Cadillacs, Dearborn, MI

William Underwood
27 Cadillacs, Sebring, FL

Robert Upshall
1 Cadillac, London, ON

Mr. John Urban
1 Cadillac, Bristol, RI

Mr. Edward J. Urbanek
10 Cadillacs, Osage Beach, MO

Mr. Morris M. Uroff
7 Cadillacs, Yorba Linda, CA

Leryes Usie
1 Cadillac, Bourg, LA

Mr. Leroy H. Utne
5 Cadillacs, Minneapolis, MN

V

Mr. Antonio Vacca
2 Cadillacs, Pittsburgh, PA

Ms. Suzanne Vacheresse
2 Cadillacs, Washington, PA

Andre Vaive
1 Cadillac, Hull, QC

John C. Valentine
1 Cadillac, Getzville, NY

Mr. John Valerio
5 Cadillacs, Hauppauge, NY

Mr. Frank J. Valka
1 Cadillac, San Antonio, TX

Mr. Gene F. Valley
3 Cadillacs, Ft. Lauderdale, FL

Mr. Charles Valvo
3 Cadillacs, Delray Beach, FL

Francis Van Antwerp, Sr.
5 Cadillacs, Cheboygan, MI

Carolyn Jean Van Buren
1 Cadillac, Flint, MI

Larry & Betty Van Eerden
12 Cadillacs, Roy, UT

Mr. Gerald Vance
4 Cadillacs, Gulfport, MS

Mr. John R. Vandegrift
4 Cadillacs, Lakeland, FL

Mr. Robert D. Vandenberg
2 Cadillacs, Plymouth, MN

Georges Vandeneynde
3 Cadillacs, Oshawa, ON

Clarence Vander Bleek, Jr.
1 Cadillac, Fulton, IL

Herman & Debby Vandevender
7 Cadillacs, Virginia Beach, VA

Mr. Cornelis Vandorp
1 Cadillac, La Habra, CA

Mae VanDyke
5 Cadillacs, Kalamazoo, MI

Mr. Cleophos Vann
1 Cadillac, Birmingham, AL

Mr. Russell Vann
13 Cadillacs, Norfolk, VA

James Vanzant
6 Cadillacs, Carlsbad, NM

Henry & Lillian Varetoni
4 Cadillacs, Denville, NJ

Ms. Norma P. Vargas
2 Cadillacs, Laredo, TX

Mr. Thomas Varner
5 Cadillacs, Roanoke, VA

Mr. Robert W. Varney
1 Cadillac, Lisbon, NH

Mr. Thomas Vasilakis
2 Cadillacs, Sn. Bernrdno., CA

Mr. Pete Vasilakos
1 Cadillac, Edison, NJ

Mr. John Vasilchin
3 Cadillacs, Las Vegas, NV

Mr. Albert Vaughn
4 Cadillacs, Lawton, OK

Mrs. Winifred A. Vaughn
3 Cadillacs, Slaton, TX

Mr. Woodrow R. Vaughn
8 Cadillacs, Greer, SC

Mr. Dennis Vawerchak
1 Cadillac, Kensington, PA

Mr. Roosevelt Veal
13 Cadillacs, Jackson, MS

Mr. David A. Veder
3 Cadillacs, Cincinnati, OH

Mr. Arthur T. Veilleux
27 Cadillacs, Danielson, CT

Mr. Gerald Velzen
1 Cadillac, Grandville, MI

Zal Venet
25 Cadillacs, Stroudsburg, PA

Mr. Michael J. Veneziano
3 Cadillacs, Nutley, NJ

Mr. Lewis A. Venters, Sr.
4 Cadillacs, Wilmington, NC

Mr. Nelson D. Ventura
5 Cadillacs, Brooklyn, NY

Mr. James M. Vereker
8 Cadillacs, McAllen, TX

G. Verwey
2 Cadillacs, Hamilton, ON

Mr. Anthony M. Vesel
7 Cadillacs, Clearwater, FL

Vertle J. Vestal
1 Cadillac, Jonesville, NC

Mr. Dalton C. Via
5 Cadillacs, Senath, MO

James Earl Vick
1 Cadillac, Harkers Is., NC

Dr. Marian L. Vick
3 Cadillacs, Greensboro, NC

Wallace Vick
5 Cadillacs, Demopolis, AL

Mr. George A. Vidrine
14 Cadillacs, Hope Mills, NC

Julius J. Vieira
22 Cadillacs, Farmington Hls., MI

Linda Dell'Arciprete Vigon
Jersey City, NJ

Mr. Lucio A. Villegas
10 Cadillacs, Trabuco Cyn., CA

Mr. N. Villella
2 Cadillacs, Welland, ON

Grace C. Vincent
12 Cadillacs, Richmond, VA

Mr. James L. Vincent
3 Cadillacs, Vinton, LA

Mr. P. Vincent
1 Cadillac, Burlington, ON

Mr. Robert V. Vincil
4 Cadillacs, N. Little Rock, AR

Mr. Richard L. Vinson
1 Cadillac, Brandon, MS

Mr. Willford C. Vinson
50 Cadillacs, Safford, AZ

Mrs. Anna R. Vitale
10 Cadillacs, E. Rockaway, NY

Dr. Thomas Vitale
10 Cadillacs, Daytona Bch., FL

Mr. Donald Vlcek, Jr.
5 Cadillacs, Plymouth, MI

Mr. Raymond J. Volluz
8 Cadillacs, Austin, TX

Mr. Lloyd Volz
3 Cadillacs, Greensburg, KS

Mr. Charles A. Voncanon
1 Cadillac, Sanford, NC

Don V. vonRentzell
3 Cadillacs, Ashland, NE

Charles R. Votaw, Sr.
3 Cadillacs, Springfield, KY

Mr. Rickey Votaw
1 Cadillac, Ashley, OH

Orrie Vraa
Wolf Point, MT

W

Mr. David F. Wade
29 Cadillacs, Santa Barbara, CA

Mr. James L. Wade
5 Cadillacs, Oklahoma City, OK

Ms. Louise A. Wade
4 Cadillacs, Raleigh, NC

Ms. Margaret Wagar
6 Cadillacs, Redondo Beach, CA

V. Wagar
9 Cadillacs, Napanee, ON

Mr. Kenneth R. Waggoner
10 Cadillacs, Charleston, SC

Mr. Curt E. Wagner
3 Cadillacs, Mandan, ND

Mrs. Janie P. Wagner
5 Cadillacs, Shreveport, LA

Mr. John A. Wagner
4 Cadillacs, Sarasota, FL

L. Wagner
1 Cadillac, Carleton, NS

Mr. Leon A. Wagner
2 Cadillacs, Madison, WI

Ms. Patricia M. Wagner
3 Cadillacs, Elko, MN

Mr. Willis W. Wagner
5 Cadillacs, Crookston, MN

Mr. Edward R. Wahlenfeld
4 Cadillacs, Oakbrook Ter., IL

John Wain, M.D.
9 Cadillacs, Vail, CO

Mr. Robert P. Wainwright
7 Cadillacs, Jacksonville, FL

Mr. Gene C. Wakefield
1 Cadillac, Scottsdale, AZ

Mr. Richard F. Walburn
7 Cadillacs, Sioux City, IA

Mr. Marvin Walden
2 Cadillacs, Montgomery, AL

Mr. Russell W. Waldo
4 Cadillacs, Saint Paul, MN

Mr. Abraham L. Walker
1 Cadillac, Smyrna, SC

Mr. Ben Walker, Jr.
2 Cadillacs, Arlington, VA

Mrs. Betty Walker
3 Cadillacs, Walla Walla, WA

Mr. Henry Walker
4 Cadillacs, Beaconsfield, QC

Mr. James Walker
3 Cadillacs, Columbus, GA

Mr. James Walker
4 Cadillacs, Lower Burrell, PA

Dr. John A. Walker
3 Cadillacs, Oakdale, LA

LaVerne & Foy Walker
3 Cadillacs, Ellaville, GA

Mr. Marvin Walker
5 Cadillacs, Mt. Pleasant, TX

Mr. Paul D. Walker
1 Cadillac, Shreveport, LA

Mr. Paul D. Walker
5 Cadillacs, Eugene, OR

Mrs. Reathel Walker
6 Cadillacs, Bristol, IN

Mr. & Mrs. Robert Walker
2 Cadillacs, Madera, CA

Mr. David P. Walkey
Kingsport, TN

MaDonna A. Walkner
4 Cadillacs, Cedar Rapids, IA

Mr. Jame O. Wall
5 Cadillacs, Saint George, UT

Mr. Clarence L. Wallace
2 Cadillacs, Olathe, CO

Mr. Earnest Wallace
17 Cadillacs, Detroit, MI

Mr. Lionel M. Wallace
3 Cadillacs, Vassar, MI

Marie Wallaert
12 Cadillacs, Mundelein, IL

Mr. Ansel W. Waller
5 Cadillacs, Sherman, TX

Lynn Waller
8 Cadillacs, Cadiz, KY

Mrs. Virginia P. Waller
8 Cadillacs, Meherrin, VA

Mr. Frank B. Wallis, Jr.
8 Cadillacs, Scottsdale, AZ

P. Douglas Wallquist
6 Cadillacs, Salamanca, NY

Mr. Michael J. Walsh, Jr.
2 Cadillacs, Holiday, FL

Mrs. Marietta F. Walter
2 Cadillacs, Hale, MI

Ms. Neva E. Walter
5 Cadillacs, Columbus, OH

Mr. Carl J. Walters
4 Cadillacs, Cincinnati, OH

Mr. Larry D. Walters
1 Cadillac, Janesville, IA

Mr. Richard B. Walters
Scarsdale, NY

Ruth H. Walters
Winston Salem, NC

Walter Walters
15 Cadillacs, Dearborn, MI

Mr. Eric A. Waltersheid
3 Cadillacs, Huntington Pk., CA

Mr. Michael J. Waltner
2 Cadillacs, Lake Wales, FL

Mr. Eugene I. Walton
5 Cadillacs, Dayton, OH

Velma & Charles Walton
1 Cadillac, Conyers, GA

Mr. Harold R. Wampler
4 Cadillacs, Springfield, MO

Ms. Nancy T. Wampler
2 Cadillacs, Charlotte, NC

Billy M. Wansley, M.D.
1 Cadillac, Biloxi, MS

Harold & Roxie Warbritton
5 Cadillacs, Danville, IL

Ms. Anna M. Ward
2 Cadillacs, Oakland, CA

Mr. Norman Ward
6 Cadillacs, Lafayette, CA

Dr. Patrick C. Ward
4 Cadillacs, Duluth, MN

Mr. Robert B. Ward
1 Cadillac, Leicester, MA

Mr. Edmond Warde
8 Cadillacs, Hampton, VA

Mr. Jesse L. Wardle
2 Cadillacs, Boise, ID

Mr. George Ware
3 Cadillacs, Brandon, MS

Mr. Morris D. Warner
2 Cadillacs, Moro, IL

Mr. Woodrow Warner
2 Cadillacs, Columbus, GA

Richard Warnimont
5 Cadillacs, Zephyrhills, FL

Alois Peter Warren, II
5 Cadillacs, Detroit, MI

Mr. Keith Warren
8 Cadillacs, Fenelon Falls, ON

Mr. Roy Warren
2 Cadillacs, Higden, AR

James Warthman
5 Cadillacs, Alma, MI

Mr. Percy Washington
3 Cadillacs, Columbus, OH

Mr. Frank G. Wasmer
17 Cadillacs, Williamsville, NY

Mr. Charles Waters
1 Cadillac, Wichita, KS

Mr. Perry L. Waters, Jr.
2 Cadillacs, San Diego, CA

Mr. Ronald E. Waters
2 Cadillacs, Buffalo, NY

Dr. David W. Watkins
1 Cadillac, Los Alamos, NM

Mr. Doyal Watkins
7 Cadillacs, Roseville, MI

Mr. Robert E. Watkins
1 Cadillac, Meadview, AZ

Ms. Betty A. Watson
1 Cadillac, Hurst, TX

Mr. & Mrs. Charles Watts
14 Cadillacs, Atlanta, GA

Claude D. Watts
6 Cadillacs, Southaven, MS

Mr. William G. Watts, Jr.
8 Cadillacs, Carrollton, TX

Mr. Robert Wavrek
1 Cadillac, Daytona Beach, FL

Mr. Richard Wayland
3 Cadillacs, Greenville, PA

Mr. Max E. Wear
4 Cadillacs, Quincy, IL

Mr. Patricia Weatherford
2 Cadillacs, Harriman, TN

Mr. Edward W. Weaver
2 Cadillacs, Columbus, OH

Jerry L. & Dorothy E. Weaver
5 Cadillacs, Decatur, IL

Jim Weaver
1 Cadillac, Climax, GA

Mr. Boyd C. Webb
4 Cadillacs, Dayton, OH

Mr. Harold T. Webb
2 Cadillacs, Webb City, MO

Mr. Herbert E. Webb
1 Cadillac, St. Mary's, GA

Mr. Joseph L. Webb
4 Cadillacs, Sun City Ctr., FL

Mr. Arthur J. Weber, Jr.
1 Cadillac, Mobile, AL

Mr. Howard L. Weber
1 Cadillac, Farmingtn Hls., MI

Ms. Mary H. Weber
1 Cadillac, Charleston, WV

Mr. Mike E. Weber
8 Cadillacs, Shreveport, LA

Arthur Webster
1 Cadillac, Etobicoke, ON

Mr. Robert A. Webster
4 Cadillacs, Cary, IL

Mrs. Fred Wedincamp
6 Cadillacs, Jesup, GA

Horton Weeks
2 Cadillacs, Vero Beach, FL

Mr. Joshua S. Weeks, Jr.
3 Cadillacs, Charleston, SC

Mr. Wallace H. Weerts
3 Cadillacs, Decatur, IL

Mr. Frederick E. Wegner
4 Cadillacs, Manitowoc, WI

Ms. Alma K. Weida
3 Cadillacs, Aurora, OH

Mr. Robert G. Weidner
2 Cadillacs, Middletown, OH

Mr. Harold C. Weiner
26 Cadillacs, Sarasota, FL

Mr. Kenneth Weingart
10 Cadillacs, Freehold, NJ

Mr. Murray H. Weinkrantz
3 Cadillacs, Lake Worth, FL

Robert Weinreich
2 Cadillacs, Fremont, CA

Dr. Frederick Weinstein
9 Cadillacs, Baltimore, MD

Capt. & Mrs. Wm. E. Weisert
3 Cadillacs, Sun Lakes, AZ

Mr. Martin Weiss
1 Cadillac, Mahopac, NY

Ms. Virginia H. Weitfle
3 Cadillacs, Cincinnati, OH

Albert Welch
7 Cadillacs, Clarkston, MI

Mr. William K. Welch
Rusk, TX

Mr. Theodore V. Weld
6 Cadillacs, Sarasota, FL

Mr. Arnold Wells
4 Cadillacs, Paintsville, KY

Mr. Irving C. Wells
15 Cadillacs, Houston, TX

Ms. Mabel Wells
5 Cadillacs, Quitman, TX

Mr. Marvin K. Wells
4 Cadillacs, Cincinnati, OH

Mary Nell Wells
6 Cadillacs, Valdosta, GA

Mr. Raymond E. Wells
1 Cadillac, Picayune, MS

Mr. Lowrie Welton
5 Cadillacs, Midwest City, OK

J. Joe Wenck
3 Cadillacs, Cincinnati, OH

Ms. Helen Wencl
2 Cadillacs, Smyrna, GA

Richard L. Wendricks, Sr.
2 Cadillacs, Green Bay, WI

Mr. William Wenner
Gloucester City, NJ

Leonard Wenninger
7 Cadillacs, Parma, OH

Mr. Jerry L. Wentz
2 Cadillacs, Tucson, AZ

Mr. & Mrs. Jerome A. Wenzel
4 Cadillacs, Abbotsford, WI

Mr. Albert F. Werner
4 Cadillacs, Holliston, MA

Mr. Robert E. Werner
17 Cadillacs, Buffalo, NY

Mr. J. Westell
1 Cadillac, Kincardine, ON

Mr. Walter Westergard
1 Cadillac, Hawarden, IA

Ms. Ella A. Westermeyer
3 Cadillacs, Superior, WI

Mr. Merritt R. Westfall
2 Cadillacs, Ballston Spa, NY

Mr. Harold L. Westhoff
5 Cadillacs, Litchfield, IL

Kurt D. Westlund
10 Cadillacs, Ozona, FL

Mr. Elijah B. Westmoreland
5 Cadillacs, Abilene, TX

T.J. Wethey
2 Cadillacs, Geneva, NY

Mr. Henry C. Wexelblatt
7 Cadillacs, E. Stroudsburg, PA

Mrs. Saroline S. Weygandt
Pinehurst, NC

Mr. Rudy G. Weyland
3 Cadillacs, Wixom, MI

Marie G. Whaley
1 Cadillac, Dunn, NC

Mr. Walter Wheatley
11 Cadillacs, Detroit, MI

James Wheeler
21 Cadillacs, Nashville, TN

Ms. Jean M. Whipp
1 Cadillac, Orlando, FL

Mr. Calvin White
1 Cadillac, Franklin, MA

Chester White
6 Cadillacs, Venice, FL

Elton R. White
1 Cadillac, Burton, OH

Florence G. White
2 Cadillacs, Statesboro, GA

Mr. Frank R. White
4 Cadillacs, Vernon, CT

Mr. Harry R. White, Jr.
6 Cadillacs, Peterborough, NH

John White
8 Cadillacs, Lockport, NY

Ms. Julia White
2 Cadillacs, Headland, AL

Mr. Nelson L. White, Jr.
3 Cadillacs, Kingston, NY

Mr. Robert E. White
6 Cadillacs, Pinehurst, NC

Russell White
5 Cadillacs, Taylor Mill, KY

Mr. Edward L. Whitfield
5 Cadillacs, Jacksonville, FL

Mr. Everett J. Whitfield
5 Cadillacs, Niles, MI

Mr. Billy A. Whitley
4 Cadillacs, Baytown, TX

Mr. John J. Whitman
4 Cadillacs, Beckley, WV

John T. & Mildred Whitmore
3 Cadillacs, Cleveland, OH

Mr. Robert Whittemore
5 Cadillacs, Augusta, ME

Mr. James M. Whitten
4 Cadillacs, Gloucester, MA

Mr. Robert M. Whittington
8 Cadillacs, Cranberry Twp., PA

Siney A. Whittington
3 Cadillacs, Cary, NC

J.C. Whittle
10 Cadillacs, Oklahoma Cty., OK

Mr. Joseph Whitworth, Jr.
8 Cadillacs, Houston, TX

Thaddius P. Wicker
3 Cadillacs, Arlington Hts., IL

Clayton Wideman
1 Cadillac, Elmira, ON

Mr. Douglas Widger-Qualls
10 Cadillacs, Vallejo, CA

Ms. Nancy C. Wiedbusch
5 Cadillacs, Shelby Twp., MI

Mr. Robert A. Wiemer
2 Cadillacs, Fair Oaks, CA

Mr. Walter C. Wiencek
1 Cadillac, Lexington, NC

Samuel Wiener
6 Cadillacs, Pompano Beach, FL

Mr. Lorenz Wiens
1 Cadillac, Edmonton, AB

Mr. William P. Wigal
1 Cadillac, Cuyahoga Fls., OH

Mrs. Anne Wiggs
6 Cadillacs, Augusta, GA

Dr. Earl B. Wigodsky
3 Cadillacs, Omaha, NE

Mr. Donald L. Wilbert
4 Cadillacs, Bountiful, UT

Ms. Louise T. Wilborn
20 Cadillacs, Tupelo, MS

Willie & Ellie Wilburn
5 Cadillacs, San Diego, CA

Andrew Wilcox
2 Cadillacs, New Church, VA

Ms. Frances W. Wildasin
4 Cadillacs, Johnson City, TN

Ms. Edith F. Wilder
6 Cadillacs, McCalla, AL

Mrs. Ruth T. Wiles
1 Cadillac, Chesapeake, VA

Mr. Bert Wiley
3 Cadillacs, Cardston, AB

Mr. Verlin D. Wilhite
1 Cadillac, Kirksville, MO

Mr. Roy L. Wilimzig
16 Cadillacs, Edwardsville, IL

Ms. Mary P. Wilkerson
4 Cadillacs, Mobile, AL

Mrs. Constance L. Wilkie
5 Cadillacs, St. Petersburg, FL

Mr. Joe R. Wilkins
9 Cadillacs, Carlsbad, NM

Mr. Ernest M. Wilkinson, Jr.
Covington, VA

Dorrence Wilkison
2 Cadillacs, Orange City, FL

Mr. Richard D. Will
1 Cadillac, Kalamazoo, MI

Crusoe Williams
1 Cadillac, Homestead, PA

Mr. Dennis Williams
3 Cadillacs, Saginaw, MI

Mr. Dominic Williams
1 Cadillac, Hobart, IN

Earl R. Williams
20 Cadillacs, Arlington, TX

Mr. Ebb Williams
Columbus, OH

Eudoris D. Williams
3 Cadillacs, Huntington, WV

Ms. Evelyn Williams
5 Cadillacs, Rogers, AR

Mr. George A. Williams
6 Cadillacs, Bridgeville, PA

Mr. Henry Williams
1 Cadillac, Mount Morris, MI

Mr. Herman Williams
5 Cadillacs, Valois, NY

James & Renee Williams
5 Cadillacs, River Rouge, MI

Jo Williams
7 Cadillacs, Marietta, GA

Mr. John D. Williams
3 Cadillacs, Murfreesboro, TN

Mr. Joseph M. Williams
9 Cadillacs, Biloxi, MS

Mr. Leo Williams
4 Cadillacs, Annapolis, MD

Ms. Lorraine Williams
1 Cadillac, Richmond, VA

Minna Lee Williams
3 Cadillacs, Glen Ridge, NJ

Ms. Ora I. Williams
4 Cadillacs, Tucker, GA

Mr. Otis E. Williams
3 Cadillacs, Danville, IL

Mr. & Mrs. Ray Williams
2 Cadillacs, Tatum, TX

Mr. Richard B. Williams
1 Cadillac, Osburn, ID

Richard Williams
10 Cadillacs, Bloomfield, MI

Ms. Thelma O. Williams
5 Cadillacs, Lehi, UT

Thomas Williams
4 Cadillacs, Fairview Hts., IL

Thomas Williams
4 Cadillacs, Broadus, MT

Mr. William M. Williams
1 Cadillac, Roosevelt, NY

Mr. William W. Williams
6 Cadillacs, Syracuse, NY

Willie L. Williams
8 Cadillacs, Detroit, MI

Dorcus J. Williamson
2 Cadillacs, Andalusia, AL

Mr. Doyle J. Williamson
2 Cadillacs, Ft. Walton Bch., FL

John Scott Williamson
4 Cadillacs, San Diego, CA

S. Williamson
1 Cadillac, Toronto, ON

Mr. Winfred Williamson
10 Cadillacs, Norfolk, VA

Mr. Benjamin Willingham, Sr.
1 Cadillac, Pontiac, MI

Mr. Elmo Willis
2 Cadillacs, Phoenix, AZ

Joseph & Mary A. Willis
1 Cadillac, Albany, GA

Ms. Sarah J. Willis
4 Cadillacs, Granite, OK

Mr. Robert D. Willits
2 Cadillacs, South Pasadena, FL

Robert D. Willits
2 Cadillacs, St. Petersburg, FL

Mr. Kenneth E. Willman
1 Cadillac, Schenectady, NY

Mr. Bernard F. Wills
5 Cadillacs, Wellfleet, MA

Mr. Zack E. Willson
1 Cadillac, Delaware, OH

Cleo & Darnell Y. Wilson
4 Cadillacs, El Paso, TX

Ms. Elizabeth S. Wilson
1 Cadillac, Pensacola, FL

Ms. Elizabeth G. Wilson
12 Cadillacs, Rock Hill, SC

Mr. Francis M. Wilson
6 Cadillacs, Columbia, MO

Mr. Hoover Wilson
7 Cadillacs, Gardendale, AL

Icelene & James W. Wilson
3 Cadillacs, Sandusky, OH

Mr. John E. Wilson
1 Cadillac, Harker Heights, TX

Mr. & Mrs. Leroy Wilson
4 Cadillacs, Thomson, GA

Mr. Melvin Wilson, Jr.
1 Cadillac, Franklin, LA

Dr. James E. Winchell
3 Cadillacs, Beatrice, NE

Tom Winchell & J.C. Pullins
3 Cadillacs, Columbus, OH

Mr. Nelson E. Windsor
Lakewood, CA

Ms. Fannie M. Wine
3 Cadillacs, Prospect, OH

Mrs. Rose E. Wing
2 Cadillacs, Atlanta, GA

Mr. Wayne C. Winslow
10 Cadillacs, Naples, FL

Mr. Glenn L. Winstead
6 Cadillacs, Cobden, IL

Clarence & Pearle Winters
10 Cadillacs, Bloomfield, MI

Mr. Emil J. Wirkus
1 Cadillac, Saint Paul, MN

Milton L. Wiscott, Jr.
3 Cadillacs, Gambrills, MD

Ms. Delphine E. Wise
1 Cadillac, Tallmadge, OH

Mrs. Lucile F. Wise
8 Cadillacs, Defuniak Spgs., FL

Harold & Sarah A. Wisecup
Grove City, OH

Mr. Harold J. Wisenbaugh
3 Cadillacs, Loveland, OH

John Wisniewski
6 Cadillacs, Scotia, NY

Mr. Albert C. Wissel
5 Cadillacs, Cockeysville, MD

Rev. Irvin R. Witcher
3 Cadillacs, Columbus, OH

Mr. Arthur F. Withers
3 Cadillacs, Sandpoint, ID

Mr. Russel R. Withrow, Sr.
4 Cadillacs, Beckley, WV

Ann S. Witkin
1 Cadillac, Fort Lee, NJ

Dr. & Mrs George J. Witkin
14 Cadillacs, Daytona Bch., FL

Mr. George J. Witkin
1 Cadillac, Fort Lee, NJ

Mrs. Elizabeth R. Witsil
9 Cadillacs, Hendersonvlle, TN

Mr. Vernon Witt
4 Cadillacs, Shawnee, KS

Roy Witte
6 Cadillacs, Inverness, IL

Mr. Gilbert F. Witzke
8 Cadillacs, Oshkosh, WI

Mr. Edward M. Woare
4 Cadillacs, Decatur, IL

Nestor Wojcichowsky
4 Cadillacs, Theodore, SK

Mr. Chester Wojcik
La Grange, IL

Mr. Walter J. Wojnar
4 Cadillacs, South Grafton, MA

Mr. Stanley W. Wojtalik
8 Cadillacs, Detroit, MI

Mr. Henry S. Wolanski
11 Cadillacs, Fort Worth, TX

Mr. George M. Wold
3 Cadillacs, Barron, WI

Mr. Bruce Wolf
5 Cadillacs, Pittsburgh, PA

Kline R. Wolf
2 Cadillacs, Howard, PA

Ms. Suzanne Wolsten
2 Cadillacs, Deerfield Bch., FL

Mr. John D. Womack
9 Cadillacs, Bonne Terre, MO

Mr. Mervin D. Womack
Sun City West, AZ

Arnold L. Womer
2 Cadillacs, Highland Bch., FL

Mr. Kenny B. Won
2 Cadillacs, Los Angeles, CA

Mr. Carlos O. Wood
5 Cadillacs, Saint George, UT

Mr. Earl J. Wood
2 Cadillacs, Fayetteville, WV

Mr. Early Wood
6 Cadillacs, Martinsville, VA

Mr. James Wood
4 Cadillacs, Marietta, GA

Lois M. Wood
8 Cadillacs, Marshall, TX

Ms. Melba Wood
5 Cadillacs, Homestead, FL

Mr. Richard C. Wood
12 Cadillacs, Crossville, TN

Mr. Richard J. Wood
5 Cadillacs, Bluefield, WV

Mr. Robbie D. Wood, Sr.
12 Cadillacs, Dolomite, AL

Dr. & Mrs. Robert C. Wood
29 Cadillacs, Clarkston, MI

Mr. Robert E. Wood
7 Cadillacs, Albany, NY

Donald W. Woodard
7 Cadillacs, Indianapolis, IN

Irene Woodard
2 Cadillacs, Gary, IN

Mr. James Woodard
2 Cadillacs, Albany, IN

Ms. Peggy S. Woodard
3 Cadillacs, Rocky Mount, NC

Mr. Rodges L. Woodard
8 Cadillacs, Richmond, CA

Mr. William B. Woodard
3 Cadillacs, Avinger, TX

Mr. Neil M. Woodcock
6 Cadillacs, Atkinson, NC

Mr. Earl Woodruff
4 Cadillacs, Pittsburg, CA

Mr. Homer G. Woods
4 Cadillacs, Morganton, NC

Lloyd Woods
14 Cadillacs, Richmond, VA

Norman & Carmelita Woods
2 Cadillacs, Pomona, CA

Mr. William F. Woods, Sr.
23 Cadillacs, Vidor, TX

Mr. Richard Woodson
2 Cadillacs, Coalinga, CA

Mr. Thomas N. Woodson
10 Cadillacs, Ocean Island, NC

Mr. Ed J. Wooten
12 Cadillacs, Cincinnati, OH

Mrs. Mary Word
8 Cadillacs, Brinkley, AR

Mr. John Wordsworth
1 Cadillac, Edmonds, WA

Ms. Theresa V. Workman
1 Cadillac, Buffalo, NY

Mr. George Worley
4 Cadillacs, Little Rock, AR

Mr. Lonny F. Worley
1 Cadillac, Nesbit, MS

Ms. Loy B. Worley
4 Cadillacs, Carlsbad, NM

Mr. Carl R. Worlund
2 Cadillacs, Salt Lake Cty., UT

Mr. Jack H. Worpell
9 Cadillacs, Novi, MI

Mr. Clinton D. Wortham
7 Cadillacs, Texarkana, TX

Kirk E. Worthington
9 Cadillacs, Tacoma, WA

Ms. Pauline Woytasczyk
1 Cadillac, San Antonio, TX

Consuella B. Wren
Oakland, CA

Mr. Alton K. Wright
1 Cadillac, Greer, SC

Mr. Bill D. Wright
4 Cadillacs, Knoxville, TN

Mr. Cleon B. Wright
7 Cadillacs, Niceville, FL

Mr. David W. Wright
19 Cadillacs, Melvindale, MI

Mr. Edward A. Wright
2 Cadillacs, Oak Ridge, TN

Mrs. Elizabeth T. Wright
1 Cadillac, Nashville, TN

Mr. Everett J. Wright
8 Cadillacs, Milton Frwtr., OR

Mr. Harvey Wright
5 Cadillacs, Las Vegas, NV

J. Wright
3 Cadillacs, Bloomington, IL

Mr. James A. Wright
1 Cadillac, Camden, SC

Mr. Jesse Wright
3 Cadillacs, Chesapeake, VA

Mr. John R. Wright
Jackson, MS

Mrs. Margaret Wright
1 Cadillac, Houghton Lake, MI

Mr. Walter T. Wright
7 Cadillacs, Pocatello, ID

Mr. Wilbert L. Wright
3 Cadillacs, Picayune, MS

Mr. Roy L. Wrightson
3 Cadillacs, Waynesville, MO

Mr. Robert Wuertz
2 Cadillacs, Edison, OH

Mr. John D. Wurdeman
2 Cadillacs, Bloomington, MN

Mr. Ralph O. Wyatt
4 Cadillacs, Findlay, OH

D. Lyle Wynn
4 Cadillacs, Ogden, UT

Y

Mr. Anthony N. Yagovane, Jr.
5 Cadillacs, Hamden, CT

Mr. Kenneth B. Yandow
2 Cadillacs, Spring Hill, FL

Mr. Edward G. Yann, Jr.
3 Cadillacs, Saint Jacob, IL

Mr. John Yarborough
4 Cadillacs, Philadelphia, PA

Mr. Michael R. Yasher
3 Cadillacs, Silver Spring, MD

Yasukazu Yasuda
1 Cadillac, Costa Mesa, CA

Mr. Denis Yergeau
1 Cadillac, Drummondville, QC

Mr. Clifford Yexley
3 Cadillacs, Bradley, SD

John A. Yocca
1 Cadillac, Pittsburgh, PA

William Yocom
8 Cadillacs, Wyomissing, PA

Mrs. Norma Yocum
7 Cadillacs, Geary, OK

Mr. John J. Yohannes
5 Cadillacs, Visalia, CA

Yoo Hoo Chocolate Co.
7 Cadillacs, Carlstadt, NJ

George & Hermie Yoo
1 Cadillac, San Antonio, TX

Mr. Vance O. York
2 Cadillacs, Zionsville, IN

Mr. Allen Yost
1 Cadillac, East St. Paul, MB

Mr. Bill R. Young
6 Cadillacs, Williamson, WV

C.D. Young
2 Cadillacs, Monroeville, PA

Mr. Charles W. Young
8 Cadillacs, York, NE

Mrs. Clemence Lucille Young
4 Cadillacs, Houston, TX

Mr. D. Young
5 Cadillacs, North York, ON

Ms. Elizabeth W. Young
5 Cadillacs, Louisville, KY

Ms. Gertrude J. Young
2 Cadillacs, Quincy, FL

Mr. Haley Young, Jr.
2 Cadillacs, Ft. Lauderdale, FL

Nell Kathryn Young
2 Cadillacs, Madisonville, KY

Nerciel Young
2 Cadillacs, Bogalusa, LA

Mr. Peter A. Young
Coral Springs, FL

Mr. Robert J. Young
2 Cadillacs, Houston, TX

Mr. Stanford Young
2 Cadillacs, Waynesboro, MS

Mr. Virgil R. Young
2 Cadillacs, St. Petersburg, FL

Mr. William H. Young
1 Cadillac, Madison, WI

Mr. Sam J. Yovanno
2 Cadillacs, Twinsburg, OH

Mr. Sang K. Yu
1 Cadillac, Cerritos, CA

David Yurk & Bonnie M. Yurk
Omaha, NE

Mr. Robert J. Yusko
1 Cadillac, Homosassa, FL

Nathan Zaba
2 Cadillacs, Baltimore, MD

Mr. & Mrs. John P. Zacharski
3 Cadillacs, Milwaukee, WI

Francis Zacherl
4 Cadillacs, Tampa, FL

Louis Zaden
12 Cadillacs, Birmingham, AL

Mr. Louis G. Zadina
7 Cadillacs, Omaha, NE

Mr. Zadorozny
1 Cadillac, Etobicoke, ON

Mr. Robert T. Zahn
1 Cadillac, Riverhead, NY

Thomas Zale
2 Cadillacs, Richardson, TX

Mr. Stanley Zaloga
21 Cadillacs, Clinton, MI

Ms. Janice Zamora
2 Cadillacs, Albuquerque, NM

Mr. James Zara
4 Cadillacs, Clarksburg, WV

Ms. Laverne Zarate
5 Cadillacs, Seagoville, TX

Ms. Geraldine L. Zarfos
1 Cadillac, Dallastown, PA

Mr. Allen Zaring
16 Cadillacs, Cincinnati, OH

Ms. Jean H. Zarth
Lakewood, OH

Mr. Joseph E. Zaytoun
6 Cadillacs, Cary, NC

Mr. Robert Zechman
10 Cadillacs, Winfield, PA

Mr. Bernard Zeiger
9 Cadillacs, Springfield, IL

Mr. Dana L. Zeigler
4 Cadillacs, Kingston, OH

Gilbert Zellan
10 Cadillacs, Rockville, MD

Mr. Albert Zellman
3 Cadillacs, Pittsburgh, PA

Ms. Joan S. Zeppetella
4 Cadillacs, Rochester, NY

Mr. Robert F. Ziebell, Jr.
2 Cadillacs, Chicago, IL

Mr. Edmund E. Zielinski
3 Cadillacs, Amherst, NY

Mr. Darrell D. Zimmer
3 Cadillacs, Sulphur, LA

Mr. Leroy Zimmerlee
10 Cadillacs, Johnson City, TN

Mr. Max Zimmerman
10 Cadillacs, Palm Beach, FL

Mrs. Mary T. Zinnerman
1 Cadillac, Ridgeland, SC

Mr. Chester E. Ziolkowski
1 Cadillac, New Britain, CT

Mr. Robert H. Zobal
2 Cadillacs, Loves Park, IL

Mr. Charles R. Zolynsky
25 Cadillacs, Allen Park, MI

Mr. Eugene E. Zorne
3 Cadillacs, Toronto, OH

Mr. Robert Zuch
7 Cadillacs, Brooklyn, MI

Ms. Katherine S. Zulauf
2 Cadillacs, Cleveland, OH

Mr. Robert J. Zuponeck
1 Cadillac, Chicago, IL

Ms. Donna M. Zylke
4 Cadillacs, Big Bend, WI

CREDITS

Author
John A. Heilig

Printer
The Kutztown Publishing Company, Inc.

Photography Credits
Sandra Appel: *page 22*
Donna H. Chiarelli: *pages 7-14, 16-20, 24-25, 28-29, 31, 33-35*
Richard W. Clark: *page 15*
Dan Donovan: *page 30*
Dave Gooley: *pages 27, 32*
John Guider: *page 23*
Keith Lanpher: *page 6*
Mary LaSalle & Diane C. Lyell: *page 21*
Michelle Ramberg: *page 26*

Historical Photographs
Automobile Quarterly Photo and Research Library
and
General Motors Corporation